C000292499

Erotic
Literature

A Connoisseur's Guide

Erotic Literature

A Connoisseur's Guide

DONALD McCORMICK

Continuum • New York

1992
The Continuum Publishing Company
370 Lexington Avenue, New York, NY 10017

Copyright © 1992 by Donald McCormick

All rights reserved. No part of this book may be reproduced, stored in a retrieval system,
or transmitted, in any form or by any means, electronic, mechanical, photocopying, recording,
or otherwise, without the written permission of The Continuum Publishing Company.

Printed in the United States of America

Library of Congress Cataloging-in-Publication Data

McCormick, Donald, 1911–
    Erotic literature : a connoisseur's guide / Donald McCormick.
        p.   cm.
    Includes bibliographical references and index.
    ISBN 0-8264-0574-6 (alk. paper)
        1. Erotic literature—History and criticism.   I. Title.
    PN56.E7M34   1992
    809′.933538—dc20
                                                                    92-6970
                                                                    CIP

Contents

Introduction

Although erotic literature has existed for much longer than two-thousand years and in many instances has been accepted as deserving the description of a classic work, it has never been easy to define. The origin of eroticism is the Greek word *erotikos*, which means sexual rather than romantic love. To qualify this, however, one must remember that the ancient Greeks raised such affairs to a somewhat higher plane by recognizing Eros as the god of love. It has been this conception of such passions that has led to the creation of a great deal of erotic literature down the ages.

Without wishing to raise any kind of prejudice, one must take note of the fact that *Erotikos* was also the title of a treatise by the Greek biographer, Plutarch, in the second century A.D. This work is clearly linked to both heterosexuality and homosexuality. In the quest for erotic literature this is something to be borne in mind, while still noting the evidence over the years that a majority of such works concern male-female relationships.

Mainly, erotic literature has taken the form of poetry in the past, not only among the Greeks and Romans, but in the *pastourelles* and *chansons* of the Middle Ages and the erotica of Marot, Ronsard, and Du Bellay of the Renaissance period. Verse of this kind even pops up in the most unexpected places such as the Anglo-Scottish vernacular of the poet Robert Burns. Yet, having accepted the definition of *erotikos*, I should say that a precise definition of the genre would be all erotic themes in books, verse, drama, and even letters and diaries that deserve to be regarded as classics of their kind. Most certainly many private letters and diaries, including those never published, come under this definition, and examples of these works will appear in this volume.

Romantic fiction can qualify, providing that it is truly erotic in a literary sense, but this would not include the novels of Barbara Cartland or Judith Krantz! Similarly, while pornography as such would be "out" (and this would include some, if not all, of Frank Harris's accounts of his prolific sexual activities), this does not prevent the inclusion in this book of certain classics and much modern work that might be considered pornographic by some puritanically minded people. Throughout my researches into this theme I have tried to remember that I need to understand other people's points of view and that what is genuinely a classic to some may fall short of this ideal to others.

Fear of being accused of supporting the propagation of pornography has from time to time caused some odd descriptions of erotica to be made. Catalogues in various auction sales of erotic literature in New York have described such works as "amatory," "*curiosa,*" "*deliciae,*" "*facetiae,*" and "*varia.*" Ralph Ginzburg has suggested that "no truly satisfactory definition of erotica (and/or pornography or obscenity) has ever been devised. The concept is entirely too subjective."[1]

In legal actions over the past century almost all definitions of the erotic have been translated differently. "A menace to literary and scientific freedoms" is how the writer Alec Craig described such actions.[2] E. M. Forster in his foreword to Craig's book, *The Banned Books of England,* cited Sir Thomas Inskip, a British attorney general in the 1930s, as saying that "the gratification of sexual appetite is an unsavory subject."[3] Certainly in this era some books included in this volume were quite absurdly banned from publication. They included *The Well of Loneliness, Ulysses,* Pepys's *Diary, The Thousand and One Arabian Nights,* and Voltaire's *Candide.* It was not until 1960 that D. H. Lawrence's *Lady Chatterley's Lover* was allowed to be published in the British Isles.

In the United States perhaps the most remarkable and drastic action taken against a book of this kind was in 1907 when Dr. C. W. Malchow, president of the Physicians and Surgeons Club of Minneapolis, was sentenced to prison for selling through the post his work, *The Sexual Life.* This was carried out despite the fact that his book had been highly praised in medical circles. It would seem that there is as big a problem in defining pornography as there is in assessing what is truly erotic and deserving of the title of a classic. Probably both questions are best summed up in these lines of Richard Aldington:

> We were right, yes, we were right
> To snatch the false idealities of the last age,
> The humbug, the soft cruelty, the mawkishness,
> The heavy tyrannical sentimentality,
> The inability to face facts, especially new facts:
> All of which linger on so damnably among us

Then Aldington goes on to say:

> I think we were right to go groping in all forbidden places,

Uncovering horrors politely forgotten
And facing them, too.[4]

This poetic comment obliquely points the way to a final verdict that what
is, or what is not erotic literature is very much a matter of personal opinion.
In selecting such material for consideration in this book one must essentially
bear in mind not just one's own opinions, but those of very many others. My
own viewpoint in seeking out what appeals to me in erotica is conditioned by
a desire to escape from what I would call "the dreary and dirty" of much of
today's fiction in quest of the joyfully erotic, welcoming any attempt to bring
sunshine and ecstasy into literature. If to find this one sometimes has to probe
into ancient literature, so be it. Meanwhile one always hopes to find it in
some new work. Seeking out erotica that appeals is like an exercise in seren-
dipity, that splendid phrase coined by Horace Walpole, or, as he put it, making
happy discoveries by accident of things one was not in quest of.

Sometimes, of course, the quest for erotica is a look into one's own past,
especially adolescence. One has only to ponder on how Orlando carved Rosalind's name on every tree in the Forest of Arden to realize how adolescent
love is invested with a certain delightful madness. One's first infatuation is
the means by which one finally becomes an adult after an exuberant display
of wild abandon to the idea of romantic love. Cloud Nine beckons in a
positive way when one is very young. Sometimes it lifts one to unexpected
heights; at other times, as many of Shakespeare's heroes suggest, it tends to
equate love with death. Or as Pandarus put it when describing the love affair
of Troilus and Cressida, indicating that the noises made by lovers copulating
were similar to the groans of the dying:

> These lovers cry O! O! they die!
> Yet that which seems the wound to kill
> Both turn O! O! O! to Ha! Ha! Ha!

Thanks in part to the more tolerant generations of the latter part of the
twentieth century, a wider and more literate public opinion today is giving
more recognition to the real artistic merits of erotic works. This is particularly
true of the United States and the United Kingdom. Nevertheless the real
centers of erotica remain in Europe and especially in Paris, where more erotica
in the English language is published than almost anywhere else in the world.
The Obelisk, Olympia, and Vendome presses have produced some two hundred thousand volumes of erotica a year, half of which undoubtedly finds its
way to the United States.

Meanwhile libraries in various parts of the world, some private, some public, have managed to preserve many of the best examples of erotica, especially
the unpublished material, of which there is a very great deal. The Library of

Congress has some five-thousand erotic works, including many taken by various past customs seizures. But by far the largest collection of erotica, including some twenty-five thousand volumes, is to be found in the Vatican Library. This may surprise those who will associate the Roman Catholic Church as being at the forefront of those banning such works. Next to the Vatican Library comes the British Museum in London, carrying some twenty-thousand volumes of the genre, while not far behind comes Indiana University's Institute for Sex Research, containing some fifteen-thousand works collected by the late Dr. Alfred C. Kinsey.

Two of the most prominent modern publishers of erotica died in 1990: Maurice Girodias, the Frenchman who founded the Olympia Press, and Charles Skilton, proprietor of one of the last of the one-man publishing houses. Skilton made a fortune from an unexpurgated version of *Fanny Hill*, which he published in the 1960s. He was alarmed to receive a telephone call the week before publication telling him that Mayflower Books was about to publish a paperback of *Fanny Hill*. He need not have worried: the Mayflower version was unexpurgated and was seized on publication by Scotland Yard. Later when Skilton published his own paperback version, it sold more than half a million copies. Girodias's father, Jack Kahane (Girodias was the name of his French mother), founded the Obelisk Press in the 1930s, and was the first to publish Henry Miller's *Tropic of Cancer*, for which at the age of fourteen Maurice actually designed the cover. In 1953 Maurice Girodias started the Olympia Press, initially making it well-known because of its publications in the English language. It was Girodias who largely revived the cult of erotica among an international readership by publishing the works of Vladimir Nabokov, Henry Miller, William Burroughs, Lawrence Durrell, Georges Bataille, and Jean Genet. Life in later years was far from easy for Girodias. He had numerous confrontations with the French censors and was at one time ordered not to publish for what would normally have been longer than his life span, but this was subsequently reduced to a mere three years. At one stage he languished in a Parisian jail for two days. Apart from this trouble Girodias had problems with some of his other authors. They, probably as much through sheer snobbishness as anything else, felt that he used their books as a cover for the publication of a great deal of pornography. His reply to all this was to quote what D. H. Lawrence said on the subject: "What is pornography to one man is the laughter of genius to another."

Conceptions of what is erotic literature not only vary from one person to another, but from century to century, sometimes from decade to decade. Occasionally humor has been the keynote, at other times wit, often the sheer magic of words and the element of pleasurable surprise. In early times the emphasis was on the poetic element and in ancient Sparta on erotic songs. In medieval England there was a special appeal for the masses, as Chaucer shows only too clearly. On the continent of Europe, however, in the same period an element of humbug crept into the presentation of eroticism as was evidenced in the works of those who professed to believe in "courtly love." Here there was an attempt to condone adultery by setting up justification for it under bogus Christian principles. The next marked change came with the introduction of the erotic novel in the seventeenth century. By that time even the intelligentsia had become bored with the poets of courtly love who dressed up their erotic dreams as a kind of crusade of the virtues against the vices. By the end of the eighteenth century there was much more self-examination in the presentation of erotic works, especially in those written in the first person.

All the foregoing views on the subject of what can be judged as erotic literature have been carefully considered in making selections of such works for this volume. There are so many aspects to assess—whether the humor or something trivial raises it to a higher plane, or often the sheer delight in juggling with words to create ecstasy. Something of the latter is evident in the end of the story of *Fanny Hill:* "If I have painted vice in all its gayest colors, if I have decked it with flowers, it has been solely in order to make the worthier, the solemn sacrifice of it to Virtue."[5]

What needs to be borne in mind—and this especially concerns the critics who disparage and condemn erotic literature—is that the genre has over the centuries not only constituted in some works an education in sexual matters, but to some extent has revolutionized sexual practices. Alan Hull Walton writes:

> The war lords of the Crusades brought back more than material goods. They had discovered that love was an art and that the sexual act could be a science. They revealed new attitudes in their approaches to their wives and traditional activity became tempered by innovation. . . . Many of our present sexual attitudes have their distant origins in Arabia, India, Greece and Rome.[6]

Walton, who has translated many ancient classics, and is an authority on such works as the *Kama Sutra* and the Arabic treatise known as *The Perfumed Garden*, makes the point that when in the nineteenth century Europeans discovered such works and eventually translated them, ultimately they benefited from learning the "niceties of erotic refinements, from the personal cleanliness essential in such refinements, to all the delights of delayed pleasure, continued and varied foreplay and the joys arising from an unselfish and applied technique."[7] In this sense it can be said that erotic literature has been positively educational, probably much more so than some of the highly dubious official sex education taught in our schools today.

There is another aspect of eroticism and that is the enhancing of a relationship by the attraction of putting love messages into code. This practice has survived for many centuries, sometimes in written works, frequently in letters and, especially in the nineteenth century, even in advertisements in newspapers. Not only the ancients, such as Vatsayayana, author of *Kama Sutra*, followed this example, but even a more recent writer such as Kenneth Grahame of *Wind in the Willows* fame. Grahame engaged in a lifelong secret language of baby talk with his wife, often in the form of letters. That serious writer Jonathan Swift indulged in baby-talk code in his letters to his beloved "Stella," addressing her and her companion, Rebecca Dingley, as "Nite deee dee logues Md," which has been variously interpreted by scholars, although the probable interpretation is "good night dear rogues." The subject of love in code is one that will be dealt with in chapter 6.[8]

Perhaps in part erotic literature owes much to the relationship of love and death. Maybe this is a needlessly depressing view to take today, but it nevertheless still exists. There is always the thought that because a love affair, whether in or out of marriage, seems so wonderful it could end in a terrible tragedy through some unforeseen accident. Romeo talks of his mind dreading "some consequences yet hanging in the stars." "Let's make it good because it cannot last" seems to be the outlook of many, whereas others just feel that a perfect love is something too splendid to last. Sometimes, especially in the past, this theme has been projected into views of what might be after death: "When I am dead, my dearest," says Christina Rossetti.[9]

Erotic literature comes in many forms and has different messages for a wide range of individuals. From it can be obtained education, pleasure, inspiration, even psychological advice and an appreciation of the varieties of love, without which that very word might mean no more than sexual intercourse. At its best erotic literature is uplifting. Or, as the poet James Thomson puts it:

> And then she sang ballads, olden ballads of love and woe,
> Love all burningly golden, grief with heart's blood in its flow.

PART ONE
. . . .

1

The Greeks and The Romans

Among the ancient Greeks and the Romans eroticism was almost the main feature of many literary works, dating back to several centuries B.C. Such works ranged from heterosexual to homosexual love, as is amply demonstrated in the works of Aeschylus, one of the earliest of Greek poets, who told of King Laius of Thebes and his love of the boy Chrysippus.

However, even in those distant days there was from time to time an element of repression in the views of some toward erotic verse. As far back as the third century B.C. Plato was on record as having demanded that certain works should be drastically edited before being told to juveniles. Pleasure, love, and wine were the main subjects of verse in the period of the fourth and fifth centuries B.C., and perhaps the most prolific of such lyric poets was Anacreon of Teos.[1] It has not always been possible to obtain absolutely accurate translations of all his works, nor has it always been possible to be sure that all works attributed to Anacreon are actually his. The truth is that there were many imitators of Anacreon and this led to the creation of a cult—Anacreonitic verse, said to cover all verse in praise of wine or women.

In his later days Anacreon addressed his mistress thus:

> Gray hairs you treat with scornful eye
> And leave me most unmannerly.
> Sweet creature, ashes do contain
> Embers that strive to flame again.
> And mountain that on top has snow
> Feels warmth and constant fire below.
> With roses white-haired lilies twine
> And in a glowing garland shine;
> They, locked in close embraces, lie
> And kiss and stir effectively.

The Greeks tended to dwell on all forms of intercourse in their verses, not only the homosexual as portrayed by Aeschylus, but of incest, too. Euripides in his tragic drama, *Aeolus,* portrayed the story of Macareus's incestuous love for his sister Canace. Almost all Greek poets or writers of this era seemed to embrace erotic subjects sooner or later, even Claudius Aelianus, author of *Varia Historia* and a work on the peculiarities of animals, *De Animalium Natura.*[2] Yet another cult was that named Cinaedic poetry, which covered all aspects of sexual perversion from pederasty to incest. Sometimes poets overstepped the mark in relating their verses too closely to living people. One such was Sotades, a Cretan, whose most notorious work was a poem that was critical of the marriage of King Ptolomy II. Despite the fact that the king was a patron of poets and had made his museum at Alexandria a center of literature and science, he ordered Sotades to be imprisoned. The poet managed to escape, but only temporarily. When he was caught the king ordered him to be drowned.

It was, of course, Plato more than anyone else who, in the third century B.C., changed the attitudes of contemporary poets by his definitions—however abstruse they may still seem to some—of various aspects of what came to be known as Platonic love. In the *Phaedrus* and *Symposium,* two of his greatest dialogues (as they were styled), Plato raises all concepts of love on to what is an exalted and spiritual yearning for the perfect and most beautiful relationship. Plato did not himself contribute to erotic literature as such except to point the way to others.[3]

Voyeurism was a subject for exploitation by writers even in those days, and even by so distinguished a historian as Herodotus. He told the story of how Candaules was so deeply in love with his wife and so enamored of her beauty that he urged his friend, Gyges, to watch how they made love. But it did not work out as Candaules intended because his wife caught a glimpse of the watchful Gyges and she was so infuriated that she gave him two choices— "kill Candaules and marry me, or die this instant, or at least shortly after."

Despite the pleas of Plato for a new vision of eroticism, other Greek scribes still took a lowlier view. Aristophanes in his comedy drama, *Ecclesiazusae,* makes great play of arguments between prostitutes, especially of one old woman haranguing a young girl who was a potential rival for men's favors. Aristophanes captures superbly the dialogue between the two. The older woman declares: "Sing as long as you like, or just peep out like a pussy lying in wait, but you can be sure no man will come to you before he has been with me first." Aristophanes goes on to describe in terms of dialogue the approaches of a young man to both these women. The older woman presents the young man with a decree that orders him to enter her house. The decree states that if a young man desires a young girl, he can only enjoy this after he had satisfied an older woman. If he refuses, then the old women are authorized to seize him.

Yet of all his works, *Lysistrata* is perhaps the most interesting in the context of such literature: its theme is the problems of sex in the life of a community. Even in recent times its production as a play has made considerable impact, not least among activist feminists. At the time Aristophanes composed this work Greece was fighting for survival in a war with Sparta. As a way out of this Lysistrata puts forward the idea that the women of Greece should refuse all intercourse with their husbands until they agree to make peace. Or, as Lysistrata herself puts it: "I shall remain in the background to encourage you to arouse your man's passions. You will do all you can to make him want you, and you can grant him every favor but the one he wants."

Naturally, Lysistrata was closely questioned as to what women should do if their husbands took them by force. Her reply was: "Yield to their demands, but with total lack of devotion. There can be no pleasure in it for them when they can achieve what they want only by force. . . . There is no satisfaction for the man unless it is shared by the woman."

Thus Lysistrata persuaded her female followers to repeat after her a series of vows—"never shall I give myself voluntarily" and "if he has me by force, I shall be as cold as ice and never let a single limb of mine move." At the same time her instructions were that her female followers should all set out "to inflame and torment" their husbands: "Grant every favor except that which is forbidden." In retrospect it all suggests that the wives concerned were almost inviting failure, unless, of course, Greek men had an unusual view of such things.

It is indeed surprising that the pleas of even so ardent a feminist as Lysistrata could succeed in an age when cuckoldry was rampant. Even in the ninth century B.C. that superb poet Homer was waxing eloquently about Aphrodite's turning her attentions away from her husband, Hephaestus, toward Ares, the god of war (book 8 of Homer's *Odyssey*). The love lives of the gods and goddesses was the subject Homer adored, not least in the *Iliad*, book 14, in which Hera, the wife of the god Zeus, plays tricks with her husband. Zeus has implored her to make love with him there and then, to which she replies: "What are you suggesting? Do you wish us to lie with one another here on the very pinnacle of Mount Ida, where all can be seen? What if one of the eternal gods should see us thus? It would be such a scandal that when I finally left your embraces I could never show myself inside your house again." To which words Zeus declares his passion in these words: "Be not afraid that god or man will see you, because I shall cause us to be hidden in a dense golden cloud that not even the sun shall pierce."

This was a world of delicious fantasy in which gods, goddesses, and human beings were wholly mixed up, when in fact man became god and woman became goddess if only for the sheer delight of putting their life patterns on some seemingly divine plane. Thus it was that Cronos, the youngest of the Titans, was in Greek mythology ruler of the gods before Zeus, and later was identified by the Romans with their god, Saturn. Myth in those days enthused and inspired men as no religion has ever done since, so much so that the Romans carried on what the Greeks had begun. No religion of any kind since then has so positively produced poetry and drama to equal the era of the multigod society. There had to be a god for everything, for every one and every need, and the Greeks certainly supplied it, not least in Pan who was the god of amorous adventures. On the whole Greek romances nearly always end with love triumphant over all odds, and to some extent the Romans continued this trend.

Nevertheless, however rewarding this may have been for literature, it tended toward highly undesirable customs among the people of that age. Strabo, the Greek historian, tells how customs among some races—the Armenians, Lydians, Phoenicians, Cypriots, and Carthaginians—included prostituting their daughters before marriage as a tribute to the goddess Anaitis.

Yet undoubtedly the one poet whose influence on those who followed him when writing on amatory themes was Ovid, or Publius Ovidius Naso as he was known. Where Plato was philosophical and vague, Ovid was practical and romantic, a quite remarkable combination for any day or age. His *Ars Amatoria*, written admittedly for a society that appreciated his motives and took amusement as well as instruction from his work, still stands out as a masterly exposition of the arts of seduction. In a superb spirit of the romantic, the practical, the amusing and even joking about love, he managed to sustain something of the element of the gods, the god Amor being introduced into his theme. Perhaps the practicality is best summed up in these words from *Ars Amatoria*:

> Go early prior the appointed hour to meet
> The fair one, and await her in the street,
> And let not Dog-star heats nor drifted loan
> Of whitening snows deter you from the road.
> Cowards, get lost! Our general, Love, disdains
> Your lukewarm service in his long campaigns.[4]

Certainly Ovid's best work was in his amatory verse—*Amores*, *Ars Amatoria*, and *Remedium Amoria*.[5] His authoritarian approach to the potential lover who seeks his guidance may seem somewhat strident at times, but what is more important is how he managed to hold medieval writers in his thrall centuries after his death. Those who wrote about love in many cases showed they were influenced by and even borrowed from Ovid. That he was, if you like, a tutor of love and not just a poet wrapped up in his own fantasies is abundantly clear from the way he presented his work. In his *Ars Amatoria*, for example, the first two books were specially directed to males on how to seduce a female and, equally important, how to keep her happy afterwards.

Yet in his third book he made it clear that he was equally eager to give advice to women in matters of love.

One typical piece of advice to women was: "Read in my looks what silently they speak, and slily, with your eyes, your answer make. My lifted eyebrow shall declare my pain; my right hand to his fellow shall complain and on the back a letter shall design; besides a note that shall be writ in wine. Whenever you think upon our last embrace, with your finger gently touch your face. If any word of mine offends you, pull with your hand the velvet of your ear. If you are pleased with what I do or say, handle your rings, or let your finger play."

This is the stuff out of which secret assignations are made; this Ovid understood and expounded well even when he became cryptic. His major anxiety was that the female should not fail to recognize when she was seriously being propositioned and how she should react to this. If Ovid had merely addressed himself to men, he might never have been banished, as he was in later years, but it is highly probable that his remarkably prescient adjunctions to women caused his downfall. In some quarters this was regarded as a man betraying men! This extract from *Ars Amatoria* gives some idea of what may have led toward his expulsion from Rome:

> Let every woman learn to understand herself, and thus enter into love's battle in the style most suited to her charms. If a woman has a lovely face, let her lie upon her back. If she prides herself on her hips, then let her display them to the best advantage. Melanion bore Atalanta's legs upon his shoulders. If your legs are as beautiful as hers, put them in the same position. If you are short, let your lover be the steed. . . . A woman who is conspicuously tall should kneel with her head turned slightly sideways. If your thighs are still lovely with the charm of youth, if your breasts are without flaw, lie aslant upon your couch, and think it not shameful for your hair to float wildly about your shoulders. If the labors of Lucina have left their mark upon you, then, like the swift Parthia, turn your back to the fray. Love has a thousand postures, and the simplest and least tiring is to lie on your right side . . . feel the pleasure in the very marrow of your bones, so share all things fairly with your lover, saying to him your loveliest and naughtiest ideas. If nature has kept back from you the sensation of total pleasure, fear not, but teach your lips to lie and say you felt every moment of it. But if you have to pretend, don't betray yourself by overacting. Let your movements and eyes deceive, and so, gasping and panting, provide the idea of a splendid climax.

To men Ovid was equally instructive: "Never speak to a woman about her defects. . . . If a woman squints, tell her she is like Venus; if she is so skinny

you would think she was at death's door, tell her she has a graceful figure. . . .
Similarly, you must disguise every defect under the name of its nearest quality. . . . Nor should it be forgotten that women of a certain age have experience. . . . They know all the different attitudes of love and will assume them
at your pleasure. Nothing can rival them in voluptuousness. . . . Learn, by
skillful dallying, to reach the goal by gentle, pleasant stages . . . then follow
gentle moanings and murmurs of delight, soft groans and sighs and whispered
words that sting and lash desire. . . . Don't go too quickly for your mistress,
but rather let her desires outstrip your own."

Nobody could better assess the various types of women who would appeal
to men than Ovid. "If she is tall, she's like an Amazon, and therefore fills the
bed she lies upon. If she is short, she lies the rounder: to speak the truth,
both short and long please me, for I love both types. . . . A white wench
enthralls me, but so do golden yellow, and nut brown girls in many respects
have no equal. If her white neck is shadowed with black hair, remember so
was Leda's, yet Leda was fair."[6]

On the other hand Ovid also warned that sobriety was essential to judge
the true talents of a woman and he also added that "Night is a cheat and all
deformities are hid, or lessened in her dark disguise. The sun's fair light each
error will confess, in face, in shape, in jewels, and in dress."

Yet another Roman who influenced such later writers as Byron and Swinburne was Gaius Valerius Catullus. Undoubtedly one of the greatest of Roman
poets, it was chiefly for his love poems and his satirical verse that he is mostly
famed. He based his style on the Greek poets, as is evident in such of his
words as *Epithalamium Pelei et Thetides, Coma Berenices,* and *Attis.*[7]

A number of Catullus's poems concern his mistress, Lesbia, whom in turn
he praises above all other women and then upbrides her:

> So loved has woman never been
> As thou hast been to me.
> No lover yet was ever seen
> So true as I to thee.
> But cruel, cruel Lesbia, thou
> Hast by thy falsehood wrought
> Such havoc in my soul, and now
> So madly it is distraught.

Somewhat different was Publius Vergilius Maro (or Virgil as he is more
generally known today). His poems were frequently of erotic encounters with
peasant girls, as in his epic on Corydon's unquenched love for Alexis:

> I wish for balmy sleep, but wish in vain:
> Love has no bounds in pleasure or in pain.

What frenzy, shepherd, has thy soul possessed?
Thy vineyard lies half-pruned and half-undressed.
Quench, Corydon, thy long unanswered fire
And on willow twigs employ thy care:
And find an easier love, though not so fair.

Quintus Horatius Flaccus (Horace) on the other hand, while still harping on the familiar theme of the Romans, unrequited love, usually wrote such verses to imaginary women. A typical example of these lyrics is:

Telephus—you praise still,
His waxen arms, his rosy-tinted neck.
Yet all the while I can but thrill
With jealous pangs I cannot, cannot check.

There was a tendency with many of these early erotic poets to mask their uncertainties, their lack of grasping some of the essentials of a happy love affair by double-talk, and often obscure symbolism. One sees a great deal of this in Titus Maccius Plautus's comedy, the *Mostellaria*, when Philolaches talks with the harlot, Philematium:

Oh, most splendid love, there's my storm which stripped me of all modesty that was my covering, when love and lust flooded my bosom, and now I can never put the cover on again. Now the walls are soaking into my heart, the house is completely useless.

One can only imagine how irritating such muddled chatter must have seemed to any Philematium! Yet Plautus was by no means unworldly. In his youth he had undertaken various menial tasks and yet found time to write his comedies and other plays, some twenty-three of them in all.[8]

It was undoubtedly Ovid who, again and again, became the educator not only of those who wished to make love and enjoy it rapturously, but for those who wished to write in an erotic vein, yet lacked the perception of how to do it. His understanding of women was quite remarkable and his advice to them was concise and absolutely lucid. But he took risks when he included names in his works: "Andromache, who was as tall as an Amazon, never comported herself in that way with Hector," he would write, and it is more than likely that his use of such names as Melanion and Atalanta, Lucina and Parthia may have aroused suspicions that he was writing about real people. His address to a mistress may well have caused some concern to husbands:

Your husband will be with us at the feasts;
May that be the last supper he shall eat.
And am poor I, a guest invited there,
Only to see, while he may touch the fair?

To see you kiss and hug your nauseous lord
While his lewd hand descends below the board?

Whether men worried more about the alleged powers of women as expressed by some poets in these times, or if the women merely decided to do all possible to advance their own authority is something one can only ponder when turning from poet to poet. Certainly Decimus Junius Juvenalis seemed to believe that Roman wives would stop at nothing in their desire to be the ruler in all amatory affairs. "Some purchase charms, some, more deadly still, Thessalian philters, to subdue the will of a husband, and make him bear blows, insults, and all a wife can dare," said Juvenalis. Then he warned what could happen to the husband: ". . . leading to that swift lapse to second childhood; hence the vapors which surround every sense and the strange forgetfulness that keeps increasing. . . . You, too, like Caligula, may be driven mad as when his Caesonia squeezed into his bowl the dire excrescence of a new-dropped foal."

Caligula, of course, was the nickname given to the Emperor Gaius Caesar who was so insane that he made his horse a consul, eventually falling victim to a conspiracy that ended in his murder.

However, Juvenalis was distinctly vindictive toward women and spoke of "the nuptial bed, still the scene of strife," and referred to a wife being as "fierce as a tigress plundered by her young, rage fires her breast and loosens all her tongue."

Rather more successful perhaps was Lucius Apuleius, the philosopher and orator who traveled widely and made a practice of finding out all that was new overseas that would enhance both the spiritual and philosophical life as well as amatory matters. He was particularly interested in the occult and especially when it was linked to eroticism, developing his fondness for this after his visits to Africa. He married a rich widow named Pudentilla whose relatives accused him of gaining her affections by witchcraft. His answer to this was to publish in his defense a tract that became famous as his *Apologia*. His most important and best-known work, however, was his *Metamorphoses* (more popularly known as *The Golden Ass*). In a peculiar way it is an autobiographical romance, for it tells the story of Lucius being turned into an ass by a woman who was practicing witchcraft—in which guise he was the better able to observe and study the follies of mankind. In many respects *Metamorphoses* is almost a novel and there is plenty of action in the story, with such fascinating characters as all kinds of women, some practitioners of witchcraft, robbers, and kidnappers. Needless to say, Lucius as an ass had his way with the wench Fotis, saying, "My sweetheart, I am happy to have such another kiss to be broiled here upon this fire, whereat I embraced her and kissed her more often and she embraced and kissed me likewise, and moreover her breath smelled like cinnamon and the liquor of her tongue was like sweet nectar."[9]

A totally different character, but in some ways more original and certainly carrying eroticism in literature much further than others among his countrymen, was Ausonius. In the fourth century A.D. he held considerable authority at the court and in various posts he held under the emperor overseas. However much he indulged in composing erotic verses and letters, he was also a stern critic of abnormal sexual practices. One of his poems contained such criticism: it was entitled *A Portrait of Crispa, a Dissolute Woman*. In this work he accused the woman Crispa of "obscene forms of love of a type that desolation at Lemnos impelled in the heir of Hercules," going on to say that Crispa "practices all the abnormalities; . . . she carries out *fellatio*, she tries by either orifice; . . . indeed, she seems desperate to try everything and every method she can think of."[10]

Anxious to learn about love, nearly always desperately anxious, the Greeks and the Romans tended either to stress the hazards and strains of such love, or to soar into the clouds with unrestrained rhetoric when all seemed splendid. It was either "Sweet and voluptuous hour, caressing hour, joyful, laughing hour of delight, of fun and whispers,"[11] or there was that premonition that what was splendid always ended in disaster and disappointment: "The god of music and the god of wine alone luxuriate in unfading bloom; fair-flowing locks around their foreheads shine—eternal beauty midst eternal gloom."[12] Nevertheless both Greek and Latin showed that the quest for the sublime even at that distance in time was worth striving for and that what had been merely mundane and often uncaring lust among primitive peoples could be raised to a much higher plane and level of enjoyment.

Some of the most vivid, lively, and occasionally coarse accounts of life in Rome in the first century A.D. came from Gaius Petronius, a member of the court of the Emperor Nero Claudius Caesar. Of all his works the *Petronii Arbitri Satyricon*, a medley of poems and prose, is perhaps outstanding, though it must be admitted that some authorities query the authorship of some of it. Certainly the piece known as *Trimalchio's Banquet* is indisputably that of Petronius.

One of the more intriguing of his characters in the *Satyricon* is Polyaemus, whose adventures with women are described in great detail. But, as so often in these early erotic tales, the prospect proved too magnificent for the male in action. At one moment it was a case of "preparing for the battle and through ten thousand kisses pressed closely to one another." Then, suddenly, "a weakness robbed me of my arms and other limbs. . . . Cheated in her expectations, she highly resented what had happened, asking if her lips, her breath or some evil smell offended me. . . . Finding my member and every other part of me without life, I could only say, 'Don't triumph over my misery. I must be bewitched.'"[13]

To translate either Greek or Latin of those remote eras into credible English is both a challenge and a hazardous adventure. Many of the translations have been toned down in the past and what remains in printed form, especially those done in the last century, is muted and pedantic. This in no way accurately reflects the spirit of the original Greek and Latin texts. On the other hand one can sometimes err in trying to be what for want of a better phrase might be called imaginatively modern. The various translations given here are an attempt to strike a balance, though even that is not always possible. With Ausonius, for example, it is essential to capture his quick-thinking, quick-fire plain speaking.[14]

However, there are occasions when the original text alone must be recorded, especially when it descends to the level, brilliantly expressed though it is, of Marcus Valerius Martialis, known to later generations as Martial. He was a master of the epigram, of which he was almost the originator in the modern sense of that word. Polished, witty, using a variety of meters in his verse, he was nonetheless frequently crude in an elegant way. This may seem a contradictory description of this poet, but it is true, as perhaps the following lines in Latin will show:

> Lingua maritus, moechus ore Nanneius,
> Summemmianis inquinatior buccis;
> Quem cum fenestra vidit a Suburana
> Obscena nudum Leda, fornicem cludit
> Mediumque mavult basiare quam summum,
> Modo qui per omnes viscerum tubos ibat
> Et voce certa consciaque dicebat
> Puer an puella matris esset in ventre:
> Gaudete cunni; vestra namque res acta est—
> Arrigere linguam non potest fututricem.
> Nam dum tumenti mersus haeret in volva
> Et vagientes intus audit infantes,
> Partem gulosam solvit indecens morbus.[15]

It is a peculiar feature of a good deal of Greek and Latin eroticism in prose and verse that, when translated into other languages, and especially into English, what was merely erotic becomes pornographic, or at least tends that way. Here again, however, it is a matter of individual points of view.

Though the *Homeric Hymns* are full of voluptuous imagery, it is extremely doubtful whether Homer wrote them. In this century there has been a tendency to rule that they cannot have been composed by Homer because they contain references to much later beliefs and customs as well as to places unknown to Homer. Quite apart from this argument, it is still impossible to pinpoint exactly the period in which Homer actually lived. According to some sources he "probably lived in the twelfth century B.C.," according to others it was "probably the tenth century B.C., while yet another source claims his *Iliad* and *Odyssey* were produced "in 850 B.C." Any scholars wishing to interpret the *Homeric Hymns* in terms of Homer's own alleged beliefs and what he really composed do so at their peril.

2

Our Oriental Teachers

*I*t should be acknowledged without almost any qualification that the supreme teachers of sexual techniques have come from the Middle and Far East. There can be no question but that such teachings have to a large extent civilized the very act of sexual intercourse to a degree that might never have been possible otherwise.

The supreme works of this nature are the *Kama Sutra*, a Hindu work by Vatsyayana; the lesser-known but equally important *Ananga Ranga* of Kalyana Malla; the *Kama Kalpa* (an ancient tract directed toward giving advice both to women and to men who wish to understand each other); and, above all, the Arabic work *Al Raud al atir wa nuzhat al Khatir*, better known in Western circles as *The Perfumed Garden*. In all these works not only are the sexual facts of life spelt out in detail, but they are raised to an art that requires study and practice. Those last three words may sound what can only be called off-putting, but in reality they are both instructive and inspiring. Let us just consider this quotation from *The Perfumed Garden*:

"The ways of doing it to women are numerous and variable. And now is the time to make it known to you the different positions that are usual." From there on the educator proceeds to detail some twenty-five variations, manners—or whatever one likes to call it—of sexual intercourse. The Shaykh Nefzawi, who was the author of this work, states quite positively in his introduction to it: "I swear before God, certainly! the knowledge of this book is necessary. It will be only the shamefully ignorant, the enemy of all knowledge, who does not read it, or who turns it into ridicule." He goes on to say, "Praise be given to God, who has placed man's greatest pleasure in the natural parts of woman, and has destined the natural parts of man to afford the greatest enjoyment to woman."[1] Certainly by that last qualification Nefzawi managed to refute any charge of sexism that might be brought against him.

Sometimes the Shaykh's name is spelt Nefzawi, at others Nafzawi and Naf-zaoui. He was Shaykh, scholar, and Imam as well as author, and as the latter he tried to fulfill what he regarded as his duties in all his other offices and capacities. There is no question but that he not only considered his book a duty to mankind, but that he was fulfilling the wishes of Allah as well. He starts off by stating, "Learn while God's blessing be upon you, that there are different sorts of men and women, that amongst these are those who are worthy of praise and those who deserve reproach."

Though to sophisticated Westerners of today a good deal of the book may seem amusingly trivial, almost at times as though he were addressing people who had no conception of what coition is, if the pun may be pardoned, nevertheless it is serious, written with a lively eye for the delights of lovemak-ing and above all contains some instructions that are as valid today as they were in Nefzawi's time. Having made this point, however, one might warn the young and inexperienced male reading this for the first time not to worry about what Nefzawi has to say on the subject of "the virile member": "To please women, the virile member must have at most a length of the breadth of twelve fingers, or three hand-breadths, and at least six fingers, or a hand and a half breadth." After this Nefzawi goes on to comment that "a man whose member is of less dimensions cannot please women." It may well be that the dimensions cited vary from race to race.

The other notable oriental work on the same subject as The Perfumed Garden is, of course, the Kama Sutra of Vatsyayana, likewise translated by Sir Richard Burton and Forster Arbuthnot into English. This work is especially interesting to the student because it has many similarities to The Perfumed Garden. Though subtitled The Hindu Art of Love,[2] much of it both in style and content reads like the Shaykh Nefzawi's work. Not only does it contain similarly styled advice to men and women on sexual techniques, but it has chapters on aphrodisiacs, amatory devices, perfumes, and postures. It would be interesting to know whether or not either book owes something to the other. Hindu poetry actually dates to 200 B.C., while Sanskrit was in general use in India by the fourth century A.D. and in 220 Sanskrit dramas were being produced. On balance one would be inclined to say that the Kama Sutra is somewhat more sophisticated than The Perfumed Garden, more formal, and less salacious. Yet even Vatsyayana remembers Hindu teachings when he writes: "This work is not intended to be used merely as an instrument for satisfying our desires. A person acquainted with the true principles of this science, and who pre-serves his Dharma, Artha, and has regard for the practices of people, is sure to obtain the mastery over his senses."

This is rather a more subdued yet still effective approach than that of Nefzawi, whose language often sounds like that of a sultan giving out orders. Some of the chapter headings of Kama Sutra suggest The Perfumed Garden all over again, others strike a somewhat different chord. Chapter headings like "The Kinds of Sexual Union according to Physical Dimension" sounds very like Nefzawi. Other chapter headings are: "On Biting, Embracing, Kissing, Pressing or Marking with Nails," "Ways of Love to Be Employed with Women of Different Countries," "Of the Sounds Appropriate to Various Kinds of Congress," "Of Ameliorating Love Quarrels," and "Of Signs of Change in a Lover's Feelings and the Way to Get Rid of Him." Vatsyayana also has a rather more romantic touch than Nefzawi on occasions, not least when he advocates secrecy as a fillip to passion and even suggesting that secret writing is one of the arts of love.

Equally important in guidance on the arts of lovemaking is the *Ananga Ranga* (a similar work to the *Kama Sutra*) by Kalyana Malla, which was also translated into English by Burton and privately printed for the Kama Shastra Society of London and Benares. Kalyana Malla wrote: "The chief reason for the separation between a married couple and the cause of the husband being driven into the embraces of strange women, and sometimes the wife into the arms of strange men is the want of variation in their pleasures, and the monotony that results from possession. . . . Fully understanding the way in which such quarrels arise, I can demonstrate how the husband, by varying the ways in which he enjoys his wife, can live with her as with thirty-two different women, always varying the enjoyment of her and for her and making repletion impossible."[3]

In other words, the message is precise and encouraging, giving the sort of sane advice that even today is ignored by large numbers in the Western world. Indeed, to judge from some of the correspondence in the agony columns of newspapers and magazines one would think vast numbers have never heard of it. It is worth noting that among the Hindus the kind of advice given principally to males in the *Kama Sutra* was offered to women, married or unmarried, in the *Kama Kalpa*, hewing carefully to women's customs and ideas in sexual relations. The *Kama Kalpa* became almost a Hindu ritual. Some of the ideas submitted in these various works were later expressed in Hindu erotic poems that have a beauty uniquely their own.[4]

The Song of Solomon was composed about 1014 B.C.—at least that is the date that a number of Bibles give it, though other sources suggest that Solomon, the third king of Israel, lived around 970–930 B.C. Solomon was an astute monarch who made treaties with all the neighboring powers with a view to preserving peace and developing trade; as a result, he became extremely wealthy. Through this wealth he increased the size of his army and his harem, but respect for his wisdom lasted long after his death and was shared by Jew and Arab alike. As to the *Song of Solomon*, regardless of the question of authorship and to what extent Solomon was helped by poets at his court in the composition of this work, nobody has ever satisfactorily explained how it came to be included in the Bible down the centuries even until the present day. Admittedly, one answer is that it is included in the Hebrew Bible, which is also non-Christian, though positively religious. But the *Song of Solomon* is equally certainly not religious, nor even remotely theological. It is a delightful lover's dream, a beautiful fantasy filled with erotic thoughts and images; in that sense it has meaning for eternity. Solomon's *Song* strikes as effective a note today as ever it did in past ages. I have no pretension to being a theological scholar, but it seems to me that if the early and medieval Christian leaders had paid more heed to the *Song of Solomon*, they could have avoided all the sexually repressive decrees that have resulted in hardship, excommunication, Puritanism, and a totally unhelpful and unsympathetic attitude toward sexual problems down the ages. For the *Song of Solomon* is uplifting, idealizing, and romantic.

It is worth quoting at some length because here is something approaching the point of perfection in eroticism:

> Let him kiss me with the kisses of his mouth: for thy love is better than wine. Because of the savor of thy good ointments thy name is as ointment poured forth, therefore do the virgins love thee. Draw me, we will run after thee: the king hath brought me into his chambers: we will be glad to rejoice in thee, we will remember thy love more than wine: the upright love thee.

It is, of course, the imagery that is the dominant feature of *The Song of Solomon*, as, for example, when the poet says,

> The fig tree putteth forth her green figs, and the vines with the tender grape give a good smell. Arise, my love, my fair one, and come away. O my dove, thou art in the clefts of the rock, in the secret places of the stairs, let me see thy countenance, let me hear thy voice, and thy countenance is comely. Take us the foxes, the little foxes, that spoil the vines; for our vines have tender grapes.

In this single work there is a dedicated attempt to place sexual intercourse on what can only be described as an Olympian height, to raise it to the level of ecstatic and aesthetic delight. This applied as much to the female as the male in the *Song*'s responses by the one to the other:

> His eyes are as the eyes of doves by the rivers of waters, washed with milk and fitly set. His cheeks are as a bed of spices, as sweet flowers; his lips are like lilies, dropping sweet-smelling myrrh. His hands are as gold rings set with the beryl: his belly is as bright ivory overlaid with sapphires. His legs are as pillows of marble, set upon sockets of fine gold: his countenance is as Lebanon, excellent as the cedars.

His mouth is most sweet: yea, he is altogether lovely. This is my
beloved and this is my friend, O daughters of Jerusalem.

The male, in summing up the female, in *The Song*, is perhaps even more
passionate:

O prince's daughter, the joints of thy thighs are like jewels, the work
of the hands of a cunning workman. Thy navel is like a round
goblet, which wanteth not liquor; thy belly is like an heap of wheat
set about with lilies. Thy breasts are like two young roes that are
twins . . . thine eyes like the fish-pools in Heshbon . . . thy nose
is as the tower of Lebanon which looketh towards Damascus.

Erotic poetry was almost at its zenith in the first few centuries prior to the
birth of Christ and for the best part of a thousand years afterwards. There
was Abu Temman, circa ninth century A.D., and among others were Al-
Nahli, who wrote *Kittab Al-Bah* (a manual that praises and recommends lust),
and in the tenth century A.D. Mohammed Ali ibn H'azm al Andalusi, an
Arab with links to Spain as his name suggests. The last named had the advantage from the viewpoint of his work, the *Risala* (The dove's neck ring), of
having been literally brought up in a harem in Cordova where the females
taught him the tricks of their mode of life. His work is an introduction to
love as he learned about it, lively and picturesquely descriptive in parts, but
the reader is always being warned about the dire penalties of the Moslems for
certain types of fornication.[5]

There were probably more treatises on the arts of love and how to make a
love life satisfactory in the Arab world in this period than anywhere else. All
of them try to raise lovemaking to an art that must be learned in detail if life
is to be worth anything at all. The message of most of these treatises is almost
as brutal as that. Perhaps *brutal* is too strong a word, but the message is fairly
clear that Allah would not have it otherwise. Always, too, did these early
erotic treatises suggest positive links between lovemaking and nature. What
was sexually delightful was invariably green and something to be compared to
flowers, plants, and trees, or an oasis in the desert. There was a work by one
Jala Al-Din Al-Siyuti entitled *Kitab Al-Izah Fi-ilm Al-Nikah* (Green splendors
of the copse in copulation).

All this kind of association of sexual intercourse with the splendors of
nature and the use of dancing not merely to win admirers but to show that
prostitution was just as sacred as other forms of lovemaking was a feature of
the Moslem world. Yet it was also practiced to a lesser degree in India and
Greece. William Flinders Petrie, a distinguished Egyptologist of the last century, when translating the *Doulaq Papyrus* made special note of the fact that
prostitution was regarded as a sacred duty. There is one quite astonishing
scene described in Petrie's translation of this work. Apparently prostitutes of

what was known as the sacred type were called a *hierodouloi* and when one such was propositioned by a man she told him: "I am a hierodule, so I am a special person. If you wish to have pleasure of me, you must arrange for your children to be slain so that they may not seek a quarrel with my children because of your possessions." Setna (he was the man involved) agreed to this quite astonishing demand and it is recorded that his children were "slain before him . . . thrown to the cats and dogs."

So besotted with the idea of the varieties of sexual intercourse were the ancient Arabs that book after book was written on the subject for several centuries. There was Omar Haleby's work, *El Ktab*, which was published in the last century in Paris under the title of *Les Lois Secrètes de l'Amour*. When the Arabs entered Spain there suddenly developed what can only be described as a Hispano-Arab literature that mainly touched on the subject of love. Ben Ammar, the vizier of Matamid of Seville, who was one such poet of the eleventh century A.D., wrote a number of poems of this kind. Yet another Hispano-Arab of medieval times was Ibn Sina, who wrote a treatise on love.[6] The emphasis was nearly always on pleasure—sometimes, it seemed, pleasure at all costs. Two further examples were *The Book of Pleasure* by Abdul Hagg Effendi, a Turkish work, and *A Summary of Pleasure* by Ibn Samsamani.[7] A work that concentrated on the subject of marriage and was both instructive and erotic was *Bridal Ceremony and Brides* by Al-Jahiz.

However, when it comes to finding the most positively arresting, stimulating, and cleverly told tales of love and adventure in ancient times from an Arab source, *The Arabian Nights Entertainments* is unsurpassed. In its original form of *Alf Laylah wa Laylah* (A thousand nights and a night) it is today accepted as an Arab translation and adaptation of an earlier Persian work entitled *Hazár Afsánah* (A thousand tales). There is still much argument as to the absolute original versions of this work. Mohammed-ibn-Ishak long ago claimed that the book was written by or for Humai, daughter of Bahman Ishak, whose mother, according to Al-Masudi, was the Jewish Esther of Hebrew Bible history. The various translators of the book all take different views. Edward Lane, who translated the work in 1838–40, maintained that the original was essentially Arab and more especially Egyptian, adding that judging from the descriptions in the book it was begun not earlier than 1475 and finished not later than 1525. Sir Richard Burton, whose translation in English best maintains the atmosphere of the book as well as keeps faithfully to the text, gave his opinion that some of the tales may have been written in the reign of the Caliph Al-Mansur (754–75), arguing that stories had been collected over a lengthy period to be added to the original, even as late as the sixteenth century.

Lane's work, while admirable, was really adapted for household consumption in the somewhat puritanical Victorian era; his version was adapted for children's reading. There had been a French translation by Antoine Galland as early as 1704–17, but this was designed for popular reading, as a result of which much of the original was toned down. Burton published his work privately in a sixteen-volume edition (1885–88). David Shumaker, who wrote a foreword to his edited selection to *Tales from the Arabian Nights*,[8] has stated that Burton's translation is "the definitive rendering of the *Nights* into English for its exceptional accuracy, masculine vitality and literary discernment, and still brooks no competition."[9]

Though the background to the *Arabian Nights* stories are generally well-known, it will perhaps be helpful to examine it again. King Shahyrar, angered almost to the point of madness by his wife's infidelity, not only executes her but decides to continue a vendetta against all women. He takes a beautiful girl night after night, sleeps with her and then orders her to be beheaded the very next morning. Then he brings to his bed Scheherazade, the daughter of his vizier. Having heard that the king likes nothing better than to be told stories late at night, she finds a way of staying his hand from making the usual dire sentence. She tells him a story right up to the exciting climax. He begs her to finish it to the last detail, and she promises to do so the following night. Thus she is spared, and so the process is carried on night after night until one thousand and one nights, after which the king is cured of his insane hatred of women. Out of her stories have come such delights as Ali Baba and the Forty Thieves and Aladdin and his Wonderful Lamp.

Some of these tales are told in a particularly salacious vein, as for instance when King Shah Zaman spies on the activities of the wife of another king and her attendants:

> Ten of them were women, concubines of the King, and the other ten were white slaves. Then they all paired off, each with each: but the Queen, who was left alone, presently cried out in a loud voice, "Here to me, O my lord Saeed!" and then sprang with a drop-leap a big slobbering man with rolling eyes which showed the whites. . . . He walked boldly up to her and threw his arms round her neck while she embraced him as warmly; then he bussed her and winding his legs round hers, as a button-loop clasps a button, he threw her and enjoyed her. Likewise did the other slaves with the girls till all had satisfied their passions, and they ceased not from kissing and clipping, coupling and carousing till day began to wane.

Naturally it was with tales of this type that Scheherazade was able to excite the king and work up to a climax at the end of the night, or as dawn was approaching. She tells how in one story there is the prospect of splendid things in "a saloon with seven doors, floored with part-colored marbles and furnished with curtains and hangings of colored silks . . . around the saloon were latticed windows overlooking a garden full of all manner of fruits . . . a jetting fountain at whose corners stood birds fashioned in red gold crusted with pearls and gems and spouting water clear. When I entered and took a seat. . . ." Here Scheherazade looks up, having "perceived the dawn of day and ceased saying her permitted say." Until the following night, of course!

The next night she continues with the story, telling how a young merchant is suddenly greeted in the saloon by a lady "crowned with a diadem of pearls and jewels; her face dotted with artificial moles in indigo, her eyebrows penciled with kohl and her hands and feet reddened with henna. When she saw me she smiled in my face and took me to her embrace and clasped me to her breast; then she put her mouth to my mouth and sucked my tongue (and I did likewise)."

Frequently these ancient Arabs seemed to have gone to excessive lengths in both describing a woman's beauty and at the same time trying to win her over. There was this story by Shaykh Nefzawi about an Arab in love with

> a woman who was all grace and perfection, beautiful of shape, and gifted with all imaginable charms. . . . Her cheeks were like roses, her forehead lily white, her lips like coral; she had teeth like pearls and breasts like pomegranates. Her mouth opened round like a ring; her tongue seemed to be incrusted with precious gems; her eyes, black and finely slit, had the languor of slumber, and her voice the sweetness of sugar. With her form pleasantly filled out, her flesh was mellow like fresh butter, and pure as the diamond. As to her vulva, it was white, prominent, round as an arch, the center of it was red, and breathed fire, without a trace of humidity; for, sweet to the touch, it was quite dry. When she walked it showed in relief like a dome or an inverted cup. In reclining it was visible between her thighs, looking like a lid couched in a hillock.

But while this Arab had great success with most other women, the one who was "all grace and perfection" seemed to elude him. When he approached her and made clear his desires, she recited to him the following verse:

> Among the mountaintops
> I saw a tent placed firmly,
> Apparent to all eyes high up in midair.
> But, oh! the pole that held it up was gone.
> And like a vase without a handle it remained,
> With all its cords undone, its center sinking in,
> Forming a hollow like that of a kettle.

The meaning of this poetic venture was lost upon the lovelorn Arab. He made other advances to her, but always she replied with the same verse. Baffled as to what she meant, the disappointed lover sought scholar after scholar to find the right interpretation. Eventually one scholar, named Abou Nouass (his real name was Abou Ali Hacene), accurately interpreted this verse. He explained that what the delectable woman most feared was that the man who doted on her might have "a member of small dimensions." Having been reassured that this was not the case, the interpreter went on to say that the "tent" in the verse represented a large vulva, placed well forward, while the "mountains" between which it arose were the thighs. The disappearance of the "pole" that held it up meant that her husband had left her "like a vase without a handle" (which meant that she was totally neglected) and "the cords are undone and its center is sinking in," revealing that she could no longer be happy. But it was in the last phrase, "forming a hollow like that of a kettle," that the woman compared her vulva to a kettle that is used to prepare an Arabian dish known as *tserid*. The fullest interpretation is given in Burton's translation of *The Perfumed Garden*:

> If the *tserid* is placed in the kettle, to turn out well it must be stirred by means of a *medeleuk* [a large wooden spoon] long and solid, whilst the kettle is steadied by the feet and hands. Only in that way can it be properly prepared. It cannot be done with a small spoon; the cook would burn her hands owing to the shortness of the handle, and the dish would not be well prepared. This is the symbol of this woman's nature. O Djoaid, if your member has not the dimensions of a respectable *medeleuk* . . . it will not give her satisfaction. . . . Finally, if you let her consume herself by her own fire, like the bottom of the kettle, which gets burnt if the *medeleuk* is not stirred upon it, you will not gratify her desire by the result.

But this was not all the advice the Arab was given. He was told to return to the woman and recite to her:

> Have patience now, O Fadehat el Djemal,
> I understand your verses and shall obey them.
> O Apple of my Eye, you thought I was embarrassed
> About the answer which I had to give you.
> Yes, certainly it was the love I bore you
> Made me look foolish in the eyes of all you know.
> . . . No other member is like mine? Here, see it, measure it!
> . . . Now kindly put it in your tent,
> Which is between the well-known mountains placed.
> It will be quite at home there, you will find it
> Not softening while inside, but sticking like a nail;
> Take it to form a handle to your vase.
> . . . If you but want a proper *medeleuk*,

A *medeleuk* to use between your thighs,
Take this to stir the center of your kettle.
It will do you good, O mistress mine!
Your kettle, be it plated, will be satisfied.

As a result of this poetic approach to lovemaking and seduction, there are more names for the sexual organs in Arabic than in any other language in the world. There are thirty-five different names for the male sexual organ and thirty-eight for the female one, each representing a different descriptive meaning. Apart from *el kamara*, which is a straightforward translation of the word *penis*, there are such variations as *el hammache* (the exciter), *el naasee* (the sleeper) and *el atsar* (the stumbler). The female variations range from *el feurdi* (the slit) and *el neufflah* (the one that swells) to *abou djebaha* (the one with a projection) and *el mokaour* (the bottomless).

While the Crusaders, when they returned home, undoubtedly brought back with them some new versions of lovemaking, it is doubtful whether they absorbed much Arabian or other literature. Curiously enough it was a Jew who was largely responsible for providing the latter. He was Petrus Alfonsi, a name he took when he converted to Christianity in 1106. He then brought out his own collection of tales from the Middle East (some of them concerning love affairs) under the title of *Disciplina Clericalis*. Some of the tales he collected were from Sanskrit collections such as *Hitopadesa* (Friendly counsel) and most of them were supposed to have a moral purpose even if only to warn men about the tricks of deception practiced by some women. Petrus Alfonsi's work was extremely popular and soon circulated widely all over Europe where other authors, notably Boccacio, borrowed from them. Yet another source into which European travelers and authors dipped in early times was an erotic work in Sanskrit entitled *Pleasures of Women*.

Finally, it is essential to take a look at the contribution made by China to erotic literature down the years. It must be remembered that records show that the first Chinese dictionary was produced in 1100 B.C. and Chinese poems were recorded as far back as 800 B.C. No fewer than forty thousand characters were recorded in this first Chinese dictionary. In Chinese calligraphy there was always a tradition that it must be beautiful, or at least attractive to the reader. In his book, *Chinese Calligraphy*, Chiang Yee writes: "The aesthetic of Chinese calligraphy is simply this: that a beautiful form should be beautifully executed." He goes on to tell how affection for the written word is instilled from childhood in the Chinese heart:

> We are taught never to tear up a sheet of paper of writing, nor to misuse any paper with writing upon it, even if it is of no practical use. In every district of a Chinese city, and even in the smallest

village, there is a little pagoda built for the burning of wastepaper bearing writing. . . . For we respect characters [i.e., writing] so highly that we cannot bear them to be trampled underfoot or thrown away in some distasteful place.[10]

Hence the Chinese emphasis on the fact that literary art is essentially something that rises spontaneously from an artistic temperament. Not for them the rules and guidance for sexual enjoyment as laid down by the Arabs and some others. Lin Yutang, that greatest of modern Chinese philosophers, said that "what is good and what is bad taste in the art of love between husband and wife in the intimacy of their bedroom is not something prescribed by rules."[11]

Nevertheless Chinese writers down the ages have frequently written reminiscences of their married lives. Lin Yutang cites three such works, which can best be described as happily erotic—Mao Pichiang's *Reminiscences of My Concubine,* Shen Sanpo's *Six Chapters of a Floating Life,* and Chiang T'an's *Reminiscences under the Lamplight.* One important point made by Lin Yutang (and this applies to a certain extent to other translations, but especially to those from Chinese) is that "one is often forced to write bad English in trying to express such Chinese aesthetic ideas or notions, as for example 'singing the wind,' 'pacing the moonlight' or 'pillowing water.'" He explains how many variations there are of the Chinese word *yi,* which means romantic and detached from life. One can be *ch'ingyi* (pure and romantic), *kaoyi* (high and romantic), or *k'uangyi* (expansive and romantic).[12]

Nevertheless on various occasions in Chinese history emperors have ordered the banning and even the burning of books, including those of Confucius. Occasionally some of those banned were erotic, such as the poems of Tschoen Koeng Ise, which touched on historical scandals. One of the most celebrated of the early erotic stories of China was *Chin P'ing Mei* (Metal vase plum blossom), a lengthy novel from the pen of a Confucian scholar, Wang Shih-cheng, in the sixteenth century. This work was enjoyed by countless readers for centuries despite the fact that until 1912 anyone doing so risked the penalty of a hundred-lash flogging.[13]

Chin P'ing Mei is the story of one Hsi Men and his six wives, of whom the wiliest is the Golden Lotus. It is erotic most especially in the instances it gives of voyeurism, descriptions of rather unique and eccentric amorous intrigues interspersed with occasional commentaries in verse. It is said that the author, Wang Shih-cheng (see A–Z section) wrote the work as a satirical and skittish comment, cleverly disguised as fiction, on the activities of one of his acquaintances. It may well be that this led to the work's being banned, first by hiding the manuscript, and then, when it was rediscovered a hundred years later and printed, again being banned because it still reflected real life too accurately.

Wang Shih-cheng did not indulge in the reticence of some Western writers of amatory escapades: he described all such activities in the plainest of language, elegant though this was, and as a result some translators of his work have been so embarrassed (unnecessarily, one feels) that they have actually put certain parts of the work into Latin, probably to avoid any risk of prosecution for obscenity. Here is an example:

> At dawn, Golden Lotus and Hsi-mên Ch'ing awoke. Golden Lotus saw that his weapon was still upright like a ramrod. "Darling," she said, "you must forgive me, but I can stand no more. *Tibi mentulam sugam.*"
>
> "*Suge,*" inquit Hsi-mên; "*si mollire poteris, bene erit.*"

Such mingling of Latin and English is fairly frequent in the translations. What is most impressive about *Chin P'ing Mei*, however, is that, despite the enormous length of the work, there is no verbosity; the story is even economically carried on without its being cluttered up with unnecessary detail and the same applies to the charming verses. Perhaps one of the best comments made on the work is that by Cordier in his *Bibliotheca Sinica:* he says of *Chin P'ing Mei* that "in it there is set before us a whole company of men and women in all the different relationships that arise in social life, and we see them pass successively through all the situations which civilized human beings can pass. The translation of such a book would render superfluous any other book upon the manners of the Chinese."

In recent times this early Chinese novel has been highly rated both in the East and the West, so much so in the former that at some date in the last century a secret society named the Golden Lotus was founded (See Glossary: GOLDEN LOTUS SOCIETY). As far as can be told the aim of this society seems to have been to propagate the idea that love should be considered the highest form of art and that members should live up to this ideal. It also set out to encourage love in all its more uninhibited and erotic forms and the idea of its being a secret society was to make love seem more romantic.

This society is referred to in the case histories of Charles Babbage, the eminent Victorian mathematician and cryptographer. Babbage, many of whose cryptological translations have been bequeathed to the British Museum, spent a great deal of time working out coded love messages, even though his interest was mathematical. When a barrister was faced with the problem of coded love messages in a divorce case (and these were quite numerous in that period), Babbage was usually asked to solve the cipher key used.[14]

Mr. F. J. Jamieson, of Hong Kong, has contributed this intriguing story:

> One of Babbage's missions is not referred to in the paper he bequeathed to the British Museum. This concerned a young Chinese

lady of a wealthy and cultured family, who had been conducting a secret affair with a young Englishman. She had written long letters to him in a code based on numbers. There would not seem to be any trace of the Englishman's letters, but only those of the Chinese girl's. For well over a hundred years these letters must have remained in the hands of a Chinese lawyer. They were only discovered a few years ago when files were being destroyed.

The letters, as translated, are certainly reminiscent of some passages in *Chin P'ing Mei* and for this reason are worth quoting. There are some lengthy descriptions of sexual practices that sound more acrobatic than erotic:

My legs seemed to be where my arms should be and my lips were everywhere they should not be, as that is how you made it all happen. . . . You really must not do this again; . . . it is not amusing or gratifying; . . . my head aches and my eyes go round and round so that I do not know where I am. . . . It is love on the [verge?] of madness. What we did last week at the same hour was much, much more, how do you say, enchanting? No, that is not the word; perhaps it should be endearing. Let us climb down out of the clouds and be content to make love more gently, slowly, so that we can still make love and whisper to each other at one and the same time.

Nonetheless, this young lady member of the Golden Lotus Society was not always as demure as she sounds. It is clear that certain words she used were not translated, presumably to spare the family's feelings, but possibly because they could not be interpreted.

Do you remember next time to keep whispering to me, whispering all those lovely, musical, naughty words which you have made up. I also want to hear you say, as we say in the Golden Lotus ritual "I will kiss you from my lips to your 4571 and then tenderly on 93270. Oh, for you to tell me of 0001 and 0002 and to keep whispering such wickedness—that is sweet to hear while I make tea for you."

Much of this goes back to *I Ching* and the ancient Taoist books on lovemaking. It is perhaps unfortunate that the illustrations to the latter have now all disappeared, but the texts show how to achieve the maximum of pleasure in various postures that are given such names as "the fluttering of butterflies," "the galloping charger," "the union of kingfishers," "the cat and mouse in the same hole," and "the wailing monkey embracing a tree." There was always a hint in this double-talk about sexual intercourse of perfect love leading to longevity, suggesting that it reflected the harmony of heaven and earth. The Taoist doctrine was that men needed to absorb a great deal of yin to conserve their own yang.

The beauty of Wu offers wine.
The beauty of Wu is fifteen years old and her hair floats in the
   breeze;
Her cup of jade invites the guest to savor the wine from the
   grape.[15]

This poem by an eighteenth-century Chinese poet gives yet another clue to the Chinese use of attractive symbols in sexual matters. Jade is regarded in China as the most precious of stones. Thus "the cup of jade" refers to the female genitals: sometimes they are known as "the gateway of jade." A man's penis is called "the flute of jade" with the suggestion that this is something that can be manipulated by fingers or lips.

Another Chinese erotic novel recently published by the Olympia Press in Paris was Wu Wu Meng's *Houses of Joy*, as it is called in English. This is a modern retelling of a Chinese erotic classic from a woman's point of view. Equally important is Eric Chou's *The Dragon and the Phoenix*, a candid description of the philosophy (yes, it is actually called thus) and practices of Chinese sex and love.[16]

Arthur Waley, an excellent translator of both Chinese and Japanese classics of this genre, produced his own version of *Chin P'ing Mei*, together with an introduction to the subject, in London in 1962. This was entitled *The Mandarin and His Six Wives*. He has also translated the tenth-century Japanese diary entitled *The Pillow Book of Sei Shonagon*, London, 1960. This last-named work was originally entitled *Makurano-Soshi*, written by Sei Shonagon, a female author who set out her thoughts and experiences in the Japanese Imperial Court. It was the first recorded example of *zuihitsu*, in which a writer sets out unconnected thoughts and ideas, *zuihitsu* being very much an ancient Japanese form of diary writing (See SEI SHONAGON in A–Z section).

Japanese art and literature have always been deeply concerned with the acts of love, and it must be remembered that phallic worship was an essential part of the Shinto religion. Giant models of phalluses, known as the August Celestial Pillar, were carried in Shinto processions. The Japanese god of love, Aizen Myoo, was said to teach that love was sacred because it developed from the sublimation of self to enlightenment. However, the Japanese tended to put most of their ideas, practices, and theories about love into paintings and sketches rather than prose or verse. Such works became known in the early eighteenth century as *Ukiyo-e* (pictures of the floating world), often with the suggestion that making love was like floating through paradise.

One of the world's earliest novels was recorded in A.D. 1004 in Japan. It was *Genji Monogatari* by Murasaki Shikibu, another Japanese woman author. Japanese literature has, in fact, as long a history of interest and solid achievement as any other literature, though it has only been in comparatively recent times that translations have been made available. In the eighth century AD there was the *Manyoshu* (Anthology of ten thousand leaves), which includes some exquisite poems about the beauties of nature and love. Lady Murasaki was a figure at the Imperial Court and her enormous tome of a novel has been compared to the work of Proust. A translation of *The Tale of Genji* (as it has been renamed in English) was published in 1976, being the really splendid adaptation by Edward Seidensticker (See MURASAKI, SHIKIBO, A–Z section).

3

Courtly and Medieval
Forms of Love

With the arrival of the Middle Ages concepts of love varied from one extreme to the other. On the one hand there was the condemnation of the Church on various forms of sexual intercourse and the creation of a list of prohibited literature. The Index Librorum Prohibitorum, vel Expurgandorum was established in 405 by Pope Innocent I, and Pope Gelasius drew up a catalogue of forbidden works. The first full Roman Index was issued by Pope Pius IV in 1557–59. Roman Catholics were ordered not to read any of these titles, while in the same period St. Jerome affirmed that all sexual intercourse, even inside marriage, was a sin unless it was for the purpose of procreation.

Despite this, as the Middle Ages developed, reactions to such extremism produced happier alternatives. It was soon evident even in devout Catholic circles that a blind eye was turned to many of the decrees of the day and the gap between antisexual principles and sexual practices was very wide and not effectively bridged by the confessional or anything else. As will be seen in the A–Z section a number of writers of erotic works were priests and prelates. The so-called Age of Chivalry related chiefly to the continent of Europe and it was here around 1170 that the traditions of what became known as Courtly Love were established. Erotic literature inevitably sprang out of this.

Languedoc is said to have been where Courtly Love started and Troubadour poetry, the verses of the itinerant minstrels, soon followed. Bernart de Ventadorn said that "the Troubadours took the view that no man is worth aught without love." From such a statement one can deduce that the importance of love was then paramount, at least in what can be called the upper circles of humanity. It was turned into a kind of religion, no doubt to make it seem highly respectable in view of the Church's attitude toward sexual intercourse.

"The sentiment," wrote C. S. Lewis, in explaining what Courtly Love was all about, "is love, but love of a highly specialized sort, whose characteristics may be enumerated as Humility, Courtesy, Adultery, and the Religion of Love. The lover is always abject. Obedience to his lady's lightest wish, however whimsical, and silent acquiescence in her rebukes, however unjust, are the only virtues he dares to claim."[1]

Out of all this a new kind of literature and poetry was created. There was the Provençal Love Song, the love poetry of the later Middle Ages and such works as *The Roman de la Rose* by Guillaume de Lorris and all the many writings of Andreas Capellanus. In England, at the court and at the stately homes of the aristocracy, the minstrels and the dance fulfilled the role undertaken by the Troubadours on the continent. The spirit of this is summed up by the English poet, Stephen Hawes, in his *The Passetyme of Pleasure*, presumably written while he was working at the court of Henry VII:

> She commanded her mynstreeles ryght to play
> *Mamours*, the swete and the gentyll daunce.
> With La Belle Pucell, that was fayre and gaye,
> She me recommanded with all pleasaunce
> To daunce true mesures without varyance.
> O Lorde God! how glad then was I
> So for to daunce with my swete lady!—
> For the fire kyndled and waxed more and more,
> The dauncing blewe it with her beauty clere.
> My hert sekend and began waxe sore
> A mynute six hourse and six houres a yere
> I thought it was.[2]

Capellanus was of course the chief exponent in his writings of the theme of Courtly Love. In fact, his work, *De Amore Libri Tres*, was more or less a manual on the whole subject (See Capellanus, Andreas, in the A–Z section). Here again the attempt was made to present love as a religion, even parallel to real religion. In *De Arte Honeste Amandi* Capellanus gives the picture of a lady pleading to be excused from making love on the quite reasonable grounds that she does not feel able to return her lover's feelings. To which the lover somewhat indignantly replies: "If that is the case, then a sinner might plead to be excused on the grounds that God had not given him grace." The lady replies that just as "charity cannot merit eternal bliss, so it will be unavailing to serve Love with love in the heart."

For a long time love was wrapped up in this somewhat tedious exchange of conversation both in real life Courtly Love and in the literature of the day. Giovanni Boccacio improved on this in the *Decameron* (1353), a collection of one-hundred stories, allegedly told among a group of young people in an abandoned villa in a mere ten days. According to what little information has been handed down about this meeting, those involved had fled from Florence on account of a severe outbreak of plague.

With Boccacio one begins to escape from medieval allegory into Renaissance-style allegory. Nevertheless much of his work lacks something of the splendor of medieval romance: Boccacio was a cynic and this shows in his frequent contempt for women. In the Middle Ages this contempt was whipped up by encouraging many ridiculous fantasies in the minds of men. Sometimes these fantasies were conjured up by suspicious husbands and lovers, at others cunningly planted by some of the priesthood. Some of these fantasies took the form of people claiming they were visited during the night by supernatural beings. Occasionally such claims were made in stories and poems, at others they came equally from men and women. The so-called supernatural being was known as an incubus or a succubus. Chaucer claimed that incubi had been heard of less since the limitours (wandering priests) appeared on the scene, suggesting that the latter pleasured the women when their husbands were away:

> For there as wont to walken was an elf
> There walketh now the limitour himself.
> Women may now go safely up and down
> In every bush and under every tree.
> There is no other incubus than he.

France, Germany, and Italy produced a number of poets and writers of erotic themes in the Middle Ages with whom in England only Chaucer and perhaps John Skelton can compare. In France Rabelais was the most outstanding, not least because he brought the common touch to his writing. Like Chaucer his appeal went to the masses as much as the courtiers. Indeed, in the prologue to the first book of the life of Gargantua, he says: "Most noble and illustrious drinkers, and you thrice precious pockified blades, for you and none else do I dedicate my writings." Rabelais may be salacious, but it is all done with a keen sense not just of humor, but of the absurd. In Italy there were rather more writers of this genre in the Middle Ages than in any other country. Apart from Boccacio, Aretino, Masuccio Salernitano, Francesco Strapparola, Angelo Poliziano, Poggio Bracciolini, and Antonio Beccatelli come to mind. Germany produced such writers later. Johannes Bruerinus was the sixteenth-century author of *De Re Cibaria*, which refers to the custom in Germany and Austria in this period of making bread and pastries in phallic and other erotic forms. Another German author was J. Hartlieb who in about 1550 published in Worms a work in Latin entitled *The Faithfulness of Harlots in Respect of Their Lovers*. Two erotic German poets of the seventeenth century were Paul Fleming and Hofmann von Hofmannswaldau.[3]

Occasionally in this era there was a writer who produced something based on experiences in the Arab world. One such was Moses Ben Maimon, who lived in the twelfth century. A native of Córdoba, this Hebrew scholar, whether because he was a Jew, or for some other reason, was compelled to leave Spain and seek a livelihood elsewhere. This he did, first in Morocco, then in Egypt. His work was translated from Arabic into Hebrew and then Latin. One of his essays on the subject of love entitled *Fi' l-jima* was translated into English and published in New York in 1961.

The Courts of Love, as the medieval custom of courtly love pronounced, played a considerable part in molding French attitudes in love affairs and to what today is called the traditional French gallantry among males. Many of the knights of ancient times devoted themselves to the service of a lady they knew only by name. In a somewhat peculiar sense this was almost the origin of the blind date. Some knights would purchase stockings for their own use and request their mistresses to wear them for a few days, by way of consecration, before they wore them themselves. This particular custom was entirely borrowed from the song of a troubadour. Again and again, when it came to the Courts of Love making their adjudications, reference would be made by the court to some writer or poet who had touched on the subject under discussion. These Courts decided all points of etiquette in gallantry, sometimes trivial and rather absurd posers, as well as settling the terms to be made use of by lovers or knights-errant to their mistresses and occasionally even between husbands and wives. Such Courts actually had the authority to arbitrate between married couples.[4]

In England the emphasis in eroticism was very much more on the common touch, and whether in verse or prose the appeal was to the masses. This was not merely the case with the immortal Chaucer, but with Skelton and many other minor writers as well. Frequently, too, there would be the feeling that lovemaking was something to joke about as much as anything else. The continental idea of courtly love never appealed to the English. What sprang up in England in the Middle Ages was a literary custom that has lasted until today— the naughtily erotic story. One example from an anonymous source—though strongly suspected to be by one Andrew Borde, medieval author of a work called *The Jests of Scoggin*—is as follows:

> When Scoggin was thus commanded [to go abroad] by the king, he got him into France into the French king's court, and there he jested. And first there was a gentleman which made a gentlewoman the promise to go to her bed at nine o'clock at night; he did promise to come to her chamber-door and would scrape and scratch at the door like a dog and would whine. Scoggin, hearing this bargain, before nine o'clock came to her door and scraped with his nails, and

did whine like a dog. Then the gentlewoman did rise and let him in.

Within a little while after, the gentleman did come and scrape and whine at the door like a dog. Scoggin arose and went to the door and said: "Arrrh, Arrrh" like another dog. And after that the French gentlewoman did love an Englishman. Wherefore in such matters let a man make nobody of his counsel lest he be deceived.[5]

It was in this period, too, that the short, terse, and wittily erotic story made its appearance in England in particular. The Scoggin story just told was a partial example of this: the same story told by a continental would probably have been extended to about four times or even longer. A collection of many of these extremely short stories (not all of them erotic, however) was contained in a book published in 1639 entitled *Conceits, Clinches, Flashes, and Whimzies*. Nearly all of these contained stories that were often more crude than funny, as for example the one about Sergeant Atthow's wife: "A woman of great boldness and audacity, the first time that ever she saw Sir John Pooly, at a great meeting, before all, proferred him to teach him an excellent way how to kiss a woman without ruffling her ruff. He desiring to know how, she told him he must set her on her head and kiss her arse."[6]

Even in the valleys of the sparsely populated Wales of that period erotic poetry flourished, as has been recently researched by Dr. Dafydd Johnston of the Department of Welsh at Cardiff University. In his book *Medieval Welsh Erotic Poetry*, Cardiff, 1991, Dr. Johnston has revealed a wealth of such verse the existence of which, except for a few scholars, nobody had previously heard. Those who had known about the poems had kept silent because, prudishly, they had regarded the works as something of an embarrassment to Wales. The poems are written in what can only be described as metrical perfection and some of them are by the greatest of all Welsh poets, Dafydd ap Gwilym. Perhaps it was because of the titles alone of some of his verses that former Welsh scholars kept quiet about them: such poems include "The Penis," "The Poet Sends His Genitals as a Love Messenger," and "Deer Coupling."[7]

These Welsh poems are much more explicit than anything written by Chaucer or Skelton, and some of the words used (especially those describing physical details) have so puzzled the editor that he has had to depend upon informed but imaginative guesswork in his translations. Dr. Johnston says he discovered the erotic poems of Dafydd ap Gwilym while working on medieval poetry: "What really startled me was the suppression involved. The poem ["The Penis"] is there in the earliest of all manuscripts, dating from the sixteenth century, where a Renaissance scholar dutifully copied it and then crossed out each line—only he didn't cross them out well enough. But this allowed modern scholars to claim it wasn't part of the poet's work, which just isn't true."[8]

There was even a female erotic poet among these medieval Welsh writers, certainly a rarity at that time. She was Gwerful Mechain (see A–Z section) and, as Dr. Johnston points out, she helps to confirm that "poetry was a national preoccupation in medieval Wales." His studies revealed that some of those early Welsh poems were satires on such European conventions as courtly love and that the women in these verses were randier than the men. During 1989 Dr. Johnston was able to lecture on Welsh erotic verse at the Celtic Congress in Los Angeles.

In the sixteenth and seventeenth centuries there was a wealth of erotic literature in Europe, much of it in the form of lengthy series of short stories. Apart from the true-life tales of that amorous adventurer, Giacomo Casanova, there were *Les Cent Nouvelles Nouvelles,* attributed to King Louis XI of France, the *Heptameron, ou Histoire des Amantes Fortunes* of Queen Marguerite d'Angoulême of Navarre, and the Abbé Prévost's story of *Manon Lescaut.*

King Louis's work was translated into English in 1899 by a British publisher specializing in erotic works, one Charles Carrington who operated in Paris. He gave his translation the lengthy title of *One Hundred Merrie and Delightsome Stories Right Pleasaunt to Relate in All Goodly Companie by Way of Joyance and Jollity.* Carrington used a secret press in Paris for his publishing, presumably to avoid trouble that could have beset him had he operated in London. In France he was described in the press as *"l'éditeur sublime des oeuvres érotique."*

There is, however, no real proof that King Louis wrote these stories either when he was king or earlier as Prince Louis. It does seem that many, if not all of the stories are based on actual incidents. One of the tales in *Les Cent Nouvelles Nouvelles,* entitled *The Reverse of the Medal,* is said by some French historians to be an account of an incident in the career of Louis, duke of Orleans. A notorious seducer of his friends' wives, the duke was nearly caught out when the husband of the woman he was secreting in his bed knocked at his door. The duke covered the woman's face with a sheet and called out to the husband to enter. In *Les Cents Nouvelles Nouvelles* this tale is told as follows:

> "Ha!" said the husband, "Master whoremonger, you have well hidden from me this good cheer; but, by my faith, though I was not at the feast, you must show me the bride."

The duke declined to allow the husband to see the face of the woman in his bed, but according to the book, "a most gracious proposal was made to him, . . . that he should be shown the backside of his wife and her haunches and thighs . . . without uncovering and beholding her face." It must have been a narrow escape both for the duke and the lady in his bed.

As for *Manon Lescaut*—along with *Aucassin et Nicolette,* and *Anna Karenina*—it remains one of the classical love stories of all time as so elegantly told by the Abbé Prévost using the Chevalier des Grieux as the narrator. There is nothing else to compare with it except perhaps that most lyrical and lovely of all early French romances, *Aucassin et Nicolette*. This is preserved for posterity in a single copy in the National Library of Paris. The author and date of this *chantefable* are alike unknown, though some authorities suggest it might date back as early as the twelfth century. It is written in the dialect of Picardy, though the setting of the story is Provence. There is that plea of Aucassin's:

> Little Star I gaze upon
> Sweetly drawing on the moon,
> In such golden haunt is set
> Love, and bright-haired Nicolette.

Sometimes the gentler romanticism of Aucassin and Nicolette is just as erotic as anything in the decidedly more erotic *Manon Lescaut*.

In a number of his plays Shakespeare dealt with the emotional and erotic weaknesses of his characters, almost analyzing some of them while putting words into their mouths. In *King Lear* the king in his madness gives a speech filled with erotic symbolism. The nurse in *Romeo and Juliet* mixes the bawdy with the erotic in her talk, as, for example, when talking of what her husband said when Juliet as a child fell on her face:

"And then my husband—God be with his soul! / . . . A merry man—took up the child: 'Yea,' quoth he, 'dost thou fall upon thy face? / Thou wilt fall backward when thou hast more wit; / Wilt thou not, Jule?' and, by my halidome, / The pretty wench left crying, and said—'Ay.' / To see, now, how a jest shall come about! / I warrant, an I should live a thousand years, / I never should forget it: 'Wilt thou not, Jule?' quoth he."

Some may claim that such prattle as Juliet's nurse keeps pouring out is irrelevant; in fact, it is such little details as these, which reveal that sense of the common touch, the realistic vernacular of everyday life, that make Shakespeare the outstanding dramatist of his time. C. S. Lewis in his *Allegory of Love* says "People find a 'likeness' or 'truth' to life in Shakespeare because the persons, passions and events which we meet in his plays are like those which we meet in our own lives." This tendency is revealed just as much in his various amatory sonnets as in his plays. One cannot imagine Spenser, that great romantic, making a lengthy poem out of the rape of Lucrece, but Shakespeare did. In a stanza from *The Rape of Lucrece* he conjures up the horrors of rape in a very realistic manner:

> His hand, that yet remains upon her breast,—
> (Rude ram, to batter such an ivory wall!)—
> May feel her heart—poor citizen—distress'd,

Wounding itself to death, rise up and fall,
Beating her bulk, that his hand shakes withal.
This moves in him more rage and lesser pity
To make the breach and enter this sweet city.

As to the identity of the "Dark Lady," to whom he wrote such a passionate sonnet, all one can say is that this is still not satisfactorily resolved. A. L. Rowse, the most recent scholar to have tackled this subject in great detail, declares with what seems like certainty that she was Emilia Lanier, née Bassano, mistress of the Lord Chamberlain. Yet there is no positive evidence that Shakespeare ever knew her. Others have claimed that the Dark Lady was none other than Mary Fitton, but portraits of her show blonde not dark hair. There is as much argument about the identity of the Dark Lady as there is of "Mr. W. H." of Shakespeare's sonnets. Some say he was the young Lord Herbert, Dr. Rowse claims that he was Sir William Hervey. Matthew Arnold wrote: "The true identities of young 'Mr. W. H.' and 'The Dark Lady' may never be known. But it is beyond doubt that William Shakespeare loved both the good-looking young man and the dark beauty to whom he addressed these sonnets . . . and that, probably, his love was more constant than was theirs."

The truth is not so much that modern scholars love to argue over who is "Mr. W. H." and whether the Dark Lady is a male or female, but that Shakespeare's sonnets still entrance as much in the twentieth century as they did in his own time. Or, as George Saintsbury put it: "Shakespeare has here caught up the sum of love and uttered it as no poet has before or since, and . . . in so doing he carried poetry—that is to say, the passionate expression in verse of the sensual and intellectual facts of life—to a pitch which it has never previously reached in English, and which it has never outstretched since."[9]

In the sonnets Shakespeare is able at last to use the first person, to put forward his own thoughts. At times he puzzles the reader, as for example in a verse such as this:

Two loves I have of comfort and despair,
Which like two spirits do suggest me still;
The better angel is a man right fair,
The worser spirit a woman colored ill.
To win me soon to hell, my female evil,
Tempteth my better angel from my side,
And would corrupt my saint to be a devil.

A major theme of the sonnets is sexual infatuation, as much the pain of it as the pleasure. Infatuation always poses riddles because it is never easy to understand, least of all to the individual overcome by it. Perhaps the wisest thing written about all these Shakespearian puzzles and riddles is the comment of Stephen Booth, editor of the Yale edition of the sonnets. In an appendix to this work he writes: "Homosexuality: William Shakespeare was almost certainly homosexual, bisexual, or heterosexual. The Sonnets provide no evidence on the matter."

British ballads from all parts of the United Kingdom have been noted for their lusty epics down the ages and none perhaps are so rich in eroticism as the *Roxburghe Ballads*, a collection of verses that is to be found in its original form in the British Museum. This collection started with the foundation in 1812 of the Roxburghe Club, an association of bibliophiles that undertook to print rare works or manuscripts as well as to preserve the originals. The club was named after John, duke of Roxburghe, a celebrated collector of ancient literature, who lived from 1740–1804. This club was the forerunner of various printing societies such as the Camden, Chetham, Percy, and Wharton in England, the Abbotsford, Bannatyne, and Maitland in Scotland, and the Celtic Society in Ireland.

Perhaps the most popular of the *Roxburghe Ballads* is the one addressed to "The Coy Shepherdess," which tells of the shepherd who comes across "Fair Phyllis in a wanton posture" and then "won her love before he went away."[10]

> Hotly he pursued the Game,
> Whilst his heart was on a flame.
> She cry'd Pish nay fye for shame in faith ye shall not do it,
> But the youth her overcame and eagerly fell to it.

Many of the love poems between the fifteenth and seventeenth centuries were known as amorets. The word *amoret* was applied not merely to love poems, but to love songs, love knots, love affairs, and love personified. One finds in Spenser's *Faery Queene* (book 3) a description of a female amoret, which in Spenser's view apparently meant the type of female loveliness that was young, unblemished, beautiful, happy, witty, and good—"soft as a rose, sweet as a violet, chaste as a lily, gentle as a dove, loving everybody and by all beloved."

The poet Thomas Heywood in his work, *Loves Maistresse* (1633), tells "he will be in his amorets and his cansonets, his pastorals and his madrigals." Many of these Elizabethan miscellanies are by unnamed and uncertain authors, and it is not certain whether or not Heywood wrote *A Praise to His Lady*, which is attributed to him.

Gradually there was a new approach to amatory stories, marked above all else by a desire to amuse as well as to intrigue. This reveals itself in all manner of ballads of the period 1500–1700 from those of Roxburghe to the poetry of Herrick and the lengthy poem entitled *The Unfortunate Miller*, the original of which is also in the British Museum. There was also a tendency at this time to use erotic stories as a form of propaganda against what was regarded as religious hypocrisy by some and religious persecution by others. One such book, published in London in 1689 was *A Second Collection of the Newest and Most Ingenious Poems, Satyrs, Songs, etc., against Popery.*

Then, of course, there was the ever-recurring theme of Don Juan that led to his exploitation by all manner of writers from the earlier Italians to Zamora, Molière, Dumas, Mozart, and Byron. Here again was a battle between those who believed in free love and the more repressive of the clergy, even though the latter had had many free lovers in their own ranks. Don Juan, or Don Juan Tenorio to give him his full name, was the son of an illustrious family in Seville. He eloped with the daughter of Comendador Ulloa and from then on his life was filled with scandal after scandal all as a result of his amorous intrigues. Eventually, so the story goes, the Franciscan Fathers enticed him to their monastery and killed him, after which they invented a tale to cover up their crime. The first person to put this tale into writing was Tirso de Molina, a Spaniard. But there is no absolute certainty that Tenorio was the only Don Juan. Some other sources suggest the model for this prototype of seducers was one Don Miguel Mañara Vicentelo de Leca.

Robert Herrick (see A–Z section) was one of the earliest writers to stress in any detail the part played by feminine clothes in arousing men's passions. In a poem entitled *Upon Julia's Clothes* he expresses this to perfection:

> A sweet disorder in the dresse
> Kindles in clothes a wantonnesse:
> A lawne about the shoulders thrown
> Into a fine distraction:
> An erring lace, which here and there
> Enthralls the crimson stomacher:
> A cuff neglectful, and thereby
> Ribbands to flow confusedly:
> A winning wave (deserving note)
> In the tempestuous petticoat:
> A careless shoe-string, in whose tye
> I see a wild civility:
> Do more bewitch me, then when Art
> Is too precise in every part.

Once the oppressive Cromwellian regime ended in England and the monarchy was restored there was an almost predictable flood of erotic poems, plays, songs, and novels. The dramatists in particular concentrated on the more piquant situations in the adulteries and other irregular sexual liaisons of the period. William Congreve in particular introduced poetic ditties into some of his plays such as the one about the soldier and the sailor, the tinker and the tailor squabbling about who should win the affections of a certain maid. This ditty occurs in *Love for Love*. An outstanding writer of comedies and perhaps the wittiest dramatist of his time, Congreve was without a rival, even in an age that included Wycherley and Etheredge. For this reason it would be ridiculous to call him a specialist in eroticism, though he suffered from the attacks of Jeremy Collier on "the immorality and profaneness of the English stage," on which subject he wrote a pamphlet in 1698. His main attack was on Wycherley rather than Congreve.

Toward the end of the seventeenth century there appeared for the first time in English a work similar to some of those instruction books of the Arabs and Hindus. However, it had a much less respectable title, being called *The Whore's Rhetoric*, and consisted of dialogues offering advice on sexual practices to a young whore. The source of this work was Italian. A new edition of *The Whore's Rhetoric* was published in New York in 1961.[11]

Perhaps Sigmund Freud summed up supremely well the psychological need for the changes in the interpretation of eroticism from the era of courtly love and medieval mysticism through the Renaissance period to the latter part of the seventeenth century. Referring to scatological and erotic jokes being published over a wide section of the world, Freud said: "Many of the most admired jokes . . . owe their exhilarating and cheerful effect to the ingenious uncovering of what are as a rule repressed complexes. . . . The jokes, both erotic and of other sorts, which are in popular circulation provide an excellent auxiliary means of investigating the unconscious mind—in the same way as do dreams, myths and legends."[12]

To put this rather more simply, to make jokes of erotic situations, to show the lighter and amusing side of love enabled people to feel freer from restrictions and ridiculous taboos on certain forms of lovemaking, while providing a balance between medieval dreams and what happens in real life. The lessons learned and fully expressed in the latter part of the seventeenth century are just as apt today.

4

The Era of Erotic Memoirs

With the coming of the eighteenth century a new trend in erotic literature developed and it lasted until the early days of the twentieth century. This was the era of erotic memoirs of all kinds. The French and the Italians had to some extent shown a fondness for such works in the sixteenth and seventeenth centuries, but they were generally presented as novels and stories rather than first-person narratives. It was in the English-speaking world that the erotic memoir came to the fore.

Some students of this genre have asserted that it was a Frenchman, however, who encouraged this trend among English writers. The man they quote was none other than Denis Diderot, best known as an encyclopedist, who in his work, *La Religieuse*, described the experiences of the nun Marie Simonin in two convents, a book aimed at exposing what Diderot regarded as the evils of convent life. John Cleland's *Fanny Hill* was one of the most popular works of this kind, but equally avidly read was William Hazlitt's *Liber Amoris*, which described the author's lengthy affair (some might call it a nonaffair) with his landlord's daughter. Jonathan Swift, of course, devoted much time to corresponding with "Stella," otherwise Esther Johnson, a girl he had known since she was nine, and in due course these letters were published.[1]

Sometimes memoirs of this type were genuinely first person, often they were anonymous; occasionally a real-life story would be put over under a false name. An example of the latter was *The Life, Adventures, Intrigues, and Amours of the Celebrated Jeremy Twicher* by one J. Brough in 1770. "Jeremy Twicher" was the nickname given to the earl of Sandwich, a notorious lecher of the period. Anonymous works of the period included *Nocturnal Revels* (1779); *Satan's Harvest Home* (1749); *Memoirs and Adventures of a Flea*, published in London in 1785 and reprinted as *The Autobiography of a Flea* by the Erotica Biblion Society of London and New York in 1901; *The Adventures, Intrigues, and*

Amours of a Lady's Maid (1822); *The Adventures of a King's Page* (circa 1750); and *The Adventures of a Schoolboy* (1866). All were concerned with amorous adventures.

Parallel to this rising tide of memoirs came the beginning of what has been called the Romantic Movement. This started sometime between 1720 and 1790: it is not easy to pin its beginning to within a few years. G. Rattray Taylor in his book, *Sex in History* (1953) claims that the word *romantic* was first used in an approving sense in 1757. Some argue that the movement really started in Germany in the last quarter of the eighteenth century and that its aim was to return to the classical formalism of the past, naming Schiller and Goethe as its sponsors. Curiously, almost cussedly, it was really stimulated in France and England by the French Revolution, with Byron and Shelley paving the way in England and Rousseau and Madame de Staël providing impetus in France.

How did the Romantic movement affect the development of erotic literature? There are those who will deny that the former had any influence on the latter and that what is romantic cannot be erotic. This is, of course, totally wrong. The marriage of romance and eroticism did not take place until late in the nineteenth century. It is worth citing a statement attributed to Anatole France. "A sad prudery reigns over literature," he said, "a prudery more stupid, more cruel, more criminal than the Holy Inquisition. . . . I want Venus from head to foot. Her face is good enough for relations and friends and children, but her body must be ready for caresses. For I hope I am not one of those fools who would limit the lover to a kiss on the face, as if she were a holy relic. Lovers can claim all the unedited places and the first editions, if I may so speak. . . . Love is now my sole and particular study."[2]

In Britain the erotic tendency progressed on much less impassioned and much more robust and humorous lines. The humor was very much like that of juveniles adapted for adults, none more so than in the works of John Wilkes, Charles Churchill, John Hall Stevenson, and Paul Whitehead. Some of this literature sprang up in the various clubs and societies (some of them secret) that were so popular at that time. Members loved telling one another stories and eventually some of these stories found their way into print. There was a myth that England was ruled by clubmen throughout the eighteenth and nineteenth centuries. This was the golden age of the English club, and many of the clubs were of a literary character even if this was enhanced by wining, dining and, in some cases, wenching. To appreciate fully the reasons for this passion for club life one must understand that it marked the birth pangs of the Romantic Movement in Britain. The seventeenth century had been one of bawdry, brawling, and nauseating brutality that not even its veneer of sophisticated manners could disguise. A reaction from this took the form of a passion for style and using one's imagination. The custom of giving the sons of the gentry what was known as "The Grand Tour" to further their education, involving travel to Italy and France, resulted in a passion for romantic love. Yet on their return home they developed this entirely in an English style, using it to fit into their club life. It could be said that most of them only half understood romanticism. They began to organize their devotions to Bacchus and Venus into a club ritual. Formal dinners, with toasts to Bacchus, and sonnets specially composed for the occasion took the place of spontaneous, drunken orgies. Those of the young bloods who had included Turkey in their Grand Tour borrowed ideas of oriental splendor and set up harems for themselves through their clubs. One such was the Divan Club that met at the Thatched Tavern in St. James's Street, London, where members wore daggers and turbans when they dined.

Romantics though some of them were, they had a mania for comparing notes both verbally and by letters and diaries on their sexual escapades and were always giving one another advice. Thus John Wilkes, writing to his friend Charles Churchill,[3] the poet, enjoined him: "you should not fail to make yourself known to Effie when at Tunbridge Wells. By all means mention my name and you will find her both pliant and pliable. She is gifted with a capacity for translating the language of love into a rich, libidinous and ribald phraseology which lends enchantment to her amoristic acrobatics."[4]

There was a tendency for many clubs to copy pagan rituals and react against organized religion. There was a spate of clubs bearing the name "Hell-Fire," chief of which was that known as the Knights of Saint Francis of Wycombe (Sir Francis Dashwood being its leader) which met in caves underneath West Wycombe Hill, Buckinghamshire. It was this club that gave birth to a great deal of erotic outpourings in books and verse, largely because it boasted so many writers among its members. This society was referred to by various titles such as "the Monks of Medmenham," "The Franciscans," "The Order of St. Francis," and "Dashwood's Apostles." Hell-Fire clubs were formed in places as far apart as Edinburgh, Dublin, and Paris, while in 1828 a society modeled on the Franciscans was started at Brasenose College, Oxford.

In 1760 a book appeared with the somewhat obscure title of *Chrysal; or, The Adventures of a Guinea*, by one Charles Johnstone. This purported to give a picture of activities in the so-called Hell-Fire Club, but it is almost certain that Johnstone's information was secondhand and not always reliable. Johnstone was a native of Ireland who in the years between 1760 and 1765 produced the series of books entitled *Chrysal*. In his later volumes of *Chrysal* there was obviously what was intended to be an account of Dashwood's society. Nevertheless, when studied against other people's versions of the society, Johnstone's account seems to be full of inaccuracies and even falsehoods, while his description of where the orgies were held relates not to the West Wycombe caves, but to the ruins of Medmenham Abbey, where the society had previously met. Charles Churchill, who was also a member of the society, provides a much more accurate portrait of activities of the Franciscans both at West Wycombe and previously at Medmenham in his poems. There has always been some mystery about those members of the society referred to as "Nuns": either whores imported from London, or women recruited from the aristocracy. In a diatribe about the Franciscans Churchill writes:

Whilst Womanhood in habit of a nun
At Mednam lies, by backwood monks undone;
A nation's reckoning like an alehouse score,
Whilst Paul the Aged [Paul Whitehead another poet] chalks
behind the door.[5]

The anonymous author of *Nocturnal Revels*, writing about the society, says:

Every member is allowed to introduce a lady of a cheerful disposition who embraces a general hilarity. The Ladies in the intervals of their repasts may make select parties among themselves or entertain one another, or alone, with reading, musick, tambour work, etc. . . . The ceremony of admission is performed in a chapel allotted for that purpose. The Ladies consider themselves as the lawful wives of the Brethren during their stay within monastic walls; every Monk being scrupulous not to infringe upon the nuptial alliance of any other Brother.

The author added that "no Lady may be taken by surprise either by her husband or any other relation. They are admitted in masks and do not unmask till all the Brethren have passed them in review, that they may avoid, if they judge it expedient, meeting with an unwelcome acquaintance . . . they may retire without making apology or revealing themselves to any but their temporary husband."[6]

Rabelais's works had made a great impression on Sir Francis Dashwood; he borrowed from Rabelais the motto over the Abbey of Thélème in the latter's stories of Gargantua and Pantagruel—"*Fay ce que voudras*" (Do as you please). This motto he had painted over the eastern porch of the Abbey Common Room at Medmenham. Rabelais made great play with the Latin word *horae* and so did the Franciscans, inventing what they called "Macaroni Latin." John Hall Stevenson (see section A–Z) punned with the word *horae*, pronouncing it in Latin, but spelling it with a *w* in front of the *h*. Quite a number of erotic verses were composed in, or made use of "Macaroni Latin," and *horae* was used to give the word its legendary meaning of three female figures. Commodore Edward Thompson expressed this in his own poem:

The winds took pity on the little whore,
And kindly puff'd her to the Cyprian shore;

The circling HORAE saw the floating car
And kindly sav'd her, for the God of War.
Eunomia, Dica and Irene fair
Made the sweet baby their peculiar care;
Taught her the deepest mysteries of love,
Then bore the Beauty to the powers above.[7]

This was also the age in which limericks—brief bawdy verses and naughty stories that were terse and to the point—began to achieve wide popularity. In one way this was both an encouragement to amorous activities and an antidote to them. This trend started in the late eighteenth century and was carried on until the early part of the twentieth century. Typical of some of them was the one about the young girl from Khartoum:

There was a young girl from Khartoum
Took a nancy boy up to her room.
She said, "Let's get this right
Before we put out the light,
Who does what, and with which,
And to whom."

Another such limerick, which suggests very much the influence of John Wilkes, was:

The King was in his counting house,
Counting out his wealth;
The Queen was in her parlour
Playing with herself.
The cook was in the kitchen,
Explaining to the groom,
That the vagina, not the rectum,
Was the entrance to the womb.[8]

This type of humor was appreciated over such a long period that it took two new forms in the twentieth century. The first was the "Knock, knock, who's there?" form which went something like this: "Knock, knock, who's there?" The reply was sometimes "Esme Percy" (the name of a well-known actor of the 1930s). "Esme Percy who?" was the question. "Ere's me purse, see, where's your fanny?" would be the reply.

The second form of this type of humor can be summed up by saying that it consisted of this approach: "She was only a so-and-so's daughter." Some examples were puerile, others deserved recognition in the erotic context, as, for example: "She was only a photographer's daughter; she was overexposed and underdeveloped, but she liked to be touched up and mounted."

It is true that between about 1750 and 1840 this type of instant eroticism prevailed and some may argue that it was not literature. Admittedly this is an arguable point, but the fact that it survived so long and that many of the stories, however brief, were put into books suggests that there is a strong case for including example of them in this guide. Even as far back as 1608 Robert Armin produced *Nest of Ninnies*, an early example of such stories.[9] In 1811 was published *The Female Jester, or, Wit for the Ladies*, while the modern author, John Wardroper, in his *Love and Drollery* (1969) had a collection of "amatory, merry and satirical verse, 1600–70 (including some versified jests)." If further proof is required of the acceptance of at least some of these brief stories and verses as a form of literature, then the Douce Collection in the Bodleian Library at Oxford provides it in some detail, as too does the Firth Collection in the same place. Not only is there an ancient ballad entitled *The Crafty Miss of London; or, the Friar Well Filled*, which describes the pranks of this pair, but an assortment of verses and very short and amusing stories, including "The Curiosities of Street Literature Comprising Cocks and Catch-pennies," as well as a nineteenth-century collection of comic tales in verse and prose.[10]

Though all this may seem to be lowering the standards by which we judge erotic literature, the fact is that it produced some real benefits. Sometimes such examples as have been given even led the way to an exchange of such jokes between male and female. When this happened and when both minds clicked in appreciation of the humor, this alone paved the way to mutual affection and understanding. There is nothing like shared understanding and appreciation of a joke for bringing people together. This is something that Sigmund Freud realized and that caused him to write *Jokes and Their Relation to the Unconscious*.[11]

Whereas the heroic and serious (classical, if one likes to put it that way) approach to erotic literature, whether in prose or verse, tended to be beyond the reach of many, this down-to-earth reaction to that brought people back to reality—the scholar just as much as the peasant or chambermaid. It slowly enabled people of each sex to enjoy the same sense of humor. Though this started quite slowly in the latter part of the eighteenth century, it was not fully accepted and understood by both sexes until the twentieth century.

In this guide there is intended to be an attempt to cover all aspects of erotic literature from the trivial to the abstruse. One cannot help feeling that some of the abstruse, especially in the nineteenth century, as expressed by Swinburne and others, caused a reaction toward the terse and easily understood verse and limericks. Yet, having made that point, one still has to consider the peculiar sexual hang-ups of the early part of the nineteenth century. In this period flagellation predominated in English erotica not only in literature but in painting, too. So much was this the case that on the continent flagellation was referred to as "*le vice anglais.*" This theme was to be found in Swinburne, in Aubrey Beardsley's *Earl Lavender,* in *The Whippingham Papers* (see SWIN-BURNE, ALGERNON CHARLES, in the A–Z section), and even in such appalling publications as *Spankers' Monthly.*

In reviewing over the ages what is and what is not erotic literature, difficult problems are sometimes posed for the student. For the purpose of this guide the author has decided to omit works that concentrate on flagellation and similarly unpleasant themes on the grounds that these are aberrations and therefore cannot come under the true definition of eroticism. Similarly the works of the Marquis de Sade (from whom we get the term *sadism*) and Leopold von Sacher-Masoch (from whom the word *masochism* is derived) are not touched upon, nor are these authors included in the biographies of authors of erotic works. This decision has been taken after much careful thought, even after researching some of the many books and pamphlets, magazines and memoirs on such themes, typified by such a work as *Lady Bumtickler's Revels, a Treatise on the Use of Flogging in Venereal Affairs* (London, 1872).

In support of my viewpoint I refer the reader to an article entitled "Literary Porn That Is One Long Yawn" by the literary editor of the London *Daily Telegraph,* David Holloway.[12] Referring to the new publication of Sade's *Juliette* as translated by Moyra Bremner, he wrote:

> I find it very difficult to believe that anyone in their right mind would wish to plow their way through the 1,193 pages of *Juliette.* As a reviewer I have been paid to do so. . . . Certainly as translated into modern English, with the use of four-letter words in preference to any of the pretty circumlocutions that John Cleland used so well in Fanny Hill, it is intensely boring. . . . I cannot recommend it to anyone and feel totally unconvinced by those who argue that it is a super-Swiftian satire on the follies of eighteenth-century France.

It is important to note the introduction of dialect into erotic verse and prose in this era. By far the most prolific of such poets was the Scottish bard, Robert Burns, and his "The Merry Muses of Caledonia," "The Ball of Kirriemuir," and "*Nine Inch Will Please a Lady*" are good examples of this kind of work. Here are some of his verses:

"Come rede me, dame, come tell me, dame,
My dame come tell me truly,
What length o' graith, when weel ca'd hame,
Will sair a woman duly?"
The carlin clew her wanton tail,
Her wanton tail sae ready—
"I learn'd a sang in Annandale,
Nine inch will please a Lady.

But for a koontrie cunt like mine,
In sooth, we're nae sae gentle;
We'll tak tway thumb-bread to the nine,
And that's a soncy pintle:
Oh, leeze me on, my Charlie, lad,
I'll ne'er forget my Charlie!
Tway roarin' handfu's and a daud,
He nidge't it in fu' rarely."

Other country dialects offered scope for writers in this period, though few seem to have taken advantage of this. An interesting book, compiled by a clergyman, no less, was *A Dictionary of the Sussex Dialect* (1875).[13] In this book the Sussex dialect meaning of the word *fornicate* is given. Surprise, surprise, it means "to dawdle," "to waste time," "to wander slowly." A *bullock* means "a fat beast of either sex." The author of the dictionary states: "I was very much astonished when I heard a farmer say, 'Yes, she's a purty cow, a very purty cow indeed, and one of these days she'll make a nice bullock.'"

Some of the Sussex dialect as employed during lovemaking is evident in the definition of *adone*. The author describes it as meaning "have done," "leave off," but he adds: "I am told on good authority that when a Sussex damsel says 'Oh! do adone,' she means you to go on; but when she says 'Adone-do,' you must leave off immediately."

Nobody could have done more to help create an entirely new type of love story than did Flaubert in the middle of the nineteenth century. It was one of the first of such novels to portray an adulterous love affair in a realistic manner, and its appeal has remained for more than a century, not only in the book, *Madame Bovary*, but in the various films made of it. Claude Chabrol, the director of a new film on the theme in 1991, stated: "For me Flaubert's novel is a high point. It is a complete universe in which I find the essential elements of what interests me: feminine dissatisfaction in particular, and human dissatisfaction in general, insatiable love accompanied by a wonderful study of one person's hopes, desires, regrets, and dreams." Suddenly, with this new film and renewed interest in the book, Emma Bovary acquired a new interest in the 1990s, not just in France, but all over the continent. The story of the rich peasant's daughter from Normandy who married a humble doctor and whose fantasies of romance and social climbing led her on to adultery, financial disaster, and ultimately suicide struck a new note. Chabrol added: "What I find particularly pleasing about this whole controversy [he was referring to the *Bovarysme* arguments the film had provoked] is that it proves that what Flaubert was writing about in 1856 is of the utmost relevance today."

The man who did most to help break through the literary Establishment's puritanism in the latter part of the nineteenth century was, of course, Sir Richard Burton. Born in 1821 of mixed English, Irish, and possibly French ancestry, he was expelled from Oxford University and went to India as a subaltern in the 18th Regiment, Bombay Native Infantry, during the war with the Sindhi. Burton, says his biographer, Byron Farwell, "was an adventurer in the purest sense of the word. . . . What made him different from most others . . . was that he extended his exploration to the realms of the intellect and the spirit."[14]

Burton's chief interest in such explorations was in his quest for sexual phenomena and customs in the Far East and also to make a study of any erotic tract he came across. He gave a logical reason for this in the *Terminal Essay* of his translation of the *Arabian Nights:* in this essay he argued that sexual education for women could benefit society as a whole and what he had in mind were works such as the *Kama Sutra* and others. Burton was used as a secret agent to gather intelligence while in India and on one occasion he was asked by Sir Charles Napier, the commander in chief, to make a report on pederasty in Karachi. The tragedy was that after his death his wife, Isobel, destroyed all his diaries and a vast amount of other papers and translations he had made. This act was condemned by the poet, Ernest Dowson, in an article entitled "Against My Lady Burton: On Her Burning the Last Writing of Her Dead Husband." "To her one God," he wrote, "sterile Propriety." Fortunately much of Burton's work survived and posterity has benefited from it.

It was that same Ernest Dowson who wrote the poem *Non Sum Qualis Eram Bonae Sub Regno Cynarae,* a typical example of verse of the 1890s, condemned as overdaring in its day, but still worthy of some study. Dowson, above all, helped to dispel some of the hypocrisy of the day:

> All night upon mine heart I felt her warm heart beat,
> Night-long within mine arms in love and sleep she lay;
> Surely the kisses of her bought red mouth were sweet;
> But I was desolate and sick of an old passion,
> When I awoke and found the dawn was gray:
> I have been faithful to thee, Cynara, in my fashion.

Another of the nineties poets was Arthur Symons whose *Stella Maris* struck another new note in the erotic:

> Child, I remember, and can tell
> One night we loved each other well,
> And one night's love, at least or most
> Is not so small a thing to boast.
> You were adorable, and I
> Adored you to infinity,
> The nuptial night too briefly borne
> To the oblivion of morn.

Ah! no oblivion, for I feel
Your lips deliriously steal
Along my neck, and fasten there;
I feel the perfume of your hair,
I feel your breast that heaves and dips
Desiring my desirous lips,
And that ineffable delight
When souls turn bodies, and united
In the intolerable, the whole
Rapture of the embodied soul.

The end of that century was marked by an attempt to make amatory verse more realistic, while still retaining its romanticism. For that reason alone we have much to thank Dowson, Symons, Richard Le Gallienne, Lionel Johnson, and others for making this important point.

That new approach to the subject was all to the good and these writers did for Britain what several French authors and poets had already done for France. At the same time there was an attempt by some writers in the latter part of the Victorian period to publish pornography under the cover of anonymity. Some such works may be listed as erotic literature by the few, but, generally speaking, the crudity of their language, the sheer exploitation of pornography, frequently at far too great a length, made them anything but uplifting. One of the most voluminous of these works was *My Secret Life* by "Walter." This consisted of no fewer than eleven volumes about the various sexual escapades of "Walter," detailing all manner of abnormal practices as well as perversions and contacts with prostitutes. The work was privately printed in 1888, but has since been published in an abbreviated form in one volume in New Jersey and New York (1966), while in London in 1967 there appeared the following work: *Walter, the English Casanova, a Presentation of His Unique Memoirs,* annotated by Phyllis and Eberhard Kronhausen from the angle of the sexual psychology of the work.

Yet another anonymous work of the period and one that deserves the adjective *erotic* rather more than Walter's *Secret Life* was *The Lustful Turk,* first published in 1828 and still frequently reprinted today. In 1990 it was printed in London under this same title. Said to have been written originally by a Greek, it is the story of an English girl who had been captured by the Turks and imprisoned in a harem. The introduction to the original work described it thus:

A history founded on facts, containing an interesting narrative of the cruel fate of the two young English ladies, named Silvia Carey and Emily Barlow, fully explaining how Emily Barlow and her servant, Eliza Biggs, on their passage to India, were taken prisoners by an Algerian pirate and made a present of to the Dey of Algiers, who, on the very night of their arrival debauched Emily.

Containing also, every particular of the artful plans laid by the Dey, to get possession of the person of Silvia Carey, etc., with the particulars of her becoming a victim of his libidinous desires. Which recital is also interspersed with the histories of several other ladies confined in the Dey's harem. One of which gives an account of the horrid practices then carrying on in several French and Italian convents by a Society of Monks, established at Algiers, under pretense of redeeming Christian slaves, but who in reality carried on an infamous traffic in young girls. Also an account of the sufferings of Eliza Gibbs, from the flogging propensities of the Bey of Tunis. With many other curious circumstances until the Reduction of Algiers by Lord Exmouth, by which means these particulars became known. The whole compiled from the original letters, by permission of one of the sufferers.

It was in 1816 that Admiral Sir Edward Pellew, Viscount Exmouth, bombarded Algiers and thereafter was able to ensure the abolition of Christian slavery in the Dey's dominions. The first publication of *The Lustful Turk* came some twelve years later.

Much of the verse of the nineties, as the period of Wilde, Beardsley, Le Gallienne, Dowson, and others became known, was eroticism shrouded in mysticism and dreams. A. J. A. Symons in his *Anthology of 'Nineties Verse* has this to say on the subject: "Condemned as over-daring in its own day, it [the poetry of the 1890s] is dismissed as overcircumspect in ours. . . . Remote corners of the spirit were explored by candlelight to make a sonnet; the music hall, the harlot's house, the artificial paradise of drugs and drink, every dream of vice and virtue were dragged into the net of literature."[15]

It was in this same period that the underground magazine catering for those who wished to escape from nineteenth-century prudery made its appearance. The first of these was *The Pearl*, the first issue of which was published in London in 1879. It was cunningly and surreptitiously marketed and soon became regular reading matter for people of all classes. Eighteen volumes of this magazine appeared between July 1879 and December 1880. Recently extracts from *The Pearl* have been published in London and New York.[16]

"Bawdy, provocative, irresistibly entertaining, *The Pearl* is a vital part of the Victorians' great literary legacy," it has been claimed. It was subtitled *A Journal of Facetiae and Voluptuous Reading* and the editor of the magazine told of some of the alternative titles for it that were suggested: "Facts and Fancies," "The Cremorne," "The All-Round," "The Monthly Courses," and "The Devil's Own" among them. While much of the fiction in the magazine does not rise above the description of pornographic, a short verse entitled "The Pleasures of Love" is lively and lyrical:

> Around my form his pliant limbs entwined,
> Love's seat of bliss to him I then resigned.
> We pant, we throb, we both convulsive start!
> Heavens! then what passions thro' our fibres dart!
> We heave, we wriggle, bite, laugh, tremble, sigh!
> We taste Elysian bliss—we fondle—die.

Striking a more humorous note, one item is a series of verses cleverly parodying Charles Wolfe's poem, "The Burial of Sir John Moore at Corunna" and it runs thus:

> Not a sound was heard, but the ottoman shook,
> And my darling looked awfully worried,
> As round her fair form I a firm hold took,
> And John Thomas I silently buried.

The Pearl was succeeded by a similar magazine, entitled *The Oyster*, but this was equally short-lived. Other undercover magazines of this period were *The Annals of Gallantry, Glee and Pleasure, The Bon Ton Magazine,* and *The Boudoir.* A complete reprint of this magazine, entitled *The Boudoir: A Victorian Magazine of Scandal,* was published in New York in 1971. Perhaps the most cunningly disguised of all such Victorian magazines was *The Englishwoman's Domestic Magazine,* which catered for a totally different market.

5

Eroticism in Code

*I*t is essential in making any study of erotic literature in all its many forms
to recall the fact that from the earliest times a considerable proportion of
it has been composed in code. Equally it is important to remember that even
in this century and continuing toward the next this trend is still evident.
Much of it, of course, may, as it has in the past, die unrecorded and even
unread save by a privileged few. The fact remains that there is a vast quantity
of such material deserving the title of literature that remains unpublished.

Even the *Kama Sutra* was composed in cipher and Vatsyayana, the author
(see A–Z section), stressed that secret writing was one of the sixty-four arts
of love. David Kahn, that foremost authority on cryptology, has referred to
the fact that Vaysyayana insisted that women should know and be able to
practice secret writing as the forty-fifth article of love decrees. This art, says
Kahn,

> begins with vocal music and runs through prestidigitation, solution
> of verbal puzzles and exercises in enigmatic poetry. The yoga is called
> *mlecogita-vikalpa*. In his commentary on the *Kama Sutra* Yasodhara
> describes two kinds of *mlecogita-vikalpa*. One is called *kautilyam* in
> which the letter substitutions are based upon phonetic relations—
> the vowels become consonants, for example. A simplification of this
> form is called *durbodha*. Another kind of secret writing is *muladeviya*.
> Its cipher alphabet consists merely of the reciprocal one with all
> other letters remaining unchanged. *Muladeviya . . .* figures in Indian
> literature.[1]

Among the ancient Romans Ovid's controversial work, *The Art of Love*,
incited lovers to correspond in code and to use invisible ink. His book was

mainly addressed to those wishing to indulge in extramarital affairs, but Ovid also felt that secrecy made love seem more exciting. One of the most passionate of coded letters of Ovid's own period was this: "I languish, I faint, I pine away, I am in torture, I am burning up, I toss and sigh and die a thousand deaths. I am vanquished, I pant, so let your lips drive out the bitter pain from my heart." What is so significant about this particular effusion of passion is that it was not written in haste, but carefully worked out in code.

Ovid was actually banished from court on one occasion by the Emperor Augustus when the latter discovered a coded love poem of Ovid's that displeased him. Ovid propounded the various primitive forms of invisible ink for use in secret communications: *"Tuta quoque est fallitque oculus e lacte recenti littera; carbonis pulvere tange leges. Fallet et umidoli quae fiet acumine lini et feeret occultas pura tabella notas."* In other words: "You can safely write a letter which cannot be visible to a stranger by writing in fresh milk. Rub it gently with coal dust and you will be able to read it. You can also deceive others by writing with a stalk of moistened flax and a pure sheet will bear hidden marks." Ovid also advised Latin lovers to use certain tricks in their letters such as addressing them to a male when they were really intended for a female and vice versa. "It is much safer sometimes to say 'he' and 'his' when you really mean 'she' and 'hers,'" he argued.[2]

Other Romans who stressed the value of coded writings in amorous matters and literature, too, were Ausonius (see A–Z section) and Andreas Capellanus. The latter believed that marriage should never be a deterrent to a little courtly (chivalrous or romantic) love on the side, and laid down a code for correspondence and signs. This principle work of his, *De Arte Honeste Amandi*, actually commended multiple love to women as well as men.[3]

His recurring theme was that secrecy was beautiful. Possibly this was due to the influence of the countess of Champagne who inspired his work and seems to have offered some ideas of her own. The countess was a clever and passionate woman who was convinced that matrimony and love were incompatible. By persuading Capellanus to compile his manual of courtly love and Chrétien de Troyes (a translator of Ovid) to rewrite ancient legends in a new romantic style, she sought to create a romantic cult. Capellanus emphasized that danger and frustration gave love its piquancy; the need to escape from a jealous husband, the frustrations of the pursuit of a loved one, and the need to make the whole business into a highly skilled game were sentiments he praised.

François Rabelais, that scatological sage of the sixteenth century, spoke enthusiastically of the value of secret inks for love messages: "No man could see the writing at first sight, therefore to find it out he set it by the fire, to see if was made with Sal Ammoniac soaked in water; then he put it into the water to see if the letter was written with the juice of Tithymalle; after that he had held it up against the candle to see if it was written with the juice of white onions."

The Chinese also used books and poems to provide the basis for a code. Some of the mandarins at their ancient courts composed secret love letters stylishly written for ladies at the imperial court, weaving the messages into love lyrics that disguised the truth. This practice reached a peak in the early nineteenth century, when the key to the mandarins' literary ciphers was often found in the ancient oracular book, *I Ching*. The origin of this book, sometimes known in the Western world as *The Book of Changes*, is obscure. It was probably compiled between 1200 and 1100 B.C. Confucius tells how its oracular devices were consulted by princes and aristocrats for advice on war, diplomacy, and marriage. The book follows the path of Chinese astrology.

Chinese lovers combined an exchange of greetings in a code using *I Ching* through the medium of a mandarin with an attempt to obtain independent forecasts as to how their love affairs were progressing. Answers to such questions would come in what seemed like coded riddles. The problem posed for the lovers was how to arrive at a correct interpretation. Lin Yutang, that notable twentieth-century philosopher, has cited the instance of a girl inquiring what the future holds for her. She was told: "The wild goose gradually draws near the summit." This could mean that for two or three years she would have no child, but that after this all would be well. Or it could be interpreted as merely meaning that in the end nothing could hinder her good fortune, or attaining her wish, whatever it was.

It should also be noted that many of the Chinese calligraphical characters lend themselves to coded meanings. For example, the character *lü* consists of two mouths linked together and many Chinese words have double meanings: *lang sheng* (sound of waves) can be construed as a pun on lewd sounds.

During the English Civil Wars of Cromwell's time the need for coded messages was acute. This much is clear from the correspondence of Lady Jane Whorwood who seems to have included in her numerous coded letters not merely information of value to the Royalist Forces, but some rather sparkling eroticism. Lady Jane was a mysterious figure and very little is known about her. She was a staunch Royalist, the daughter of a man named Ryder who was surveyor of the Royal Stables to King James I. A red-haired beauty, she was married at nineteen to Brome Whorwood, the eldest son of Sir Thomas Whorwood of Holton, Oxfordshire. In 1647–48, when Charles I was in prison, she tried to arrange his escape. She is often referred to in the king's correspondence under the cipher *N* or *715*.

To create her cipher Lady Jane took a fairly simple and established code, known as the pigpen cipher, and turned it cleverly into a cipher of her own. This code, originally developed by John Wilkins, had the great advantage of being simple to construct and taking up very little room, while being difficult to detect as it consisted of dots, short lines, squares, half squares, and three-quarter squares. In the jargon of the cryptographers this is known as a nine-cell diagram as dots are substituted for letters of the alphabet.

In one of the coded letters Lady Jane signed herself "Your love-hungry Ariadne." It is not clear to whom this letter was addressed, but it was sent by William Lilly as intermediary and it is possible he passed it on to an imprisoned Royalist. So much one could deduce by the reference to Ariadne. This mythical daughter of Minos of Crete, who fell in love with Theseus, gave him the clue he needed to extricate himself from the labyrinth where he was in danger of being destroyed by the Minotaur. This seems a reasonable conclusion to draw when one reads that a "Master of Witches named N-b-ad [probably Neobad]" had found a messenger "who would acte as guide to shewe you which corridors to take for leaving this maze of a place."[4] The letter goes on to suggest that Lady Jane and the recipient of her letter would meet at "Sir William Maxie's house in Essex and there those cochineal-flecked breasts which you never before dared touch you may now graspe without asking my leave and kisse the sweetnesses thereof til all below dissolves."[5]

There is then a gap in the letter: the code was written at an angle of forty-five degrees and the whole alphabet was distorted. But further on it appears that "to the tunes of the fiddlers of Coggeshall we may play a score of games and you may practice upon me all the hocus-pocus tricks you so desire. Tops will be below and belowe will be on toppe."

All of which suggests that Lady Jane Whorwood was quite a girl.

The harshness of the Puritan ethic both in America and Britain must have forced many lovers to keep their affairs secret and their amorous correspondence coded. The Puritans' aim was to make immorality an offense against the laws of the state. In England this was achieved in 1650 when the Parliament of Praise-God-Barebones made the punishment for fornication three months' imprisonment and for adultery, death. In New England the Puritan colonizers were even more ruthless. They took the view that a bachelor was a menace to all women and that he should be pressed into marriage. So unless a bachelor had special permission to live alone, he was fined one pound a week. It is little wonder that Senator William Byrd of Westover, Virginia, kept his diaries in an ambiguous kind of shorthand. Nevertheless he led a much more circumspect life in America than when he was abroad (see BYRD, WILLIAM, in the A–Z section).[6]

Another American who resorted to code for writing his love letters was John Winthrop, the Younger, later governor of the Massachusetts Bay colony, who in his early twenties fell in love with his orphan cousin, Martha Fones, a ward of his father, the first governor of that puritanical colony. It was in Massachusetts that the extreme breakaway Puritans sought to create a life-style in accord with the Book of Leviticus, making life impossible for all young courting couples. Even to walk innocently hand in hand was deemed to be "sinful dalliance" and an offense against the law.

Young Winthrop somehow managed to marry his beloved secretly when he was twenty-four, but as he had to go to England to petition a charter from King Charles II, communications posed a serious problem. Not only were mails irregular, but the wax seals on letters made them far from safe from prying eyes. Yet over a long period John and Martha somehow managed to keep up a transatlantic correspondence by adopting a simple substitution code. John Winthrop wrote:

> Martha, three times Martha, and then one very long and specially savored MARTHA. So it is that I say this verie deare name to mine selfe everie time before I address thee. My pulse beats like the tapping of a drum as I speake this verie name. The thought of your beautiful ancilla is just to raise me uppe into the heavens there to gaze down on the most wondrous sight of all. Though we are by time manie weekes apart and by miles almost half waye round the world, yet I still am enthralled by thinking of you waiting for me and trust in God that this poore but truthfule missive may cause you to remember me.[7]

The reference to "ancilla" is interesting. In one of Senator Byrd's letters the following reference appears: "Alas, she treasures her ancilla as though it were the sacred buckler itself." Byrd, Winthrop, and even Samuel Pepys, the English diarist, all used the word *ancilla* in a sexual sense. But as Byrd was a classical scholar he probably used the term as a simile, comparing woman's most precious jewel with the *ancile* that was said to have fallen from heaven in the reign of Numa in Rome. To prevent this sacred buckler from being stolen, Numa caused eleven others, exactly the same, to be made and entrusted them to the guardianship of twelve priests.

Restif de la Bretonne (see A–Z section), who was a prolific writer of amorous activities, composed a great deal of his work in codes of his own, not all of which have even yet been fully deciphered. He was so fascinated by the varied sexual habits and fetishes he observed in Paris that he made notes about them in hieroglyphics. One curious code mark of his was that of a dove, beside which was a crutch, and on the other side a church, a bottle of wine and a key, alongside which was written the word *Grecque*. The dove almost certainly meant a woman named Colombe (dove) who was a cripple and who could be found in the crypt of a church where she would welcome a bottle of wine. The last sign, the key marked *Grecque* is more puzzling. As churches were then open day and night it is unlikely that the key refers to the church.

But the word *clitoris* is derived from the Greek for key, and Restif may have used it in this sense, to indicate the key to sexual joy.

Restif's work, *Monsieur Nicolas*, ran to sixteen volumes and the original material consisted of coded graffiti, drawings, and hieroglyphics.[8]

Maria Edgeworth, the English novelist whose sense of characterization was so acute, while spending her school holidays at Northchurch in Hertfordshire between 1776 and 1780, conducted a lively correspondence with a young schoolfriend named Antonia, whose name she changed to "Antony" when writing highly colored and imaginative love letters that involved an unusual code. The letters would start quite normally, such as "My ever beloved Antony" and exchange fond greetings in a relatively innocent manner. Suddenly there would be references such as "page 48, paragraph 3," or "page 104, line 27." The mystery of Maria's code seems never to have been solved, or, if it was, then it must have been hushed up through Victorian prudery.

Mrs. Walter Edgeworth, a descendant of Maria's family, said:

> We never managed to discover what the clue was to this code. There seems no doubt that both Maria and Antonia had in their possession copies of a book which would have supplied all the answers and one must presume it was some romantic novel. Antonia died quite suddenly at an early age and it would seem that Maria carried on writing these letters even after Antonia's death, as years later they were found tucked away in a neat bundle in a cupboard. Obviously they had never been posted. It was a sad but touching little story of make-believe.[9]

There was also a tendency in the later Victorian period for baby-talk to be used as a kind of code, frequently in letters but sometimes in actual literature. Some of the baby-talk was used to convey sexual thoughts acceptably. For example, what is one to make of this letter written by the teenage wife of Henry Brooke, the Irish novelist? "Be sure you cherish My Beanstalk while you are away. I shall expect it to be just the same as when last I set eyes on it. Remember it is Jill's to climb and not Jack's."

Henry Brooke, whose best-known work was probably *The Fool of Quality*, belonged to the eighteenth century (1703–83), but his works were revived by the Victorians. He married his ward when she was only thirteen years of age and attending school. This letter was composed when she was barely fifteen.

Charles Kingsley, the clergyman author of *Westward Ho!* and *Hereward the Wake*, revealed a penchant for baby-talk in *The Water Babies*. Curiously, Kingsley also had a fondness for the work of Henry Brooke and he republished *The Fool of Quality* in 1859. In her book, *The Erotic World of Faery*, Maureen Duffy saw in *The Water Babies* something of a secret essay in eschatology, a concealed parable about masturbation. Duffy's work is an important guide to certain works containing disguised eroticism, and it is almost a Freudian interpretation of fairy tales, showing them in terms of sexual symbolism.[10]

Lady Susan Chitty, Kingsley's most recent biographer, agrees that "in one of her interpretations of the story Miss Duffy falls not so far short of the target."[11]

There were at least two, maybe even four saints named Valentine, but although two of them were supposed to have been either born or martyred on February 14, the custom of sending cards or other mementos on that day has traditionally been linked with a pagan festival based on the legend that the birds of the air chose their mates on this day. The custom of sending valentines and using them for secret messages was prevalent in prosaic England long before it reached France, where it has never been very popular. The French poet, Charles d'Orléans, who spent twenty-five years as a prisoner in England, introduced the valentine to France on his return in the middle of the fifteenth century. Quite a number of his poems were love messages encoded in valentines.

In Victorian times, when valentines were highly popular, one valentine specially drawn for a certain young lady from a baker who wished to provide a hint as to his identity read:

> Oh, thy sweet flesh is soft as dough,
> And I shall knead thee soon, I know

Such a sentiment was probably more innocent in those days than the erotic thoughts conjured up by such a message today. The early Victorian usually expressed the anguish and heartaches of love rather than anticipated pleasure. Take for example this valentine in which the sender's name was coded:

> Since first we met, I
> am no longer myself. Oh, Love,
> unhappy Love! I am lost. I neglect my
> everyday occupation. I pass my nights in ceaseless sighs,
> lying wretchedly in bed. My poor heart!

The first letters of each line give the name of the sender, i.e., S-A-M-U-E-L.

Valentines may not be literature, but there is undoubtedly literary talent in some of them. If a search for such gems is to be made, then there can hardly be a better place for study than the Hallmark Museum in Connecticut. Here is a huge collection of valentines purchased by Mr. C. A. Means, of Connecticut, who gave them to the museum. The original collection was made by one Jonathan King, of Islington, London, who offered twelve tons of these cards to the British Museum in his will. The offer was declined on the grounds of lack of space. Thus the United States benefited when the valentines were eventually sold.

It was about 1800 that coded love messages began to find a regular place in the columns of both newspapers and magazines. Such advertisements usually led to an exchange of coded letters, though these were rarely sent by post. The object of such secrecy was, of course, to keep the love affairs of young people from the eyes and ears of their parents. Fortunately for posterity some of these coded agony column notices attracted the attention of two friends, Lyon Playfair and his neighbor, Charles Wheatstone, who were both enthusiastic cryptologists. Lyon Playfair, writing about his friend, explained: "On Sundays we usually walked together and used to amuse ourselves by deciphering the cipher advertisements in *The Times.*[12]

Lyon Playfair was also the inventor of the Playfair Cipher, which was ultimately adopted by the British Admiralty, though in fact it is credited to Wheatstone. However, the foremost of decipherers in the nineteenth century was a scientist, Charles Babbage (1792–1871). The precursor of a number of eccentric dons who have made mathematics their favorite science, he actually designed the forerunner of today's computer, which he called the "Second Difference Engine." More than this, Babbage was a detective of nineteenth-century love affairs, as his papers in the Manuscripts Department of the British Library reveal. He seems to have been regarded as a kind of Sherlock Holmes in the field of cryptography, especially in dealing with coded love letters and messages, being frequently consulted by all manner of people from cabinet ministers and lawyers seeking information either to solve divorce problems or on behalf of frantic parents in quest of a runaway daughter.

Among the Babbage Papers in the British Library is a letter that states: "I am counsel in a case which has some curious features in it and there are a quantity of writings in cipher which it is deemed impossible to have interpreted." Yet another letter from the solicitors claims that Babbage had "triumphantly enabled us to establish the truth."[13]

Some of the letters and notices that Babbage deciphered were certainly extremely amorous and erotic, yet occasionally acquired a literary quality. The following section of one very lengthy coded letter gave Babbage immense trouble, as the gaps and queries in his interpretation show:

> Beloved, with the most sweet and beautiful cunt hair. I have just been reading about you . . . arkosh is what I sd and as regards the D it shall be what you and Lord Bdom wish. I have only the objections I have to D . . . tell you of . . . The ———— which is on my faithful word I do not dive [?]. I wish however . . . for it really does make it less sweet . . . not so *molto* and always did. If all the world was to make love to me, I do not think they would make me love

you less. You are my dearest Seraph [sometimes this was spelled "Serat"], my Dearest best segt [sic] and beloved. I don't know if the Duchess of Cambridge knows anything of me, but if she does give her my best respects. My regards 45–150. . . . I understand very sweet but very wicked, and my darling what is your wish I do agree fully . . . what you wish *molto*, I cannot refuse. . . . I do not like all these things.[14]

Such language is certainly somewhat mystifying and almost in the realms of *Through the Looking Glass*. The word *seraph* can be applied to angels, but *serat* is a different matter altogether and would seem to imply that a woman was being addressed. *Serat* or *Al-Sirat* is in Moslem mythology the bridge over midhell leading to paradise as a land of houris and sensual delights. *Serat* might be a term of endearment.

Turning to more recent examples of coded diaries of an amorous kind, one of the best is contained in the 1960s diaries of an American woman, Loretta, who kept her diary in a code she invented herself that included many astrological signs. Loretta died in 1969, aged thirty-seven, almost certainly through a combination of drink and drugs. She had traveled widely in the Americas, Europe, and Morocco, and from her diaries it is evident that she was cultured, well-educated, affectionate, wayward, superstitious, and adventurous. Like the Elizabethan John Dee and some other diarists, Loretta marked each occasion on which she made love with the sign of Pisces. When she died her diaries were presented to a member of the Astrological Association in the hope that it might be deciphered.

It took five years to work out the key to Loretta's code, especially as parts of the diaries were written in an almost undecipherable scrawl.[15]

She was at her best when painting a verbal picture of a young man in a couple of succinct sentences: "He's creamy and luscious and groovy. He has hearts painted on his jeans and he plays the harmonica like he's in bed with you." Three days later she wrote: "Out here in the shade of the trees all looks sexy and beautiful. But Leo, who has just come along, is the most beautiful of all. He talks as well as he plays." A month later she was describing how she and Leo were "hooked up and unhookable on our own colored glass minds. For once I don't need hash, or speed. Here we sit, under the trees, peaceful in each other's minds, unprogrammed and therefore able to tap out our own private jargon like a couple of detached robots, while we watch other people unfold."

One of the longest entries was:

Made love . . . wearing a bathing dress . . . sandwich love with the bathing dress as bread, but the sky dancing a waltz and the trees letting in little sparks of light that matched the stars inside the sandwich. . . . The July wurzles effervesce in glorious chunks of blue, and, laughing at her bathing dress, the Persian cat cries out "tishoo" . . . laminated love . . . kaleidoscopic love . . . Venus on wheels skiing on sand . . . must get [indecipherable for about three words] . . . as in Bimini . . . winging to the moon with Leo, hopping from Cloud Nine to the supreme heights of Cloud twenty-one, then back to earth in an hour to go and drink sangria at Fountain Café. Oh, happy Bethesda!

The reference to "happy Bethesda" is to the Bethesda Fountain created out of the open sewer that existed in New York's Central Park in the middle of the last century. The fountain was intended to be a convenient place for people to meet, with its circular walk, its terrace, and its steps. The picture of Central Park that emerged from the diaries was built up over a period of several early summer weeks in staccato fashion. Diary extracts have been checked by a member of the curator's staff who can recall Central Park in 1963. "It is an accurate picture," he said, "but, because it appears to concentrate on certain areas of the park, it is more typical of what Central Park became like in, say, the early seventies than the park as a whole in 1963. But, as far as the details go, the stuff she writes is identifiable."

Though she experimented with drugs and drinks, Loretta only described her mental experiences and never went into details of how she indulged herself, except for one entry that reads: "Belladonna and mescaline = aphrodisiac happiness minus the rats and spiders." Sometimes she and Leo would row on the lake and "pretend it's just a far-off lagoon, skg a quiet corner into which we can drift away from the voyeurs and make love without being bugged."

Reading through the diary is like looking at Central Park through a long-range telescope. But it isn't all happy. Loretta mentions seeing "a boy of thirteen on t strangest trip, hvg convulsions under a tree. Asked if I cd help, but he just says 'yellow fly, yellow-yellow fly.' What is it? God knows." There are thumbnail sketches of the very earliest of the flower children when they were genuinely gentle and had a benevolent communal spirit. Loretta welcomed and praised the trend, adding that it made "just the right background for Leo and me, so much in need of this kind of peace." She saw them as "people who might hv come out of Camelot more naturally than any o t Kennedy Clan and much more graceful in their sheepskin vests and Indian headbands." She said that Leo called the flower children "our bridesmaids and attendants." Later Loretta was to lament the deterioration of the flower-power cult into "an unloving and unlovable, politically motivated, vandalizing bunch of hoodlums."

Leo is always the "Great Bright Star" who shines through the whole of her diary. Never is he criticized in the slightest degree. Whatever Loretta suffered from in her bleak moments, these were never linked to Leo. Intermittently there were astrological commentaries in Loretta's diary. Apparently she went in for astropalmistry, the study of the hands in relation to astrological as well as palmistic principles. "I find I have a low set little finger which means sexual difficulties relating to my parents," she wrote. "Does this pose problems with Leo in the long run? Tried the Tarot cards again, but aspects not good. I feel like someone watching a superbly conceived play, with climax piled up upon climax, and getting the feeling that it's coming to an end. Can Leo sustain it? Can he make the play go on and on, forever and forever?"

There was, alas, no neatly rounded end to Loretta's diaries. During 1964 the entries became increasingly incoherent and indecipherable. By 1965 there were long meaningless squiggles against some days of the week and many blanks against others. Leo remained the central figure in the diary. What emerges so distinctly, despite all Loretta's escapades and incursions into what she once called "the Land of Mother-Judge-of-all-Drugs," is that there was real devotion on both sides. Their love survived not only in Central Park, but on a transatlantic trip, sleeping under the stars in England and again in Morocco. "What is so wonderful w Leo is how he can b deliciously mad and gently cosseting alternately," Loretta once commented. "This is love wh blends Don Q with St Anthony. Leo, too, cd charm a bird off a tree and often does."[16]

Much of the coded diaries, correspondence, and other epistles that are mentioned or cited in this guide can be called instant literature. Yet while this is true, the description should not be taken in a derogatory sense. It has a feeling of honest expression about it and in this sense the eroticism of the coded word has an advantage over that of, say, the novel, and most certainly over the poem set in meticulous meter.

6

Through the Maze of Modern Erotica

The title of this final chapter may puzzle, or even disturb some readers, the suggestion being that I am trying to lead them through the maze. The natural question will be: does he know his way? The answer to that is quite simple: yes, I think I know *my* way, but you must understand that my way may not be *your* way. The maze of modern erotica is, in fact, a maze with more than one exit.

I could have made this task simpler by choosing a maze with only one exit: in other words, by doing it entirely my way. I have deliberately rejected that plan because today it is harder than ever to agree on what is or is not erotic. Remember, originally in the Greek sense of the word (and one should never forget that it is of Greek origin), eroticism meant something uplifting for many. That trend lasted through the medieval and Renaissance periods and only began to change in the latter part of the seventeenth century. The most marked feature of that change came with the insistence of some writers to change the language of eroticism from the subtle to the blatant. Partly this was done with the object of bringing some humor to bear on the subject, but also as a defiant gesture against the prim literary taboos of the day. There is, of course, a case to be made out in favor of such literary tactics, and few could do this better than the poet, Robert Burns, who introduced eroticism for the masses. But there is always a very real danger that unless these tactics are skillfully employed they will result in nothing more than pornography. This is where the individual reader or student must decide for himself. To give readers a chance to make up their own minds I have included in this guide some examples of writers whose work is on the borderline between genuine eroticism and downright pornography.

In the early part of this century the French Symbolists undoubtedly inspired many English writers to adopt new techniques; this applied especially to James Joyce and Samuel Beckett. Sometimes these techniques worked well; at other times they merely resulted in meaningless mumbo jumbos of prose. Even when Beckett was asked by the director of his play, *Waiting for Godot,* "who or what does Godot mean?", he replied, "If I knew, I would have said so in the play." Very often *Godot* adds up to little more than a prolonged and boring string of crude words and jokes about smelly feet and going to the lavatory. This, I submit, is hardly eroticism.

In the 1950s Kenneth Tynan quite frankly admitted that he wanted to stage what he called "elegant pornography," maintaining that if it "didn't turn you on, it wasn't working." In the same period in the literary field a new market for pornographic books was opened up in Paris by the establishment of the Olympia Press by Maurice Girodias in 1953. He has been described as "the man who made the world safe for pornography."[1] This is somewhat unfair because although he published some inferior works, he was also responsible for the publication of work by Vladimir Nabokov, Henry Miller, William Burroughs, J. P. Donleavy, Lawrence Durrell, Georges Bataille, and Jean Genet.

Rather more disturbing in this author's opinion was a tendency in this period to cater to those who reveled in stories of sadism and masochism, or what Girodias called "the British market for whipping, nannies and so on."[2] One of the worst features of the underworld book trade has been a marked increase in this type of book not merely with new works, but frequent reprints of de Sade and Sacher-Masoch.

Many writers who try to be erotic fail lamentably—and this especially applies to those who write in English—because they fail to find any elegant language to describe various parts of the anatomy. In this respect it is as well to ponder on Oscar Wilde's advice that "the man who calls a spade a spade, deserves to use one." This observation leads me toward another problem in this modern maze, making decisions as to who are and who are not erotic writers. It seems to me that unless an absolutely sound case can be made out for describing a modern author as an erotic writer then he or she should be omitted from the A–Z section. To include such a writer on the strength, say, of just one erotic novel or poem, would be totally unfair when most other works by the same author were of a different genre.

Today it is possible to see erotica in a different light: one can often find a single sentence in a nonerotic book that stands out as a splendid example of the genre. Here is one such example, though it comes from an author's first detective story, *The Dead Butler Caper* by Frank Norman, London, 1978.

> Black Satin Hotpants had a wiggle that could fry a man's eyeballs
> at fifty yards. She was a sizzling little hooker just the right side of

> the age of consent, and only too well aware of the fortune to be made from the meter that ticked away in her knickers. She plied for hire, on wicked pencil thin high-heels, on a short stretch of pavement between Piccadilly underground station and the first set of traffic lights in the Haymarket. The view from my third-floor office window in Regent Chambers exactly overlooked the limits of her beat. Watching Black Satin Hotpants mincing up and down was not, however, without discomfort. All but the bottom six inches of my window was blacked off by a giant hoarding that advertised Hankey Bannister's Scotch Whisky and it was only by adopting a position of prayer that I was able to catch a glimpse of her. Business had been slack of late and ogling Hotpants had given me housemaid's knee.

That was the opening paragraph of Norman's novel, and what a belletristic beginning to a book it makes. The prose is attractive and there is not a hint of pornography. Yet it would be unfair to both author and readers to include Norman in the A–Z section, splendid detective story writer that he is.

Female readers of this guide may say that as a male I am merely picking out a paragraph that appeals to males only, and that the tastes of female readers should also be catered for. Indeed they should, and one of the benefits of eroticism in literature in modern times is that ideally it should be something that can be shared by male and female together and enjoyed together. This is absolutely true and it is equally true that people of opposite sexes can be brought closer together through sharing an appreciation of erotic works. There have been countless cases in modern times of a love affair, or even a marriage, developing out of two people's enthusiasm for a single book. Probably nobody realized this better than Dickens when he wrote that "'tis love, 'tis love, 'tis love that makes the world go round."

The late H. E. Bates wrote in 1954:

> Our age is an anxious one. It has been, artistically, a bony, wiry, unbending time, in which the application of the word charm to a work of art has been tantamount to damning it in all serious eyes forever. . . . Literature . . . has been terrified of happiness and the candid attempt to make us laugh. We have been prone to make a fetish of plays with buried spiritual meanings and have been fed—I now suggest to the teeth—with films and literature in which no act or word, however gross, is spared.[3]

Bates suggested that one might usefully turn to Raymond Peynet's creation of *Les Amoreux* (*Elle* and *Lui*) because they "are undoubtedly the nicest lovers in the world."[4] It is true that Peynet is first and foremost a cartoonist and that to study his works, notably *The Lovers' Pocketbook*, *The Lovers' Bedside Book*, and *The Lovers' Weekend Book,* is to revel in his pictorial effects that are superb. Yet I was very nearly tempted to include Peynet in the A–Z section if only for the splendid captions to his pictures. It is the combination of his sketches of Elle and Lui in various situations and the superb if terse captions that together provide erotic delight of a kind that ensures shared happiness between two people reading them together.

One example will suffice. Peynet has drawn a sketch of Lui in the bath, still turning on the water with Elle standing coyly outside, totally nude, but very coy and with her hands held across her nether parts. Obviously Lui is begging her to enter the bath with him. All shy Elle says is "I can't swim."

To me, obviously in danger of taking some very risky bypaths inside the maze of modern erotica, this is erotic literature with a small *l* cleverly enhanced by the artist. If I seem to have gone slightly astray, I can only say that I am in good company. H. E. Bates, a splendid novelist and no mean literary critic, comments on *The Lovers' Pocketbook:*

> Where else do the tears of love make garlands, and the garlands of autumn make tresses of hair? Nowhere except in Peynet. . . . Just as the lovers themselves are quite the nicest lovers in the world, so are these the nicest bosoms. Is there anything nicer than the scene of tender detachment on the park seat, when a lover nurses the apples of his delight. . . . Peynet, without a doubt, is a poet. His world of lovers, of parks, of birds, of cherry time, of daisy chains and daisy clocks . . . is intensely lyrical."[5]

One would certainly hesitate to describe John Fowles, the author of those highly popular novels, *The French Lieutenant's Woman* and *The Magus* as an erotic writer and he, too, will not be found in the A–Z section. Yet in his novel, *The Collector,* he includes in a work of fiction what is really an analysis of some of the problems that an obsession with erotic thoughts can bring about. In this book he often delves into the psychology of eroticism seen through the words and actions of his characters. It is not that this is an erotic book in any joyous or uplifting sense, but it gives a completely new look at what constitutes erotica from the trivial to the intense, from the perils of a lonely but intense imagination to a longing to escape to a new relationship.

The Collector has been called "a psychological thriller" that explores the relationship between the sexes and especially the kind of relationship that can exist between the few and the many. Published in London in 1963 as a first novel, it has only two characters, Fred Clegg, who divides his time between collecting butterflies and daydreaming, and the attractive Miranda Gray, a doctor's daughter. Fred wins a handsome sum of money on the football pools, buys a country cottage, kidnaps Miranda, and holds her there. The first part of the story is told by Fred, the second by Miranda, and Fred finished off the story.

What makes *The Collector* so realistic is that the novel is actually based on a true-life story. In June 1957 a twenty-six-year-old woman told Bow Street magistrates in London how she had been held prisoner for three months in an underground room beneath a shed.[6]

When I wrote to Mr. Fowles to ask him if he could confirm that there was a link between this case and his book, he kindly replied: "*The Collector* was indeed based on the incident you referred to. Of course books spring from countless things and another important source in my case was Bartok's opera, *Bluebeard's Castle.*"[7]

When Miranda is in captivity she keeps a diary and in it she records thoughts and actions. "I think, perhaps, I'll just try putting my arms round him and kissing him," she writes. "No more. But he'd grow to like that. It would drag on. It's got to be a shock." The next day she acts:

> I made him sit down and then I sat on his lap. He was so stiff, so shocked, that I had to go on. . . . In a nasty perverted way it was exciting. A woman-in-me reaching out to a man-in-him. I can't explain. It was also the feeling that he didn't know what to do. That he was sheer virgin. . . . I had to force him to kiss me. He made a sort of feeble pretense of being afraid that he might lose his head. I don't care if you do, I said. And I kissed him again. His mouth was sweet. He smelled clean and I shut my eyes. It wasn't so bad.

The Collector analyzes brilliantly the minds of both kidnapper and kidnapped and the fantasies of both. Thank God, too, that, unlike reading Joyce and Beckett, one doesn't get tangled up in the mind of the author. John Fowles also wrote to me saying that "a French woman novelist got on to the real life case even before I did, although I didn't know this until some time after my own book came out. In some ways she kept even closer to the original than I did."[8]

The French author was Simonne Jacquemard and her novel, *Le Veilleur de Nuit* (The night watchman, in the sense of the night watcher), was published in Paris in 1962. Anyone wishing to study the subjects envisaged in *The Collector* should certainly read her book, too. In this story a young man creates a hiding place in his garden to which he lures a young girl.

Today eroticism can be found in nonerotic works, sometimes, as in *The Dead Butler Caper*, in a single paragraph, but also in an oblique way by providing enlightenment on psychological problems as in both *The Collector* and *Le Veilleur de Nuit*. One must remember that eroticism can be hidden in prose and verse just as much as it can be blatantly exploited in the same forms of art. In the twentieth century it has been the blatant pornography of a few best-selling authors that led to a reaction in the development of a new, low-key, and much more subtle form of eroticism among a new school of writers. Often such works are as much concerned with sexual frustration as sexual triumph. One recent example of this was Melvyn Bragg's *A Time to Dance,* London, 1991, about a fifty-four-year-old retired bank manager who is embroiled in the most passionate love affair of his life with a girl young enough to be his granddaughter. The story is told in the epistolary form in which the male writes as follows: "You said words that made me so confident and insatiable that our lovemaking could go on for more than an hour—you know that I do not exaggerate—stop, because of satisfaction—often for both of us—and then, quite soon, begin again, this time for longer. And then yet again for hours."

But such thoughts, fantasies—call them what you will—are damped down when the retired bank manager reads Hazlitt's *Liber Amoris*[9] when that Victorian writer had a hopeless passion for a teenage girl: "Dreadful, second-rate, disgraceful suspicions flooded through my mind. . . . I tried to order them away."

Sometimes the attempt to be different from other writers goes astray even when it makes amusing reading. It was certainly an idea with great possibilities to make a novel out of the true life story of Wallis Simpson and the former King Edward VIII who was relegated to the title of duke of Windsor. Then one reads this account of Mrs. Simpson seeing the future king [he was then only prince of Wales and heir to the throne] stark naked for the first time:

"His testicles, Wallis noted, seemed trapped within his body. This must have given him a great deal of sexual difficulty through the years and was probably responsible for the lack of hair on his face and chest. An erection could not be easy." This paragraph might cause one to look up a medical textbook for more information on such a problem, but, put as bluntly as this, it is more a letdown than a turn-on in a literary sense.[10]

Oh, for more Peynet! Even just his brief captions! The danger in many of today's attempts to try to be erotic and at the same time original in expressing it is one we come across again and again. Mario Vargas Llosa is a skillful writer, but when translated into English one feels that his attempts to say something different occasionally fail to convince. In his book, *In Praise of the Stepmother,* for example, he becomes a bit too pretentious in a discussion about a picture by Fernando de Szyszlo: "We were a woman and a man and now we are ejaculation, orgasm, and a fixed idea. We have become sacred and obsessive."[11]

The book is the story of how one Don Rigoberto fantasizes while making love to his new wife, Lucrecia. His schoolboy son spies on his stepmother from the roof of her bathroom and eventually makes love to her when his father is away. When all is discovered Don Rigoberto boots out his wife and abandons sex in favor of meditation on sexlessness, corresponding to Fra Angelico's "Annunciation" in San Marco in Florence.

There has been much discussion over the past few years about the desirability or otherwise of reprinting the Marquis de Sade's work, *Justine,* in the English language. Susannah Herbert, a most perspicacious critic, has declared that "the Marquis de Sade has a lot to answer for. It seems that ever since he made it unexceptionable to be sex-obsessed *and* an intellectual, avant-gardists have felt obliged to be both. Could it be that the sadomasochistic orgy has ousted the creative writing course as a preparation for publication?"

This apt comment was made by Herbert in the course of reviewing three 1991 novels that might be said to come under the heading of erotic or mildly erotic. One of these was *Women,* by Philippe Sollers (London), telling the story of Will, a philandering American writer with limitless sexual expertise who believed that women run the world, are "allied to death," and that they have banded together in an organization called WOMANN (World Organization for Male Annihilation and a New Natality). Herbert describes this work as "pseudoeroticism," citing the author as saying on page 279, "Lady reader who by some miracle has got as far as this, if you possess a pair of panty hose, you're not worthy to read this book."[12]

Therein lies one of the literary problems of the 1990s: the debasing of the erotic novel by the introduction of pseudoeroticism, sadism, masochism, avant-gardism, call it what you will. This is shown in such works as *Two Girls, Fat and Thin,* by Mary Gaitskill, and *Absolute Hush,* by Sara Banerji, both published in London in 1991. It is surely no coincidence that the thin girl is named Justine and that she grows up in Middle America fantasizing about torture and then goes to New York and ends up half-strangled and tied to her bedposts by a male she met in a bar. As for *Absolute Hush,* this is the story of incest resulting in pregnancy for one of two thirteen-year-old twins.

Another factor in this trend of pseudoeroticism is that of the feminist school of writing. The feminist movement has undoubtedly created a tendency for women to write about sex, stepping into the male arena, some would call it. There is of course every good reason why they should, but as Virginia Woolf pointed out "when a woman comes to write a novel, she will find that she is perpetually trying to alter the established values—to make serious what appears insignificant to a man, and trivial what is to him important." In this context Erica Jong comes to mind. She has somewhat unfairly been called "the Frank Harris of the fairer sex," but a recent novel of hers, *Any Woman's Blues,* raised just this question. In all this work Erica Jong seems to suggest that perhaps after all women must accept men as they are: "The male ego, the rush of testosterone and most of society's rules dictate that man must be central or he will sulk."

One sinister factor in the gradual debasement of erotic literature in the present age has, of course, been the development of what is known as commercial erotica and the exploitation of it by video. This unhappily applies across the world from the Far West to the Far East. In Japan today *roman poruno* (which can loosely be called romantic porn) is the successor to the earlier *erodakushun* (erotic production). *Roman poruno* is a predominant form of present-day Japanese cinema. It should be noted, however, that Japanese work of this kind is not as pornographic as much that is produced in Europe since the Japanese Criminal Code prohibits public display of obscene materials as well as close-up explicit shots of the sexual act. Admittedly this refers mainly to plays and films, but it has had some effect on Japanese novels, too, and, though the film is not quite literature, in any study of eroticism today the influence of the film needs to be taken into account. One must remember that a film requires a script and a script is a form of literature.

A recent report in the *Japanese Interpreter* (a serious journal) on a movie belonging to the new *roman poruno* category read: "Summary: seven fornications, one masturbation, one fellatio, one fetish, and one sadomasochistic act. Nudity throughout, breasts and butts galore, but no front shots below the navel and no public hair."[13]

However, Japan has not thrown away its past traditions of producing some of the most superbly written erotic literature. Much of this ancient work like that of Baroness Murasaki Shikibu and her extremely lengthy *The Tale of Genji* is still being printed as well as being translated into other languages. Japanese erotic literature still owes much to the talent of earlier generations for creating an erotic vernacular that is far more elegant and actually upliftingly pleasant than similar language in the Western world where the tendency has been, alas, in modern times to exploit the crudest of works and phrases rather than attempt imaginative invention of something new and better. Even today there is still a tendency among some in Japan to recall the distant past when lovemaking was viewed as a complicated exercise and people were urged to study its intricate procedures and the special language of love. The male in those distant days had to learn the "nine styles of moving the jade stalk" and the female had to be aware of such exercises as "the wailing monkey embracing a tree," or "the cat and mouse in one hole."

A particularly instructive book on this and other erotic themes in Japan is *Pink Samurai: The Pursuit and Politics of Sex in Japan,* by Nicholas Bornoff, London, 1991. He reveals how even the prevalence of endearing names for sex organs has recently led to controversy. Japanese feminists have objected to the fact that the word *ochinchin* ("honorable tinkle-tinkle") existed for men, while there was no equivalent term for the female organ. It was, therefore, suggested that to put matters right women should have their own word, *ware-*

me-chan ("dear little slit"), but Nicholas Bornoff suggests that the idea has not caught on.

The late Georges Simenon was, of course, essentially a writer of detective and crime stories, yet even he produced one novel that has been judged as coming under the category of the erotic by some critics. This was *The Stain on the Snow*.[14] Maybe Simenon wanted to break new ground. He openly boasted about the thousands of women he claimed to have bedded. The chief character in *The Stain on the Snow* is a young man who is equally obsessed with making careful note of how many females he slept with in each week of his life. In that sense Simenon might have been almost autobiographical. This is not a pleasant novel and, needless to say, there is crime as well as sex in the story. Indeed, I am almost tempted not to follow the Simenon path in this maze of modern erotica. But, as others have dubbed the work erotic, I feel it is a duty to explore it. For here is yet another example of an attempt to introduce erotic analysis into modern novels.

Most of this work consists of confused ideas and fantasies pouring out of the mind of Frank Friedmaier, whose mother runs a bordello. One paragraph early in the book says that "when Frank did kill his first man, at nineteen years old, his initiation into murder was hardly more exciting than the earlier initiation into sex had been. And, like the earlier one, it was quite unpremeditated. It was an event without context."

Frank's early life had been spent with a foster mother and he only received occasional visits from his mother. When he lived in his mother's brothel (his father was unknown) he became quite the boss and went to bed with any of the whores as and when he liked. To them he was "Herr Frank." Suddenly he becomes fascinated in a most curious manner with sixteen-year-old Sissy, a neighbor's daughter. He takes her to the cinema and occasionally out for a meal. She is quite pathetically fond of him: "Have you thought about me, Frank?" or "Do you think I'm ugly, Frank?" As for Frank, "He didn't fumble her. He just slipped his hand inside her blouse for a second. Yesterday, at the Lido, he hadn't thought about her breasts, and he had no idea what they were like. The thought had struck him during the night, while he was in bed with Minna, who was almost flat-chested."

The curious effect this book has on a reader is first that one is attracted to the character of Sissy, despite her inept childishness, while at the same time surprisingly sympathetic to the revolting Frank, hoping he will mend his ways, cure himself of his fantasies, and come to love Sissy. In this respect the author has been quite clever. But what happens? Frank arranges for the virgin Sissy to sleep with a pal of his unbeknownst to her. Sissy is lured to his bedroom at night and the lights are out: the idea is that she will climb into his bed and make love with Frank. But it is Frank's friend Kromer who awaits her, while Frank hides outside the bedroom. But Sissy, having climbed into the bed, puts her hand out and switches on the light, screaming out when she sees who is there. Then she rushes out of the apartment.

What was Frank trying to prove by this escapade? Or what was Simenon trying to say? Not even at the end of the story when Frank is in prison and a forgiving Sissy is allowed to visit him do we really understand quite what has happened. All Simenon records is "She had come. She was there. She was in him. She was his."

Both *The Collector* and *The Stain on the Snow* reflect how sophisticated and complex erotic themes in novels are today. What is almost certain is that fifty years ago such works as these would not be regarded by the most discriminating of critics as erotic. That path of the maze would have been deliberately avoided. Nevertheless it should now be quite clear that the work of James Joyce, D. H. Lawrence, Aldous Huxley, Miller, and Beckett has led in this new direction. Their themes never quite succeeded in creating new forms of eroticism- that was what some of them, consciously or unconsciously, were trying to do. Chiefly, especially Lawrence and Beckett, they were revolting against the crassly stupid censorship rules of the day, especially those of the British.

Since victories have been won in the courts over extreme forms of censorship, as in the case of *Lady Chatterley's Lover,* and the abolition of the powers of the lord chamberlain to ban plays because of a single sentence to which he and his office objected, there have been some unfortunate developments to take advantage of these changes. These have applied more to the stage than to the world of books. Often what happens today is that some reputable classic is distorted in presentation. One example was the production in 1991 of the eighteenth-century comedy, *The Dispute,* by the French dramatist, Pierre Marivaux. An East European company produced this originally elegant play at the St. Bride's Centre in London and turned it into what one critic, Charles Spencer, described as "an uproarious piece of soft porn."[15] Spencer also referred to the same company's production of Bertolt Brecht's first play, *Baal,* as "a potent reminder of what a thoroughly nasty piece of work the German dramatist was even before his conversion to hard-line Marxism."[16]

Spencer's further comments on *Baal* will perhaps be some justification for my not including Brecht in the A–Z section.

> The play has a central character who is clearly a dark personification of young Bertolt's adolescent desires. . . . Baal is irresistible to women. He mauls them, beds them, humiliates them, and kicks them out. After that they try to commit suicide. He brawls in bars, kills his best friend, and writes terrible poetry. . . . Baal's an artist, you see, rebelling against the repression of bourgeois society. And

because he's an artist, anything he does is permissible, even admirable. Lucky old Baal. Lucky old Bertolt. Poor old audience. . . . If it weren't for Brecht's ludicrously inflated reputation, the piece would have disappeared into the oblivion it so richly deserves long ago.

Brecht's work is perhaps the best example of what can be regarded as the bogus, deliberately unpleasant, and often politically left-wing erotica of modern times. It is part political, but aimed to shock in a crude kind of way. Inevitably it ends up by being neither genuinely political or even remotely erotic. Edna O'Brien makes the point rather effectively when she writes that "surprise is everything. It is often confused with sensation, though the two could not be more different. Sensation is a trick and short-lived. Surprise is a little lance to the psyche."

Occasionally such experiments—for that is the only way to describe them—come off. James Joyce's *Ulysses* was, perhaps, one such case. But Joyce was clever: he set people pondering for so long as to what he really meant, or whether he meant nothing of importance at all that it led to the creation of a James Joyce industry for scores of academics. There was the task that Professor Hans Walter Gabler, a textual scholar at Munich University, set himself when the West German Government gave him three-hundred-thousand dollars to prepare a fresh edition of *Ulysses* in 1977, one that would correct all the typographical errors and deletions that had made their way into previous printings of the novel (see JOYCE, JAMES, in the A–Z section). Gabler labored for seven years at his self-imposed task, eventually claiming that he had "fixed" no fewer than five-thousand mistakes. Meanwhile the Joyce industry continues to flourish, quite recently through the work of Bruce Arnold: *The Scandal of Ulysses*, London, 1991, and the establishment by John Kidd of the Boston University James Joyce Research Center.

Perhaps Bernard Shaw summed up the *Ulysses* problem best, or at the very least as well as anyone else. In a letter to Sylvia Beach the playwright wrote:

> I have read several fragments of *Ulysses* in its serial form. It is a revolting record of a disgusting phase of civilization, but it is a truthful one, and I should like to put a cordon round Dublin, round up every male person in it between the ages of fifteen and thirty, force them to read it and ask them whether on reflection they could see anything amusing in all that foul-mouthed derision and obscenity. To you, possibly, it may appeal as art: you are probably a young barbarian beglamoured by the excitements and enthusiasms that art stirs up in passionate material.[17]

In the wake of the feminist movement female writers have at last entered the field in pursuit of erotic themes. Outstanding among such writers is, of course, Erica Jong (see JONG, ERICA in the A–Z section). It is worth noting what Jong has to say about herself. "I'm the most feminist woman you will ever meet," she told one interviewer, Martyn Harris. "Though I don't want to be part of any movement where I can't dance." "But," insisted her interviewer, "you suggest men need to dominate and that women have to go along with that." Erica replied: "Every smart woman knows that. We know men are focused on their sexuality, on measuring themselves against other men in battle and in bed. But we always hope it isn't true."[18]

What was remarkable about Erica Jong's best-seller, *Fear of Flying*, was that it was esteemed as much by men as by women. Anthony Burgess praised it lavishly and it may well be that this explains why ever since she has taken the view of herself as a Writer with a capital *W*. "I believe that the Writer is healing the reader," she says. "Writing is a sacramental act. . . . The Writer has to write in order not to go mad."[19]

The Eastern world even in modern times has had some outstanding female writers who have tackled the kind of subjects that for far too long were left chiefly to males. One such was Uno Chiyo, hardly known at all in the West, but whose extraordinary life story has recently been dramatized for Japanese television. Her books included *Confessions of Love* and *The Sound of the Wind*, both of which have been translated into English and published in London. In a review of her works in the London *Times* she was described as "the Japanese combination of Colette and Elinor Glyn." Rebecca Copeland has traced the whole story of Uno Chiyo from her early life as an adventurous, unconventional young woman to the time when she became one of her country's leading novelists: *Uno Chiyo: A Biography*, London, 1991.

Yet another of the new and enlightened school of female authors entering the erotic lists is Ann Oakley (see OAKLEY, ANN, A–Z section). When her first novel was published in 1988 its implications were not perceived by most reviewers. *The Men's Room*, as it was entitled, turned out to be something of a delayed literary time bomb that finally went off when it was turned into a television film by the British Broadcasting Corporation in 1991. Views on that particular transformation of novel to screen varied markedly and Ann Oakley drew much criticism somewhat unfairly as a result of her cooperation with Laura Lamson in producing the film scenario. The idea behind *The Men's Room* was to provide an exposé of our male-dominated society, but the dialogue given to this film did little to uphold such a theme. One critic, Richard Last of the London *Daily Telegraph*, said of Laura Lamson's scenario, "It had aspects which suggested its author—by which I mean Ms. Lamson, not Ms. Oakley—didn't intend to be taken entirely seriously. As her characters rampaged around, changing alliances, tearing each other apart, and sticking themselves together again, I felt she was, at least marginally, taking the mickey both out of us [i.e., putting in one's place] and the feminist ethic."[20]

Here again we come to one of those more dubious paths of this intricate maze of modern eroticism. It is the path that brings one to the modern erotic film, sometimes based on books and occasionally ruining them, but more often simply the screening of soft-porn twaddle. The warning must be given that any student of modern eroticism should read the book before seeing the film and most certainly watch for sheer cynicism without a care for what is either artistic or beautiful in the works presented as films alone without any book behind them. Danger signals should certainly be hoisted over such pictures as *Wild Orchid*, Zalman King's sequel to *9½ Weeks* and *Two Moon Junction*. These films all tended to make "rot" rather than Eros the current emphasis in erotica. In this *Wild Orchid* epic Mickey Rourke plays a depressingly inadequate male and Jacqueline Bisset is a foul-mouthed virago who not only dominates her man, but on occasions dresses in a man's suit to conduct a business deal. Whether this is done to clinch the deal, or to convince the man she deals with that she is a transvestite is anybody's guess.

By this time one has reached the final and, hopefully, correct exit from this literary maze and needs time to ponder, to absorb and sift through all that has been seen and heard. What is certainly true beyond any doubt is that today there is not just one single genre of erotic literature, but several and they seem to be multiplying all the time. They range from Stephen Fry's novel, *The Liar*, with its hero for whom "love was his guilty secret, sex his public pride" to the Maly Theater of Leningrad's production of *Gaudeamus* in London, described by one critic as "a mix of the erotic, the grotesque, and the beautiful."

PART TWO
· · · · · · · ·

A–Z
Author Entries

ABÉLARD, PIERRE
Born 1079. Died 1142.

Philosopher, teacher, and theologian, Abélard was born at Pallet near Nantes, in which area he was known even in his youth as "Dr. Palatinus" on account of his scholastic talents. He studied under Roscellin first and later under William of Champeaux. At the age of thirty-six he was acclaimed as the outstanding teacher in the whole country and was as well highly regarded beyond the borders of France. His school at Nôtre Dame was full of students from all over Europe.

Suddenly tragedy changed Abélard's whole life. He had fallen in love with Héloise, the niece of Canon Fulbert of Nôtre Dame. The canon was so outraged that he ordered his niece to become a nun of Argenteuil convent while procuring the right to have Abélard castrated. Abélard thereafter became an inmate of a hermitage known as the Paraclete. It was the amatory correspondence between Abélard and Héloise that in part led to the destruction of this love affair, rightly considered to be one of the most romantic of the age. These love letters, still extant, reveal the most intimate passions as well as spiritual worries.

In the meantime Abélard also suffered imprisonment for heresy by a judgment of the Synod of Soissons in 1121. Later he was called to take charge of the Abbey of St. Gildas-de-Rhuys in Britanny, while Héloise directed a sisterhood at Paraclete. Eventually Abelard's reputation as a great teacher was restored, though his enemies continued to try to thwart him. Finally, he went to Rome and died in the priory of St. Marcellus. His body was taken to Paraclete where Héloise was buried alongside him in 1163. In 1817 both their bodies were reinterred at Père-la-Chaise in Paris. The first of Abélard's books to be printed was *Scito te ipsum* in 1721. For further insight into Abélard's life and his relationship with Héloise and their correspondence see *Peter Abélard* by Helen Waddell, London, 1933; *The Epistle of Eloisa to Abélard*, Alexander Pope, London, 1717.

AELIANUS, CLAUDIUS
Lived (circa A.D. 250)

A native of Praeneste in Italy, Aelianus was the author of two books that have survived, the *Varia Historia* and *De Animalium Natura*. The latter concerned the peculiarities of animals, but both works include some erotic stories. These books were edited by Hercher in what was known as the Teubner Series, 1864–66.

AESCHYLUS
Born 525 B.C. Died 456 B.C.

The son of Euphorion, Aeschylus was one of the earliest of the great Athenian tragic poets and dramatists. In 490 B.C. he fought against the Persians at Marathon, and repeated these efforts in 480 and 479 B.C. at Salamis and Plataea. In 476 B.C. he went to Syracuse at the request of its ruler, Hiero, and he seemed to have spent most of the rest of his life in Sicily. He died at Gela and was buried there. He was chiefly responsible for developing Attic drama, which had previously consisted of monologues divided by choric songs, by introducing a second and third actor as well as scenery and stage props. Altogether he wrote ninety plays, including *Prometheus Bound*, *Agamemnon*, and *Eumenides*. See chapter 1 of this guide for reference to some of his erotic work, and also translations of his work in English by Anna Swanwick in 1881, also by Henry Sidgwick, 1887–92.

ALDINGTON, RICHARD
Born 1892. Died 1962.

Most discerning literary critics would perhaps raise their eyebrows at the suggestion that Richard Aldington should be included in this book. Nevertheless for one single, short work alone he justifies this choice by his superb demonstration of the joyful and elegantly erotic in his *A Dream in the Luxembourg* (1930). In his early days Aldington, who married the American poet, Hilda Doolittle, in 1913, wrote vehemently on antiwar themes, as for example *Images of War* and *Death of a Hero*. Later he became a controversial biographer when he wrote of the lives of the duke of Wellington, D. H. Lawrence, and Lawrence of Arabia.

A *Dream in the Luxembourg*, naturally referring to those delightful Parisian gardens with their long avenues, was published in London and dedicated in the most unostentatious manner possible "For B," with the comment "*Si vis* amari, ama." In developing his theme Aldington writes, "For who can be in love in Paris in June, / And the lady of his thoughts in another country, / Without daydreaming under the trees in the Luxembourg?" There are fifty-three rather small-sized pages of print of this poem, which is one of the most splendid narrative poems of love of the twentieth century. There is love at a distance with happy thoughts, love in imaginative dreams, then a swift message, and an invitation to meet. Eventually the narrator meets his love again and they have dinner together, when he comments:

> I was still too excited to eat much,
> And of course I wasted so much time looking at her
> When I thought she wouldn't notice it,
> That I was always miles behind with my course.

Later that same night he is told to go to bed and rest. But he tells himself, "If I do not love her tonight it is treason, / Treason to Love, to her, to myself, to the miracle." And so he plucks up courage and taps at her bedroom door and she says, "Come in." He does so.

"Is there anything the matter?" she asks him. "Has Antoinette forgotten something?"

The poem continues:

> I shall say no more,
> Nothing of how we were lovers,
> How I was her lover and she was my woman.
> Though once I meant to tell her—the real her—
> How in the dream she was so beautiful
> And so ardent a woman lover,
> And all we did and all we said.

The whole poem is a gentle treatise for all lovers and perhaps especially first-time lovers.

ANACREON OF TEOS
Born circa 563 B.C. Died circa 478 B.C.

A poet of pleasure, love, and wine, Anacreon had many imitators, so many in fact that it is not always possible to trace what is actually his work. About 544 B.C. he moved to Abdera in Thrace, but later he lived with Polycrates, the despot of Samos, until the latter's death in 522 B.C. After that he lived with Hipparchus in Athens. From his name comes the unusual adjective anacreonitic as applied to a certain type of verse. Some of his original work as well as some imitations are contained in Poetae Lyrici Graeci, by Theodor Bergk, Leipzig, 3 vols., 1943. See ANACREONITIC in the glossary, also chapter 1.

APOLLINAIRE, GUILLAUME [WILHELM DE KOSTROWITZI]
Born 1880. Died 1918.

This French poet, who was born in Rome, will always be associated with the Symbolist movement and even as one of the founders of surrealism. His verses took poetry into new paths as was shown in his best-known works such as *Alcools* and *Calligrammes*. He was also the author of a number of erotic tales. Two of the latter were *The Debauched Hospodar*, published by the Olympia Press, Paris (1962) and *Les Onze Milles Verges*, a French text published in Holland in 1948, which is described as "the most explicit and violent erotic novel ever written in French," though this claim is somewhat exaggerated.

Apollinaire was also fascinated by the life story of the notorious Comte de Mirabeau, and in *L'Oeuvre du Comte de Mirabeau*, Paris, 1921, he provided an introduction and bibliographic essay on the man. He also wrote *L'Oeuvre Libertine Des Conteurs Italiens*, Paris, 1910. This work consisted of selections of Italian erotica including the anonymous *Nouvelles de Masuccio*, *Proverbes en Faceties d'Antonio Cornazzano*, and *Le gros Menuisier*. Apollinaire wrote an introduction to this work along with bibliographical essays. It will be noted that many of his works were published long after his death. One of the other many tasks he set himself was that of sorting out the genuine from the dubious or forgeries of the Italian sonnet writer, Pietro Aretino. In his *Essai de Bibliographie Aretinesque* (1909) Apollinaire largely succeeded in separating the one from the other and he listed editions of Aretino's works from those originating in Venice in 1556 to those published in Paris (1757), another Venice edition (1779), and those of Rome (1792), Leiden (1864), Paris (1882), and Berlin (1904). See ARETINO, PIETRO, in the A–Z section.

Though a French citizen, Apollinaire had a Polish mother and an Italian father. When he was young his mother brought him to London where he had a governess who was extremely circumspect. Many of Apollinaire's verses were written about his various mistresses, but his first, long, rhyming if unpunctuated poem was about his hopeless passion for Annie, his governess. This was entitled *La Chanson du mai-aime*, Paris, 1903, and in an esoteric way it conjured up all kinds of moods, dreams, images, and sometimes just symbols. Apollinaire was also an influential art critic; by this work too he influenced French painting. Also worth studying is *Le Poète Assassiné* (1916), which was translated into English in 1923. A more recent translation into English of Apollinaire's work has been *The Amorous Exploits of a Young Rakehell* (originally *Les Exploits d'un Jeune Don Juan*), published in Paris in 1953.

APULEIUS, LUCIUS
Born circa A.D. 123.

Though the date of Apuleius's death remains unconfirmed, it has been established that he was born in Madaura in North Africa and educated at Carthage and Athens. Thus equipped, on the death of his father, who left him a large fortune, he traveled widely, visiting the Middle East and Asia. He had an acquisitive mind, especially for the furtive practices and strange rituals that he came across in his travels. He was specially interested in all erotic cults and what he called "priestly irregularities" in various parts. His most important work was *Metamorphoseon seu de Asino Aureo*, which is better known today as *The Golden Ass*, a satire on the manners and customs of his day. English translations of his work are *The Golden Ass*, Sir G. Head, London, 1851, and *Eros and Psyche*, R. Bridges, London, 1885. This latter work provided the inspiration for Raphael's frescoes on the story of Psyche in the Villa Fannesina in Rome. See also chapter 1.

ARETINO, PIETRO
Born 1492. Died 1556.

This Italian poet was one of the most celebrated satirists of his day and he possessed a keen eye for the erotic, especially if it lent itself to humorous writing. Born at Arezzo, from whence he was banished on account of his lampooning against the practice of indulgences, which had been gravely abused by the Catholic church in the latter part of the Middle Ages, he sought support for his work from others. Prior to this he had worked as a bookbinder at Perugia and had actually been favorably received by Pope Leo X in Rome in 1517. That patronage was eventually lost not only by his lampoon on indulgences, but by the publication of sonnets denounced as obscene.

Gregarious and adaptable as he always was, Aretino found little difficulty in obtaining patronage elsewhere, particularly from King Francis I of France and King Charles V of Germany. The latter part of his life was spent in Venice in such luxury and ostentation that he kept a veritable seraglio of mistresses. The latter were known by the nickname of "Aretinies" by the Venetian populace who had a fondness for the poet on account of his sense of fun. His humorous and erotic verses won him many admirers. Donald Thomas, in his work *Master of Renaissance Erotica*, London, 1970, has described Aretino as being "like some Italian Falstaff, he lied, cheated, drank, and whored his way through sixty-four years of his country's history." Aretino was painted by Titian, showing him as dressed in doublet and cloak. Pope Julius III made him a knight of St. Peter early on in his life and it was even suggested that at one time he was nearly made a cardinal! Somewhere there is supposed to exist a complete copy of his *Sonetti lussuriosi di Pietro Aretino*, which is believed to have been published in Venice in 1527. It contained both erotic verses and erotic engravings of copulating couples. In 1802 a book entitled *The Amours of Peter Aretin* by James Aitkin resulted in the author's being prosecuted by the Society for the Suppression of Vice and given a six-month jail sentence. There have been various attempts to trace the Aretino sonnets and to separate the genuine from the clearly bogus plagiarism of the poet. The most consistent effort to achieve that was made by Guillaume Apollinaire (see APOLLINAIRE GUILLAUME, in the A–Z section).

There was an attempt to reproduce the Aretino sonnets in English in the latter part of the last century. *The Lascivious Sonnets of Pietro Aretino* was published privately in London. It has been suggested that Oscar Wilde was the translator. Though this is far from being confirmed, it would seem that the translation was reasonably well done. In what is called Sonnet Number Four we have this version in English:

> Place your leg, dearest, on my shoulder here,
> And take my truncheon in your tender grasp,
> And while I gently move it, let your clasp
> Tighten and draw me to your bosom, dear.
> And should I stray from front to hinder side,
> Call me a rogue and villain, will not you?
> Because I know the difference 'twixt the two,
> As stallions know how lusty mares to ride.

Among Aretino's many works were his dialogues, called *Ragionamenti* (1535–38); five prose comedies, *Il Marescalco, La Cortigiana, L'Ipocrito, La Talanta,* and *Il Filosofo;* a tragedy, *Orazia* (1546) and some volumes of letters and sonnets, the last of which were translated into French under the title of *Académie des Dames.* See also chapter 3 and an English edition of Aretino, *The Works of Aretino,* translated by Samuel Putnam, New York, 1933, and *The Divine Aretino: Pietro of Arezzo 1492–1556: A Biography,* by James Cleugh, London, 1965.

ARISTOPHANES
Born circa 450 B.C. Died circa 388 B.C.

Unquestionably the first and greatest of all the early poets, Aristophanes, the son of Philippus, was born in Aegiua, a fact that later was to tell against him when his entitlement to being an Athenian citizen was challenged. The Greek statesman, Cleon, made a number of attempts to deprive Aristophanes of his civic rights. This enmity toward the poet can in part be explained by the fact

that his verses contained bold criticism of leading statesmen as well as carica-
tures of them. He never hesitated about using the names of real people in his
comedies, including such as Cleon, Nicias, and Demosthenes (all mentioned
in the work, *Knights*), Socrates in *The Clouds* and Euripides in *Archanians*.
The fact that he used real names in his works has given them a historical
value and greatly added to the knowledge of the period.

As will be seen in chapter 1, Aristophanes introduced some lively erotic
sequences in such of his works as the comedy *Ecclesiazusae* and *Lysistrata*,
which took as its theme the power of sex in the life of a community and more
especially during war, in this case the war against Sparta. Aristophanes very
cleverly took the women's part and in some ways developed the idea of mili-
tant feminism before anyone else had thought of it. One of Aristophanes'
favorite gimmicks in writing was what he called the unexpected joke, for
example, ending a sentence with a quite unexpected word, a trick that worked
much more easily than one would think. He also created extraordinary com-
pound words, sometimes extending to as many as 170 letters. His work, *The
Women in Parliament,* was in effect a caricature of Plato's *Republic* that had set
out a plea for the absolute equality of the sexes.

ARMSTRONG, ANTHONY [ANTHONY ARMSTRONG WILLIS]
Born 1897. Died 1976.

The son of a naval captain, Anthony Willis adopted the pen name of Anthony
Armstrong for his various books and plays. Educated at Uppingham School
and Cambridge University, he joined the Royal Engineers in the British Army
in World War I, and while in World War II he served in the Royal Air Force
with the rank of squadron leader. In between the two wars he pursued writing
as a career after having been wounded in action in the first war in which he
also won the Military Cross. He first contributed weekly to *Punch* magazine
under the byline of "A.A." His writing was prolific, including five historical
romances between 1920 and 1925, a variety of novels and such plays as *Knight
of a Night* (a farce), *Ten Minute Alibi* (a thriller), *The Running Man* (a comedy
thriller), and such radio plays as *For Love of a Lady,* and *The Black King.*

However, it is for one particularly original and delightfully low-key erotic
book, *The Naughty Princes,* that Armstrong deserves credit in these biographies. He described this work as "humorous fairy stories"; in fact they were
fairy stories for adults and the best of them all is probably "The Princess and
the Frog," a work that Armstrong himself chose to be published in an anthology of stories entitled *My Naughtiest Story,* London, 1934. It is the tale of
how one Christmas morning a certain Princess Columbine stopped by a lily
pond into which she dropped her vanity case. Up springs a frog, promising

to retrieve the case for her if she will "promise to grant my request whatever it may be." His wish is granted and the princess wants to know what it is.

"My request," says the Frog, nothing if not businesslike, "is to dine at your table and sleep in your bed this night!" When the princess's Great Aunt Grizel hears this story she is duly shocked, but Princess Columbine replies: "What harm is there in keeping the promise? After all, *I'm* the person that's got to have a nasty cold frog in my nice warm bed on Christmas night." The whole story is delightful, surprising, and has a happy ending. (The Frog turns into a prince: at least that's the implication.)

One of Armstrong's World War II activities was founding the Tee Emm, the RAF Training Memorandum.

ASHBEE, HENRY SPENCER
Born 1834. Died 1900.

A wealthy businessman who made a lifelong hobby of collecting erotica, Ashbee acquired some 15,229 volumes of such work that he bequeathed to the British Museum at his death. He was also the most thorough and meticulous British bibliographer of erotica of any age, and between the 1870s and 1880s he compiled a three-volume bibliography of such, sometimes using the non de plume of Pisanus Fraxi. These works were *Centuria Librorum Absconditorum*, *Catena Librorum Tacendorum*, and *Index Librorum Prohibitorum*, all of which were privately printed. His collection of works in the British Museum includes such oddities as *My Secret Life; or, The Modern Casanova*, by "Walter," *Venus Schoolmistress; or, Birchen Sports*, and *The Pearl, a Journal of Facetiae and Voluptuous Reading*.

AUBREY, JOHN
Born 1626. Died 1697.

John Aubrey was born in Wiltshire, England, and originally made a name for himself by contributing to Dugdale's *Monasticon Anglicanum* while at Trinity College, Oxford. Later he was engaged by King Charles II to write an account of megalithic remains at Avebury in Wiltshire, where there is the largest stone circle in the world. Largely as a result of this he was in 1663 admitted as a member of the Royal Society. His work, *Miscellanies* (1696) is a storehouse of anecdotes of all kinds, including reference to some supernatural studies. *Minutes of Lives* was given by him to Anthony à Wood and was not published until long after his death under the title of *Letters by Eminent Persons* (1813). In the ordinary sense of the word Aubrey was not a writer of erotic literature, but he collected a considerable number of true-life stories of what can be described as erotic incidents and these he left to the Ashmolean Museum at Oxford, where some of his unpublished work can still be seen. An example of this can be found in his uncensored work, *Brief Lives,* in which he writes about Sir Thomas More, the Tudor statesman who was canonized by the Roman Catholic church and was the author of *Utopia.* Aubrey, referring to this, stated: "In his utopia . . . young people are to see each other stark naked before marriage. Sir William Roper, of Eltham in Kent, came early one morning to Sir Thomas, with a proposal to marry one of his daughters. My lord's daughters were then both together abed in their father's chamber asleep. He carried Sir William into the chamber and took the sheet by the corner and suddenly whipped it off. They lay on their backs, and their smocks up as high as their armpits. This awakened them and immediately they turned on their bellies. Quoth Roper: 'I have seen both sides,' and so gave a pat on her buttock he made a choice of, saying 'Thou are mine.'"

AUSONIUS, DECIMUS MAGNUS
Born circa 310. Died 390.

A native of Bordeaux, where he practiced at the bar until he was thirty, Ausonius then became a teacher of rhetoric and was a tutor to Gratian, the son of the Emperor Valentinian I. The emperor gave him the title of count and later Ausonius became prefect of Latium, Libya, and Gaul, eventually being made consul. He was a writer of both prose and verse, his most notable erotic work *Cento Nuptialis.* He had an erotic code of his own and, when composing both poems and letters in Latin, he used letters of the Greek alphabet to denote various positions of the male and female sexual organs in lovemaking. The recipient of such verse had to know exactly what he meant, as some Greek letters made the postures fairly obvious, but others were more difficult to interpret. An example of this was:

> *Enus Syriscus inguinum liguritor,*
> *Opicus magister (sic eum ducet Phyllis)*
> *Muliebre membrum quadriangulum cernit:*
> *Triquetro coactu Δ litteram ducit.*
> *De valle femorum altrinsecus pares rugas,*
> *Mediumque, fissi rima qua patet, callem*
> *Ψ dicit esse: nam trifisslis forma est.*
> *Cui ipse linguam cum dedit suam, Λ est:*
> *Veramque in illis esse Φ notam sentit.*
> *Quid imperite, P putas ibi scriptum*
> *Ubi locari I convenit longum*
> *Miselle doctor, 8 tibi sit obsceno,*
> *Tuumque nomen H sectilis signet.*

Translated into modern English, this reads approximately as follows:

> Enus Syricus, the licker of genitals and Oscan master (that's what
> Phyllis will think of him) sees the female organs as four-cornered:
> with triangular pressure he draws them into a letter Δ. Talking of
> the hollow of the thighs, he says that the equal wrinkles on either
> side, and the middle of the passage where the cleft opens, together
> make a Ψ: for it can be parted in three places. When he gives his
> tongue to it, it becomes a Λ; and he feels that there is a real letter
> Φ in there. You ignoramus, why do you think P was written there,
> where it is convenient to put a long I? Silly little teacher, try a
> disgusting 8, and let H, which can be cut, stand for your name.

BALZAC, HONORÉ DE
Born 1799. Died 1850.

A native of Tours, descended from a family of laborers whose real name was
Balssa, Balzac was educated at Vendôme and left school to take up a career
in the law. There was a brief period at the Sorbonne, but after three years,
to his parents' disgust, he decided against a legal career. Hoping to bring him
to his senses, his parents gave him a very meager allowance on which he lived
in a garret for a considerable time. For several years he existed in a state of
penury and it was not until 1829, when his work, *Les Derniers Chouans*, was
published that life began to improve for him. From then onwards he poured
out novels with astonishing rapidity, some historical but most based on contemporary French life of which he was an astute observer. It was his talent as
a novelist who could so brilliantly analyze character that made his name as
one of the outstanding French writers of his day. His *Contes Drôlatiques*, about
life in provincial France in the sixteenth century, contain some of the best-
written erotic stories of all time. They were first published in 1833: the original
plan was that there should be a hundred of these stories altogether, but Balzac
did not produce more than the third series of ten.

This was not caused by any indolence, however. Far from it: Balzac's
method as a writer was to start his work at midnight and he carried on far
into the following day. It was not unusual for him to work as long as fourteen
or fifteen hours after midnight. Despite such strange hours for working, Balzac
had a full life with many lovers. As a result of an exchange of letters in 1832
one of the chief loves of his life was the Polish Countess Evelina Hanska: she
became his wife for the last few months of his life. His death occurred in Paris
only shortly after he had returned from a lengthy honeymoon. "Observation
and imagination were his greatest assets as a writer," declared his friend,
Victor Hugo, at his funeral. He might have added one other asset—Balzac's
quietly effective sense of humor. There is, for example, this cleverly amusing

sketch of a young married couple on their wedding night, neither of whom is sure how to set about enjoying matrimony:

> Then came the innocent, gliding into the bed, and thus they found themselves, so to speak, united, but far from you can imagine what. Did you ever see a monkey brought from across the seas, who for the first time is given a nut to crack? This ape, knowing by high apish imagination how delicious is the food hidden under the shell, sniffs and twists himself about in a thousand apish ways, saying, I know not what, between his chattering jaws. Ah! With what affection he studies it, with what study he examines it, in what examination he holds it, then throws it, rolls it and tosses it about with passion, and often, when it is an ape of low extraction and intelligence, leaves the nut. As much did the poor innocent who, towards the dawn, was obliged to confess to his dear wife that, not knowing how to perform his office, or what that office was, or where to obtain the said office, it would be necessary for him to inquire concerning it, to have help and aid. "Yes," said she, "since unhappily I cannot instruct you." In fact, in spite of their efforts, essays of all kinds— inspite of a thousand things which the innocents invent, and which the wise in matters of love know nothing about—the pair dropped off to sleep, wretched at having been unable to discover the secret of marriage.

This story comes from the *Contes Drôlatiques*. Among the best known of Balzac's other works are *La Peau de Chagrin* (1831), *L'Auberge Rouge* (1831), *La Femme de Trente Ans* (1831), *Eugénie Grandet* (1833), *Le Père Goriot* (1835), and *Les Parents Pauvres* (1849). See Théophile Gautier's *H. de Balzac*, Paris, 1859. Of the numerous translations of Balzac's work one of the best and fullest is that by Katharine P. Wormeley, London, done 1890–93,

BANDELLO, MATTEO
Born 1485. Died 1561.

This Italian novelist was born at Castelnuovo (Tortona). He entered the Dominican Order and became a tutor to Lucrezia Gonzaga of the Italian family who ruled Mantua from the fourteenth to the eighteenth century. He dedicated a poem in eleven cantos, which he had written, to Lucrezia in 1545. A merry monk indeed was Matteo who, despite a lifetime of amorous adventures and escapades of various kinds, went to France and was appointed bishop of Agen by King Henri II in 1550. In many ways he was yet another of the various literary disciples of Boccacio, though he lacked the former's humor. His work, *Novelle*, was published in 1573 after some years of gathering his material together. Good editions of this work were published in London in 1740 and Milan in 1813–14, but there was an excellent English translation made by Sir Geoffrey Fenton in the sixteenth century called *Tragical Discourses*, which was reprinted in 1898 in a work named *Tudor Translations*.

His erotic stories are told with a certain amount of restraint, and many later writers made use of his material. His erotic tale of the duchess of Malfi was used as a source for the English drama of that title by John Webster. Bandello died at Agen, but his works were still presented in Italian, as were most of the books written about him such as *M. B. Studj*, Morellini, 1900, and *M. B. e le sue Novelle*, V. Spampanato, 1896.

BARKER, GEORGE (GRANVILLE)
Born 1913. Died 1991.

"The only subjects for poetry are death and sex—some people call it love. Since we know nothing about death, I write about sex." So declared this English poet who composed his work in the neo-Romantic manner and was more appreciated in America than in his native country. His obituary writer in the London *Daily Telegraph* said of him: "Whether or not his rebellious strain of Roman Catholicism had anything to do with this is hard to say, but certainly there was an extravagance and exoticism about much of his work that reflected the rich dull blaze of medieval color associated with his Church." His father was a butler at Gray's Inn, London, and his mother was an Irish Catholic from Drogheda. Educated at the Regent Street Polytechnic, which he left at the age of fifteen, he started writing poetry early on while working as a garage mechanic, wallpaper designer, and a writer of advertising copy for John Betjeman at Shell. Later he traveled widely, eventually becoming a professor of English at the Imperial University of Japan. Then from 1940–43 he taught in the USA. In 1965 he was professor at New York State University and in 1974 he was visiting professor at the Florida International University.

His volume *Thirty Preliminary Poems* was published in 1933 and *Calamiterror* in 1935, but the works that drew attention to him most in these early days were *Lament and Triumph* (1940) and *Eros in Dogma* (1944). *The True Confession of George Barker* (1950) created somewhat of a scandal when it was broadcast on the radio and was denounced in the House of Lords as "pornography." The work was not actually published until 1965 when Barker explained that he wanted this work "to be thoroughly vulgar because I was sick of chichi verse." Nevertheless the construction of his verses was meticulous and lyrical. Later works were *Dreams of a Summer Night* (1966), *The Golden Chains* (1968), *Poems of Places and People* (1971), *The Alphabetical Zoo* (1972), *Dialogues* (1976), and *Villa Stella* (1979), which he explained as being an attempt on his part "to describe the changing colors of the memory." His final work was

Anno Domini (1983), while various volumes of his collected poems were issued in 1987—this last being the most complete.

Barker married Jessica Woodward in 1933 and Elspeth Langlands in 1989. He was a swashbuckling character in his early days in Soho, London, wearing a huge Spanish-style hat and a long blue cloak and his bosom companion was the Scottish painter, Robert MacBryde, to whom he composed a poem. Throughout his life he was a compulsive womanizer, and one of his many female partners, Elizabeth Smart, said of him that "there was no man as witty, as intelligent, as passionate" (*By Heart: Elizabeth Smart*, Rosemary Sullivan, London, 1991). Barker's widow, Elspeth, actually reviewed this book for the *Sunday Independent*, London, commenting: "Her passionate love affair with George Barker, whose poetry she had loved for years with equal passion, needs no documentation from me, his widow. Its guilty, grim and glorious consequences, literary and physical, have become the stuff of legend. . . . She had her great love affair and did not want another one."

BARTHELEMY, JEAN JACQUES
Born 1716. Died 1795.

This French scholar and writer was born at Cassis in Provence. In 1753 he was appointed keeper of the Royal Cabinet of Medals. His best-known book took him thirty years to complete: it was the four volume *Voyage du jeune Anacharsis en Grèce* (1787). Barthélemy also wrote a number of erotic poems and one of his books, *La Cantatrice Grammairienne*, also published in 1787, aimed at teaching French by means of erotic songs.

BATAILLE, GEORGES
Born 1897. Died 1962.

"*La petite mort*" is how Bataille has described eroticism in his work, *Les Larmes d'Eros*, Paris, 1904. He went on to say that the violence of the spasmodic joy of orgasm was at the same time the heart of death—"*de la douleur finale et d'une insupportable joie.*" Though in writing about this subject and often mixing up existentialism and surrealism in expressing his views Bataille made eroticism seem even more confusing than before, he was one of the first of the modern writers to seek an adequate definition of the word. The son of a tax collector, he was born in Billom, Pay-de-Dôme, France, and after taking his degree became an archivist. He married and had two children and eventually became deputy keeper at the Bibliothèque Nationale in Paris.

Two subjects kept him fully occupied for some years—surrealism and the culture of the Aztec Indians. His first big work was *L'Histoire de l'oeil* (1928), published in Paris under the name "Lord Auch." It was eventually reissued under his own name in 1967 and afterwards published in London in translation as *Story of an Eye*, as well as in California. Bataille's theme in so many of his novels was sexual excess among middle-class adolescents. In *Blue of Noon*, recently published in the USA and Britain, the reader is taken on a dark journey through the psyche of the prewar French intelligentsia torn between identification with the victims of history and the glamour of its victors. A reviewer in the *Detroit Free Press* described the book as "daringly imaginative . . . the writing is superb."

Bataille was both a novelist and a philosopher and he also established the review *Critique* in 1946. In *Eroticisme*, Paris, 1957, and the translation *Eroticism*, London, 1966, he dealt with the subject of eroticism in art and literature. Sometimes he tended to lose himself in his own ideas as when in *Eroticism* he says, "The passage from the normal state to that of erotic desire supposes within us a relative dissolution of the constituted being—the term dissolution recalling the familiar expression dissolute applied to erotic activity. For what is at stake in eroticism is always a dissolution of constituted forms." On another occasion he bluntly stated that "eroticism is assenting to life even up to the point of death."

Yet Michel Foucault has called Bataille "one of the most important writers of this century." Much of his fiction was written in an era when Europe was slowly slipping toward fascism and war, and his novel *Blue of Noon*, London, 1979, very much reflects this for it examines the ambiguity of sex as a subversive force and tells of one Tropman moving from country to country searching for spiritual comfort in a miserable world. *My Mother, Madame Edwarda, and the Dead Man*, London, 1989, comprised three short pieces of erotic prose in which he told of a young man's sexual initiation and corruption by his mother.

Other works by Bataille are *L'Abbé C*, London, 1983, the story of twin brothers, one a modern libertine and the other a devout priest; *Literature And Evil: a Literary Study*, with chapters on Sade, Kafka, and others, London, 1985. Worthwhile reading for an independent study of this author and his works is *The Violent Silence: Celebrating Georges Bataille*, edited by Paul Buck, London, 1984. This book was produced for the Georges Bataille Event held in London in 1984. It contains photographs, translations, and various appreciations of Bataille.

BAUDELAIRE, CHARLES-PIERRE
Born 1821. Died 1867.

"The unique and supreme pleasure in love lies in the certainty of doing evil. Both man and woman know from birth that evil lies at the root of all pleasure," declared Baudelaire in *Fusées* in his *Oeuvres Complètes*. Yet sometimes out of the depths of perversity and sorrow have come grace and form. In Baudelaire's *Les Fleurs du Mal*, decadent as many critics consider it, there is something of the beauty of the parable of the Prodigal Son, and thus one realizes that Baudelaire really did cry to God:

> O Seigneur, donnez-moi la force et le courage
> De contempler mon corps et mon coeur sans dégout.

Born in Paris, Baudelaire began his career as an art critic and later became editor of a short-lived conservative journal. He translated Edgar Allan Poe's tales in three volumes and then, under the influence of De Quincey's *Confessions of an English Opium Eater*, he published in 1861 *Les Paradis Artificiels*, which describes the sensations of an eater of hashish. It was in 1857 that he published the volume of verse known as *Les Fleurs du Mal* that caused him to be prosecuted for an offense against public morals. He also wrote *Petits Poèmes en Prose (Le spleen de Paris)* and a collection of critical essays entitled *L'Art Romantique*. Certainly he was one of the "Decadent School" of French writers, but this was a reaction to the stultifying atmosphere of religious reactionaries in which many artists found themselves encompassed at that time.

Baudelaire, like many other writers in the nineteenth century, linked much of his verse to prostitutes, and it was largely because of this that he was so attacked in his lifetime. Baudelaire also had a fascination for lesbianism that manifested itself in many of his poems. In modern terms what Baudelaire was trying to say was that love or lust is to some extent a preoccupation with naughtiness. But he put this much more elegantly.

There is an interesting biography of Baudelaire that includes a discussion of *Les Fleurs du Mal* and the obscenity trial that resulted from it: see *Baudelaire*, by E. Starkie, London, 1971. See also *A Une Courtisane* by Baudelaire, Los Angeles, 1972, and *The Flowers of Evil*, London, 1955 (the latter gives the text both in French and in English and all three of Baudelaire's prefaces).

BEARDSLEY, AUBREY VINCENT
Born 1872. Died 1898.

Best known as an artist rather than a writer (and of highly erotic sketches, too), Beardsley was one of a group of writers and artists associated with the period now known as fin de siècle or the "naughty nineties." When the *Yellow Book* was started in 1894 he became its art editor. He also created the designs and illustrations for Oscar Wilde's *Salome*. Born at Brighton, England, while his drawings and other works were much admired, he was also much criticized for his affectations and his fondness for what his critics called "an unsavory life." In his work, *Under the Hill*, London, 1894, published after his early death from tuberculosis, he indulged in what he himself called "a rococo eroticism with peeps into the exotic underworld of amorous fantasy." Here is an example of such "peeps" in this book:

> Poor Adolphe! How happy he was, touching the Queen's breasts with his quick tongue tip. I have no doubt that the keener scent of animals must make women much more attractive to them than to men; for the gorgeous odor that but faintly fills our nostrils must be revealed to the brute creation in divine fullness. Anyhow, Adolphe sniffed as never a man did round the skirts of Venus. After the first interchange of affectionate delicacies was over, the unicorn lay down upon his side, and, closing his eyes, beat his stomach wildly with the mark of manhood. Venus caught that stunning member in her hands and laid her cheek along it; but few touches were wanted to consummate the creature's pleasure. The Queen bared her left arm to the elbow, and with the soft underneath of it made amazing movements upon the tightly strung instrument. When the melody began to flow, the unicorn offered up an astonishing vocal accomplishment. Tannhauser was amused to learn that the etiquette of Venusburg compelled everybody to await the outburst of those venereal sounds before they could sit down to *déjeuner*.

With Beardsley, both in his sketches and his writing there are two distinct and sometimes parallel objectives—the pursuit of decadence, in which he seemed to delight, and art for art's sake, the creed of the avant-garde of the 1890s.

Under the Hill, by Beardsley and John Glassco, was published in New York in 1959.

BECKETT, SAMUEL BARCLAY
Born 1906. Died 1989.

This remarkable Irishman became a lecturer in English at the Ecole Normale Supérieure in Paris from 1928–30 and then a lecturer in French at Trinity College, Dublin, in 1931. In the early 1920s he had been associated with James Joyce, but in 1938 he settled in Paris and thereafter wrote mainly in French, translating his own work back into English when required to do so. He produced both novels and short stories. Two of his earliest works were *Whoroscope* (1930) and *Murphy* (1938). His most erotic novels were published by Olympia Press of Paris, including *The Unnameable, Malone Dies*, and *Molloy*.

Gradually Beckett turned his attention to play writing and he is, of course, still best remembered for *Waiting for Godot*, which was first produced as *En*

Attendant Godot. Beckett liked the idea of one-act plays, preferably with one single actor. He was encouraged in his work by Kenneth Tynan as a result of which *Waiting for Godot* (1955) was a great success. In 1969 he was awarded the Nobel Prize for Literature.

In return for the encouragement that Tynan had given him, Beckett provided a sketch for Tynan's production of *Oh! Calcutta!* This sketch was the only publicly identifiable work in the show, as Tynan had offered anonymity to the other sketch writers. It was a curious piece of work: Beckett had given instructions that a faint light should reveal a stage littered with miscellaneous rubbish "including naked people." After about five seconds there was to be a faint cry and a slow increase of light. Then a decrease in light for ten seconds and another cry. Used as a prologue to the show in New York, it was dropped when performed in London.

BEHN, APHRA
Born 1640. Died 1689.

The first Englishwoman to become a professional writer, Aphra Behn (her original name was Ayfar Amis) was born at Wye in Kent, England. She sailed to Suriname in Dutch Guiana with her father, who died on the voyage to take up his appointment as lieutenant governor. Aphra remained on the island long enough to obtain material for her eventual novel, *Oroonoko; or, The History of the Royal Slave* (published after her death in 1698). She became a staunch supporter of slaves: Swinburne wrote of her as being "the first champion of the slave in the history of fiction." She married a wealthy Dutch merchant and on her return to England became a spy for Charles II, being sent to Antwerp to spy on the Dutch. After her husband's death in 1665 Mrs. Behn made her living from writing. Prior to this Charles II's government was so dilatory in paying for her espionage work that she spent some time in a debtor's prison. Her writing was robust and coarse in the spirit of the times, but she had real talent, to which tribute was paid by such of her contemporaries as Dryden and Otway. Her most successful play was *The Rovers*, which was performed for many years after her death. An edition of all her *Works* appeared in London in six volumes in 1871.

Altogether between 1671 and 1689 Aphra Behn wrote fifteen plays and a number of poems of which perhaps the most outstanding was *Love in Fantastic Triumph Sat*.

BELLAY, JOACHIM DU
Born 1522. Died 1560.

Perhaps best known today for his poems praising the glories of the past, du Bellay was born at Lyré, near Angers. In 1548 he met the poet Ronsard and together with the aid of other poets they formed a society known as the Pléiade that aimed at setting up a school of French renaissance poetry. He was a romantic and a patriot, writing in one poem of *"France, mère des arts, des armes, et des lois, Tu m'as nourry long temps du laict de ta mamelle."* This led to his writing a prose work, *Defense et Illustration de la Langue françoise* (1549). Much of his verse is what one could call subdued but nonetheless refreshing erotica. Most of his poetic work is contained in his *Recueil de Poésie* and *L'Olive* (1550).

BOCCACCIO, GIOVANNI
Born 1313. Died 1375.

The illegitimate son of a Florentine merchant, this Italian poet was born in Paris. In 1334 he himself fell in love with the illegitimate daughter of King Robert of Naples. He always claimed that this love affair had inspired him to write verse and that it was primarily responsible for such of his works as *Rime, Filocolo, Filostrato, Teseida, Amorosa Visione,* and *Faimmetta.* His father recalled him to Florence in 1340, but from 1345–47 he lived in the Romagna, returning again to Florence after his father's death. Here he entertained the celebrated Italian poet Francesco Petrarch, who thereafter became a great influence in his life.

It was *The Decameron* (1471) that brought Boccaccio everlasting fame. This is supposed to have been based to a certain extent on an incident in real life (see chapter 3). In *The Decameron* seven maidens and three youths of noble birth have escaped from the plague that has been raging in Florence and make their temporary home in an abandoned villa outside the city. The ten young people tell ten stories each, thus comprising the one hundred stories of *The Decameron,* the first edition of which appeared in 1470. Nearly all the stories are of amorous incidents, told in erotic detail but never obscene. It is noticeable that in some of these stories the women take the initiative in no uncertain fashion as is the following story of Calandrino:

> As soon as she [Niccolosa] was within she shut the door and taking Calandrino in her arms, hurled him down on the straw on the floor of the barn; then, climbing astride him and holding him with her hands on his shoulders, without letting him come near her face, she gazed at him with lust in her eyes and said: "O sweet Calandrino, my treasure, my beloved comforter, how long have I desired to have thee and to be able to hold thee at my wish. Thou has drawn all the thread from my shift with thy playfulness; thou has tickled my heart. . . . Let me first take my fill of looking upon thee; let me drink in thine eyes and that sweet face of thine."

See *Boccaccio as Man and Author,* J. A. Symonds, London, 1895.

BONDI, CLEMENTE
Born 1742. Died 1821.

An Italian poet, born at Mezzano in Parma, Bondi became a member of the Jesuit order. When that order was suppressed he gave his time to writing and in 1797 was appointed librarian to the Archduke Ferdinand at Brno in Moldavia. Later he was professor of history and literature at Vienna where he died. His poems, including the erotic *La Cacaiuola*, and various translations of Ovid and Virgil, were published in three volumes in 1808.

BORDE, ANDREW
Born circa 1490. Died circa 1550.

"There is nothing, beside the goodness of God, that preserves health so much as honest mirth . . . therefore I publish this book to make men merry," wrote Borde in his prologue to his work, *The Jests of Scoggin*. Born at Borde Hill, near Haywards Heath, Sussex, England, he was admitted to the Carthusian Order while still in his teens. Accused of intercourse with women, he was relieved of his vows in 1521 and he made a study of medicine first at Oxford and then at the University of Montpelier. In 1547 he published *Introduction of Knowledge*, which was one of the earliest English travel guides. But it was his *Jests of Scoggin* (the earliest copy of which is in the British Museum), printed in 1626 by one Francis Williams, which is his masterpiece. Some scholars have tried to deny that this was Borde's work, but the copy just referred to has as its title *The First and Best Part of Scoggin's Jests, Gathered by Andrew Borde, Doctor of Physicke*. There had been a previous edition of this work and others followed, this probably being one reason for doubts about the authorship. As to the character of Scoggin, he is reputed to have been at court in the reign of Edward IV, who died in 1483 before Borde was born. The seventy-six stories about Scoggin therefore have either been based on gossip or Borde's lively imagination: they are droll, sometimes erotic, always lively and full of laughs. Even in his other work, *A Dyetarie of Health* (1542), Borde has to introduce a touch of humor: he advises as a cure for lust "to leap into a great vessel of cold water, or to put nettles in the codpiece about the yard and stones."

Latterly Borde was once again a practicing priest at Winchester and was mixed up in yet another scandal. Recording this, one John Ponet stated that "a holy man named Master Doctor Borde, a physician, thrice in the week would drink nothing but water who under the color of virginity kept three whores at once in his chamber at Winchester to serve not only himself, but also to help the virgin priests about in the country." Borde's death is somewhat of a mystery: he is reputed to have made a will in 1549 and died some little time after this and, say some sources, as a result of taking poison.

BOSWELL, JAMES
Born 1740. Died 1795.

Best known as the biographer of Samuel Johnson, Boswell was the eldest son of Lord Auchinleck, a Scottish judge, and was born in Edinburgh. It was a trip to London when he was twenty years old that set him on his lifelong path thereafter of exploring the night life of the British capital city. Shortly after this he was introduced to Dr. Johnson and from then on they became close friends, with Boswell accompanying the doctor in his travels. His first literary work was a contribution to *A Collection of Original Poems by Scotch Gentlemen* (1762). From 1777–79 he wrote a series of papers entitled *The Hypochondriac* for the *London Magazine* and in 1785 his *Journal of a Tour of the Hebrides* was published as a result of his trip to those islands with Dr. Johnson. *The Life of Samuel Johnson* appeared from his pen in 1791 and was such an instant success that a second edition was published in 1793. But Boswell did not have long to enjoy his triumph. After his wife's death in 1789 he became an alcoholic and died without ever overcoming this ailment.

Yet in modern times perhaps Boswell is studied more for his *London Journal: 1762–63* than for his biography of Johnson, even though this is still regarded as one of the best biographies ever written. Boswell had entrusted his papers, letters, and diaries to his literary executors. His accounts of his amatory adventures were so frank that they hesitated to publish anything for fear of bringing any embarrassment to Boswell's children. Some of his papers were reputed to have been burned in Scotland. For years attempts to find and obtain the various papers and diaries of Boswell were made in vain. In 1949 negotiations were concluded by which Yale University, through a gift from the Old Dominion Foundation established by Paul Mellon, and through the sale of the publication rights of the papers, purchased the entire collection from Lieutenant-Colonel Ralph H. Isham, an American collector of eighteenth-century rareties. As a result *Boswell's London Journal* was published by Yale University Press in 1950.

These journals certainly reveal Boswell as a man who reveled in picking up women on the streets of London; he gives detailed accounts of what followed such episodes. Even in church attending a service he ruminates on which female he will next select for his amours. Occasionally he ventures to try his luck with a beautiful lady of his own class, but with a certain diffidence: "I approached Louisa with a kind of uneasy tremor. I sat down. I toyed with her. . . . I felt rather a delicate sensation of love than a violent inclination for her. . . I thought myself feeble as a gallant. . . . Louisa knew not my powers. She might imagine me impotent." Alas, later one learns that, following an affair with Louisa, he has acquired "Signor Gonorrhoea" and "What! I thought, can this beautiful, this sensible and agreeable woman be so sadly defiled?"

Later on he seems to have taken precautions in his amorous adventures, for he talks of going to "the Park [presumably St. James] and in armorial guise performed concubinage with a strong, plump good-humored girl called Nanny Baker." Possibly it was not only alcohol that caused Boswell's early death!

BOUFFLERS, STANISLAS-JEAN, MARQUIS DE
Born 1738. Died 1815.

Usually better known under the title of the Chevalier de Boufflers, this French poet was born at Nancy. He traveled widely, had a passion for adventure, and an imaginatively romantic attitude toward amorous affairs. His earliest work was *Aline* (1761), followed by *Voyage en Suisse*, a collection of letters (1770). In 1784 he was made a marshal and the following year governor of Senegal. In 1778 he was appointed a member of the French Academy.

From the viewpoint of this guide perhaps the most fascinating of his works is *La Reine de Goloconde*, a slender book published in 1763, highly evocative of the "cottage love" pastimes at Fontainebleau and other royal palaces (see Cottage Love in the glossary). This work was translated by Eric Sutton, and, with an introduction by Hugh Walpole, was published in London in 1926. Queen Marie Antoinette, who was very much involved in the game of "Cottage Love," delighted in de Boufflers's book. Making a habit of using codes in her love letters, it is recorded that she underlined certain words in *La Reine de Goloconde* and added just one word herself—*Ariel*, obviously a code name and intended for one person's eyes alone.

This was the passage underlined:

> *Trouver de vrais plaisirs dans les plus douces illusions. . . . Le ciel serein, la terre encore brillante des perles de la rosée. . . . Je voudrais bien être votre frère, (ce n'était pas cela que je voulois dire) . . . et moi je voudrais bien être votre soeur, me repondit-elle. . . . J'avais quinze ans. . . . C'était à cet âge et dans ce lieu que l'amour nous donner ses premières leçons . . . quand arrivé à l'issue du bois. . . . J'oublais la Reine de Goloconde . . . Trouver des charmes dans un leger travail, de douces reflexions et de tendres sentiments.*
>
> [To find real pleasure in the sweetest illusions. . . . The tranquil sky, the earth still shining with beads of dew . . . I wish I could be your brother (that's not what I wanted to say) . . . and I wish I could be your sister, she replied. . . . I was fifteen. . . . It was at that age in that place that love waited for us to give us our first

lessons . . . when I arrived at the end of the wood. . . . I forgot the
Queen of Goloconde . . . to find charms, sweet reflections and
tender feelings in light work.]

No doubt Marie Antoinette's *Ariel,* whoever he was, would be expected to
recognize the implications of the passages underlined and to follow up the
particular proposals. It would seem that he was being invited to meet the
queen at the entrance to one of the wooded parks in the environs of Versailles
at the first light of dawn. She would like him to pretend she was only fifteen
and ready for her first lessons in love, to revel in the "sweetest illusions."

The Marquis de Boufflers moved to Berlin when the French Revolution
started and did not return to Paris until 1800. His *Oeuvres Complètes* were
published in various editions in 1817 (4 vols) and an edition of his *Poésies
Diverses* was published in Paris in 1886.

BRACCIOLINI, POGGIO
Born 1380. Died 1459.

An Italian humanist scholar, Bracciolini when still a young man is credited
with having invented the early italic-style handwriting known as humanist
script. As a result of this he was taken on as a secretary in the Vatican and
during his lifetime he served as such to a number of Popes. He spent some
time in Switzerland and Germany searching for classical manuscripts and as
a result rescued some of the work of such as Cicero and Plautus. He is said to
have visited England in 1418 as a guest of the bishop of Winchester, but in
1420 returned to Rome and settled down to write what he called "my book
of merry stories" in Latin. This later became known as the *Liber facetiarum.*
The stories are both funny and erotic and there seems to be no doubt that
Bracciolini thought that people would tolerate certain jests and naughtiness
in Latin whereas they might object to it in another language. He wrote simply
under his first name of Poggio and he used to tell people that most of the
stories emanated from the papal secretariat in a retiring room that he called
the *bugiale* or lie factory. From 1470 onwards (after his death) this book was
translated in most countries in Europe, Caxton actually having printed one
version in English.

His stories are essentially intended to make people laugh and, needless to
say, they appeal to men more than women. There is the story of the bride
who was "misled" by a donkey, though this has been omitted from some
translations. There is another tale of a clergyman who, in his sermon, denounced husbands who, "in the cause of pleasure" placed pillows under their
wives' buttocks (*natibus uxoris pulvinum subjicerunt*). The husbands who had
not thought of this matrimonial couch device previously then went home to
put it into practice.

Poggio, despite his service at the Vatican, led quite a merry life of his own. He had six children by a young wife and another fourteen by his mistress. He ended his days at Florence.

BURNS, ROBERT
Born 1759. Died 1796.

The son of a gardener, Burns was born at Alloway, near Ayr, Scotland. Originally the family spelled their name Burnes, but Robert dropped the e. His father, in order to keep his family together, took a small farm at Mount Oliphant about two miles from their home. Burnes employed no servants and his sons had to work day and night, and this applied to Robert, even before he was in his teens. Such hardship damaged his health and made him tend toward hypochondria, not to mention fostering a resentment against his father for being a harsh taskmaster.

It was a youthful love affair that prompted him to turn to poetry as much for consolation as anything else. After the death of his father he and his brother took another farm some few miles distant, but, as in the case of their father, this proved to be a losing game. As a result Robert turned increasingly toward poetry as a means of livelihood, precarious as that was. The birth of an illegitimate child brought him under ecclesiastical discipline and impelled him to use the satirical element in his verse to attack the old, hard school in the Church of Scotland, known north of the border as the "Old Lichts." Ever a philanderer, he wrote verse of an erotic kind, telling amatory tales in a Scottish dialect such as "Gie the Lass her Fairin'," "My Handsome Nell," and "Bonnie Peg." In 1786 he was involved in yet another amatory scandal that more or less forced him to acknowledge Jean Armour as his wife. As a result of this he made plans to go to Jamaica to seek a living and to raise funds for the passage he produced a volume of verses that was published later that same year. Jean Armour made him a father, his poems were widely praised, and Burns was received into both literary and fashionable society, so the Jamaica project was abandoned. However, it was not until 1788 when Jean Armour again made him a father that he actually married her. In the meantime he had had an affair with a Mrs. Maclehose, conducting correspondence between them under the names of Sylvander and Clarinda. In 1791 he gave up farming altogether and spent the rest of his life at Dumfries, working for the Excise.

By far the greatest of the vernacular poets of Scotland, Burns is still celebrated as a national hero, Burns Night dinners still being an annual feature not only in Scotland, but in other parts of the United Kingdom as well. Many of his poems, such as "Auld Lang Syne" have been set to music. But love was the subject about which he most enthused, as is so aptly shown in "Green Grow the Rashes, O!"

> Green grow the rashes, O!
> Green grow the rashes, O!
> The sweetest hours that e'er I spend
> Are spent among the lasses, O.
> There's nought but care on ev'ry han',
> In every hour that passes, O;
> What signifies the life o' man,
> An' 'twere na for the lasses, O?
> . . . But gie me a canny hour at e'en,
> My arms about my dearie, O;
> An' warl'y cares, an warl'y men
> May a' gae tapsalterie, O.

Some of his best work was written during his stay in Edinburgh at the time he was being received by such people as the duchess of Gordon and the earl of Glencairn. There are various editions and collections of his poetry such as *The Life and Works of Robert Burns*, by Robert Chambers, 1896, but perhaps the best was an early nineteenth-century version, *The Merry Muses of Caledonia: A Collection of Favourite Scot Songs*, compiled by "Robert Burns, the illustrious Scotch poet." See also Leslie Stephen's account of Burns and his life in the *Dictionary of National Biography*.

BURROUGHS, WILLIAM
Born 1914.

This American author, who also writes under the name of William Lee, has had a varied career. At various periods of his life he worked as a journalist, private detective, and bartender. His best-known novels have been *Naked Lunch*, *Dead Fingers Talk*, and *Nova Express*, and some of the themes are at least marginally erotic. In one of his works, *The Ticket That Exploded*, Burroughs made the somewhat depressing comment that "death *is* orgasm *is* rebirth *is* death in orgasm." He has been linked to the Beat movement and some of his novels are an unusual mixture of realism, exotic daydreams, and analysis of thoughts. He wrote with great skill on the hallucinations of people taking drugs. He has also written some poetry, "The Third Mind" and "The Exterminator."

In *The Algebra of Need* (1977), which had as its subtitle *William Burroughs and the Gods of Death*, Burroughs presented the story of his career up to 1976. Professor Eric Mottram, formerly professor of American literature at King's College, London, a well-known poet and latterly a visiting lecturer at various American, German, and French universities, has helped in the production of a new enlarged edition of this work, due to be published in 1992. He says of this work that "the author incorporates substantial additions which no serious critical study can afford to omit: the complete and unexpurgated version of the early *Junkie*, new novels from *Port of Saints* (1980) to *Western Lands* (1988)." The additions to this new edition are substantial and they include *Letters to Allen Ginsburg, 1953–1957* and *Interzone* (1989).

BYRD, WILLIAM
Born 1674. Died 1744.

Like Samuel Pepys, William Byrd kept his diaries in an ambiguous kind of shorthand, presumably because he lived in a time when the Puritan ethic was very much to the fore. His home was in Westover, Virginia, and his diaries are preserved in the Huntingdon Library and the Library of the Virginia Historical Society. Many passages of these diaries have been brilliantly deciphered by Louis B. Wright and Marion Tinling, who admit that "the identification of proper names, which Byrd always wrote in shorthand, has proved particularly baffling."

Over a long period Byrd persistently recorded the minutiae of his sexual adventures on both sides of the Atlantic, omitting nothing. Unfailingly Byrd noted in his diaries whether he had said or neglected his prayers. Sometimes he went in quest of women in the parks and gardens, and not even recurring attacks of venereal disease seem to have deterred him from wenching. On June 16, 1718, he recorded that he

> sat with Mrs. Cole, a milliner, and ate some cherries. Then I went to Chelsea and saw Mrs. A-l-c for the last time because she had played the whore. However I drank tea with her and about 8 o'clock returned to London and went to Will's where I read the news and then went to the Union Tavern to meet a young woman who supped with me and I ate some roast chicken and then we went to the bagnio in Silver Street, where I lay all night with her and rogered her three times and found her very straight and unprecocious and very sweet and agreeable. I slept very little.

Sometimes Byrd's dreams were better than his actual adventures. In 1718, when he was hopelessly in love with a certain Miss Smith in London, he related: "I dreamed that Miss Smith called me dear and was in bed with me. . . . I dreamed this night that I kissed Miss Smith very much and that her father would die this morning. God's will be done." A few nights later he came home "in the chair and said my prayers. I dreamed that I saw Miss Smith almost naked and drew her to me." In between these dreams he was also solemnly recording on more than one occasion that he "kissed the maid till I committed uncleanness, for which God forgive me."

Once back in America Byrd appears to have led a rather more circumspect life. He was in bed earlier and saying his prayers more frequently. A typical entry in his diary regarding his night life in this period explains that he went to a ball "where I danced four dances and ate some plum cake. We stayed till 10 oclock and then I walked home and said my prayers."

See the Byrd Papers: William Byrd's shorthand notebook. MS 5, i B 9964 I in the Library of the Virginia Historical Association. Also *Another Secret Diary of William Byrd of Westover*, translated by Marion Tinling, by Maude H. Woodfin, Richmond, Virginia; and *The London Diary (1717–1721) and Other Writings of William Byrd of Virginia*, New York, 1958.

BYRON, GEORGE NOEL GORDON, LORD
Born 1788. Died 1824.

The son of Captain John Byron, nephew of the fifth Lord Byron, this outstanding poet of the nineteenth century was born in London. At the age of ten he succeeded to his granduncle's title as the sixth Lord Byron and, with his mother, left Scotland where they were living to take up residence at the Byrons' family seat of Newstead Abbey in Nottinghamshire. Educated at Harrow, he made his experiences at that famous school the subject of his work, *Childish Recollections*. In 1805 he went to Trinity College, Cambridge, where his Bohemian conduct and fondness for wild revels caused the authorities some concern. In 1807 he published *Hours of Idleness*, which was harshly criticized in the *Edinburgh Review*. Byron retaliated by writing the satirical essay, *English Bards and Scottish Reviewers* (1809).

On coming of age Byron went abroad, visiting Greece, Asia Minor, Albania, Spain, and Turkey. In 1812 he published the first two cantos of *Childe Harold*, which brought him instant success. Byron was essentially a rebel, albeit a romantic rebel, and his own views on the subject of eroticism are perhaps best summed up by his statement that "the mixture, or rather contrast of tenderness, delicacy, obscenity, and coarseness in the same mind is wonderful." This comment was made in a letter he wrote in 1813, quoted in *The Horn Book*, New York, University Books, 1964. This single sentence almost sums up the character of the poet himself, not least in his fickle and sometimes bizarre love life. In 1815 he married Anne Isabella Milbanke, but a year later she left him and returned to her parents. After this Byron spent some time in Switzerland, where he wrote *The Prisoner of Chillon* and other works. Two women entered his life, first in Switzerland, a dalliance with Claire Claremont, and then in Venice with the Countess Guiccioli. *Don Juan*, a satirical and erotic mixture of verse, began publication in 1819 and ended in 1824. In one part of this work Don Alfonso unexpectedly enters his wife's bedroom, suspecting that a male is hiding there. His wife's maid "Contrived to fling the bedclothes in a heap, / As, if she had just from out them crept." The husband, still suspicious, searches the room:

Under the bed they search'd, and there they found—
Nor matter what—it was not that they sought!
They open'd windows, gazing if the ground
had signs or footmarks, but the earth said nought!
And then they stared each other's faces round:
'tis odd, not one of all these seekers thought,
And seems to me almost a sort of blunder,
of looking in the bed as well as under.

Byron's life of rake and libertine resulted in a number of privately printed books about his notorious life: *The Secret Loves of Byron*, *Byron's Intrigues with Celebrated Women*, and *The Connections of Lord Byron with Ladies of Rank and Fame* were among the titles. But cynic and rake though he was, there were some splendid traits in Byron's character—his passion for justice, as when he took up the cause of Greek independence, and a deep sensitivity in some of his verse. The poet who could write "Hell is a city just like London, / Where there is little or no fun done," could also tell in "She Walks in Beauty":

One shade the more, one ray the less,
Had half impair'd the nameless grace
Which waves in every raven tress,
Or softly lightens o'er her face;
Where thoughts serenely sweet express
How pure, how dear their dwelling-place.

To help the Greeks in their fight for freedom Byron set out for Missolonghi in 1824, but, worn out by his efforts, he died of rheumatic fever in that same year. His body was taken back to England where he was buried in the church of Hucknall-Torkard, near Newstead Abbey.

CABELL, JAMES BRANCH
Born 1879. Died 1958.

This American novelist was born in Richmond, Virginia, and educated at William and Mary College. After teaching French and Greek for a period he became a reporter on the *New York Herald*. Then, after a spell free-lancing as a writer, he was appointed genealogist of the Virginia Chapter of the Sons of the Revolution. His first major writing work consisted of two or three genealogical studies of his ancestors. His early novels were *Eagle's Shadow* (1904) and *The Line of Love* (1905), followed by *Figures of Earth*, *The Rivet in Grandfather's Neck*, and an essay on literary values, *Beyond Life*. In 1913 he married Priscilla Bradley. For many years his books were either neglected or treated with contempt: one of his books was described by a critic as "worse than immoral—dull." It was *Jurgen: A Comedy of Justice* (1921) that suddenly brought him into prominence. Not only was this probably his best work, but because of the part that sexual activities played in it throughout there were attempts to censor it. For a short while the sale of the book in America was illegal (incidentally, when it was in its third edition), but eventually critics came to Cabell's aid and the censorship campaign failed.

Benjamin de Casseres called Cabell "the Debussy of prose, the Spinoza of word magic." Hugh Walpole, the British novelist, wrote a sympathetic article on *Jurgen* in the *Yale Review* saying that "no writer, new to us in the last ten years, has revealed in English so arresting a personality as Mr. Cabell." As there was a touch of Rabelais in some of Cabell's narratives a new word was invented to describe his style of writing—*Cabellaisian.* Hugh Walpole wrote an introduction to later editions of *Jurgen* in which he said "some thought it indecent . . . some were puzzled by it . . . others again, and these, almost without exception, the best critics in modern America, delighted in it as an original work of beauty of which their country had every reason to be proud." This introduction appeared in the London edition of the book.

There was a certain magic about this controversial story of Jurgen, the middle-aged, henpecked pawnbroker who journeys through the land of man's imagination and his desires. He meets Queen Guinevere and Helen of Troy, becomes the lover of a hamadryad and a vampire, and visits both heaven and hell. One of the typical love passages in *Jurgen* tells how he "kissed the girl. Her lips parted and softened, and they assumed a not unpleasant sort of submissive ardor. Her eyes, when seen thus closely, had languorously opened, had viewed him without wonder, and then the lids had fallen, about halfway, just as, Jurgen remembered, the eyelids of a woman ought to do when she is being kissed properly. She clung a little, and now she shivered a little, but not with cold; Jurgen perfectly remembered that ecstatic shudder convulsing a woman's body; everything, in fine, was quite as it should be. So Jurgen put an end to the kiss, which, as you may surmise, was a tolerably lengthy affair." One might describe such prose as endearing, but it hardly seems to have come under the category of pornography as alleged by the New York Society for the Suppression of Vice.

A rather interesting feature of the book is Jurgen's search for enlightenment on the whole range of love practices: "Jurgen went back to the Library and the *System of Worshipping a Girl,* and the unique manuscripts of Astyannassa and Elephantis and Sotadeand the Dionysiac Formulae, and the Chart of Postures and the *Litany of the Center of Delight,* and the Spintrian Treatises and the *Thirty-two Gratifications.*" In this "library of Cocaigne," as he called it, Jurgen found "every recreation which ingenuity had been able to contrive for the gratifying of the most subtle and the most strong-stomached tastes."

Other notable books by Cabell were *The King Was in the Counting-House* (1938) and some adaptations of medieval poetry.

CALDWELL, ERSKINE
Born 1903. Died 1987.

This American writer on the "Deep South" spent all his early days in various Southern states from Virginia to Florida. The son of a Presbyterian minister, he described how he acquired an almost eccentric wanderlust at an early age. "I actually slept in my clothes so as to be ready to travel elsewhere at a moment's notice until my mother discovered this and stopped me from doing it," he used to say. He went to the University of Virginia and then had a variety of jobs including that of a professional footballer and a cub reporter on the *Atlanta Journal*. Afterwards he specialized as a writer of realistic novels on the poor white communities of the Deep South both in *Tobacco Road* (1932) and *God's Little Acre* (1933).

This second book concentrated on the fact that sex was almost the only recreation that seemed to be available to such communities. Caldwell vividly displayed the problems that ignorance, lack of culture, and sometimes the gnawing of conscience had on the various lovemaking episodes of which he writes. There are many passages in *God's Little Acre*, which show how inexperienced were these country lovers of the Deep South. There is Griselda of whom he wrote: "It was only when she could find his hands that she lay still against him. One after the other she kissed his fingers, pushing them between her lips and into her mouth, but after that, she was still not satisfied." Equally, of course, there were passages where the lovemaking was much more positive and arousing, but perhaps Buck summed up some of their problems when he wrote:

> There was a mean trick played on us somewhere. God put us in the bodies of animals and tried to make us act like people. That was the beginning of trouble. If He had made us like we are, and not called us people, the last one of us would know how to live. A man can't live, feeling himself from the inside, and listening to what the preachers say. He can't do both, but he can do one or the other. He can live like we were made to live and feel himself on the inside, or he can live like the preachers say, and be dead on the inside. . . . God made pretty girls and He made men, and there was enough to go around. When you try to take a woman or a man and hold him off all for yourself, there ain't going to be nothing but trouble and sorrow the rest of your days.

Caldwell married Helen Lannigan in 1925 and they had two sons and a daughter. In 1940 he and his wife were in Moscow when the Germans invaded

Russia. He stayed on for a while as a newspaper correspondent and his wife as a photographer. *All Out on the Road to Smolensk* (1942) was a result of this experience. Later Caldwell and his wife were divorced. *Claudette Inglish* was published in 1959.

CALLIMACHUS
Born circa 305 B.C. Died circa 240 B.C.

One of the oldest composers of erotic poems, this scholar and poet was born at Cyrene and lived in Alexandria, where he was in charge of the celebrated library there from about 260 B.C. Aristophanes was one of his pupils. He was a prolific writer, producing some eight-hundred works in all, many of which have since been lost, notably his most important work, a history of Greek literature. The Romans regarded his work highly and they translated such of them as *Aetia*, a volume of elegies, and *Hecale*, an epic. Some of his works were translated into English by Alexander Fraser Tytler in 1793.

CALVINO, ITALO
Born 1923. Died 1987.

For those who seek for a corrective influence to enable them to avoid the risk of fantasy taking over from reality in the quest for true erotic literature, one man to supply it most effectively is Italo Calvino. This Italian author was an arts graduate at Turin University who joined the Resistance Movement during World War II and became very popular in left-wing intellectual circles. His stories have been collected in English translation with the titles of *The Path of the Nest of Spiders, Adam, One Afternoon and Other Stories*. Few other authors can so effectively blend reality and fantasy. His place in this guide is deserved if only for his work, *t zero*. This is really a collection of brief science comedies told by Calvino's versatile narrator Qfwfq. He remembers himself back to the unicellular stage. The world of DNA, genes and chromosomes, and the double helix come to life as a protozoan love affair. This is first mitotic, therefore autoerotic and finally, with the emergences of sexual differentiation, becomes an affair with the multicellular Priscilla Langwood ("red coat, little black boots, bangs, freckles"). This affair is visualized as a meeting of two encoded messages from the past, a merging of chromosomal information and, only in a transitory sense, copulation. The lead-up to all this is an abstract "romance" of "about fifty trillion cells" and Qfwfq makes his ultimate comment: "This is in itself enough, Priscilla, to cheer me, when I bend my outstretched neck over yours and I give you a little nip on your yellow fur and you dilate your nostrils, bare your teeth and kneel on the sand." Suddenly they became camels.

CAPELLANUS, ANDREAS
Lived circa twelfth century.

Andreas Capellanus, also known as Andreas the Chaplain, can justly claim to be one of the founders of the code of *Courtly Love*, for, about 1186 he worked out and wrote down the elaborate rules of such in his work *De Arte Honeste Amandi*. At this time he was a chaplain at the court of Queen Eleanor. Some sources put the date of this work as late as early in the thirteenth century. It is in effect a manual that outlines what the conduct of married and unmarried relationships should be, and Andreas added to this in a further treatise entitled *De Amori Libri Tres*, giving certain hints as well as rules as a code of what might be called amorous chivalry. That word *chivalry* was sometimes used to cover up all manner of dubious affairs. Addressing a certain "Walter," Andreas in his treatise says: "Be careful therefore, Walter, about seeking lonely places with nuns, or looking for opportunities to talk with them, for if one should think the place suitable for a wanton dalliance, she would have no hesitation in granting what you desire . . . and you could hardly escape the worst of crimes, engaging in the work of Venus."

The truth is that Andreas's conception of *purus amor* (pure love) is far from Platonic. In his writings he uses the technique of presenting his arguments and codes in the form of dialogues. By this means, through imaginary conversations, he manages to convey how a nobleman should woo his female equivalent, how such approaches should be made by those lower down the social scale, and even how one of the lower orders should woo one of the nobility. The presentation of such information in this form is fascinating, but it sometimes leaves one a little unsure as to what Andreas really thought himself. However, generally speaking, the message seems to be that the lover must hope to win favors by his eloquence and his probity while at all times being courteous, and from this Andreas drew a picture of there being "no good thing in the world and no courtesy which is not derived from the fountain of love." There is also the implication in his code of love that the female should be allowed free choice in her acceptance or rejection of a lover so that she may reward the merit of the best. On the other hand Andreas suggests that she must not use this right merely to gratify her own fancies. Finally, in his last book, Andreas comes up with what must have been somewhat of a shock for the imaginary "Walter": "You must read all this, my dear Walter, not as though you sought to embrace the life of lovers, but that, being refreshed by its doctrine, and having learned how to provoke the minds of women to love you, you may yet abstain from such provocation and ultimately deserve a greater reward." This is typical of the humbug that lay behind much of the code of Courtly Love whether it came from Andreas or other disciples of this cult. What a mixed-up philosophy it all was: "love endures best when it is secretive," "marriage is no obstacle to Courtly Love," "jealousy makes love endure," and "abstinence offers a rich prize in eternity." See *The Art of Courtly Love*, Columbia University Press, 1941.

CARCO, FRANCIS
Born 1886. Died 1958.

This French writer concentrated on themes associated with the underworld of Parisian life and he also translated a number of works. Born at Nouméa, he wrote both poems and novels. His most notable novel was *Jésus la Caille*, a study of homosexuality, published in Paris. When World War II broke out Carco was living at L'Isle Adam near Paris. During the German occupation he published nothing and eventually fled to the South of France where, short of funds, he sang in nightclubs. Later he managed to escape into Switzerland, staying in Geneva until the war was over. His other best-known work was *L'Homme Traqué*. Returning to France to live the rest of his life there, he was awarded the Académie Goncourt prize, on which occasion tribute was paid to "the finesse of his writing" and "the hallucinatory technique of his prose."

CASANOVA, GIOVANNI GIACOMO
Born 1725. Died 1798.

Few compulsive adventurers and men of action, as well as being incessant libertines, can have found the time to write so much as did Casanova. In this respect he was unique, traveling as he did all over Europe from capital to capital. Yet he made a translation into verse of the *Iliad* and in his old age produced twelve volumes of his *Memoirs*. These were originally written in French and given to his grandson, Carlo Angiolini, who in 1820 forwarded them to a German publisher who produced them between 1828–38 from Leipzig. They gave such a lively account of Casanova's travels, adventures, and especially his amorous activities that interst in them became worldwide. Many translations and private editions of the work have appeared throughout the last and the present century, one of the best being the English translation by Arthur Machen, *Memoirs of Casanova*, 3 vols, New York, 1961.

Casanova always declared that his interest in females was first aroused when, as a boy, he translated a salacious piece of verse in Latin. He came from a distinguished family and moved in aristocratic circles all over Europe, wenching, gambling, and seeking adventure in any form. He was expelled from a seminary where he took minor orders and it was after this that he started his travels. His acquaintances included princes, ambassadors, cardinals, and lawyers as well as rogues and thieves, and as a result became a free-lance mercenary, sometimes ending up in prison as a result. Nothing ever seemed to daunt his spirit or his appetite for both adventure and the pursuit of women.

He was quick to seize on the merest hint as an excuse for an affair. Once, having given a female two kisses, he received a note that said, "My aunt will invite you to supper: don't accept. Leave as soon as we are at table, and Mariton will carry a light as far as the street door, but don't go out. As soon as the door is closed, with everyone thinking you gone, go upstairs carefully to the third floor. . . . It will only remain for Angela to give you, the whole night through, her company and may it be to your taste."

On another occasion Casanova records that "four hours of voluptuous ecstasy passed with extreme rapidity. Our last bout would have been prolonged if my charming mistress had not taken it into her head to change places with me, and to reverse our roles."

Casanova is, however, important to study from the viewpoint of analyzing the whole wide question of love. He makes this statement: "I have read numerous ancient writings on this theme. I have also read most of what the moderns say. But neither all that is said about it, nor all that I myself have said about it either when I was young or now that I am no longer young, nothing, absolutely nothing will make me admit that love is a trifle or a vanity. It is a kind of madness, agreed, but one over which philosophy has no power. It is a sickness to which man is subject at every age, and it is incurable if it extends into old age. Love, being, sentiment that cannot be defined. . . . In the midst of a thousand tortures that you inflict upon life, you implant so much pleasure in human existence that but for you being and nonbeing would be united and conjoined!"

In his old age Casanova wrote on all kinds of subjects from mathematical problems to poetry. It is worth recording that Frederick the Great, king of Prussia, said of him: "He was a fine figure of a man." Two other texts of Casanova worth consulting are *Memoires*, a Dutch text, Amsterdam, 1950, and *Casanova; Les Amours*, including ten erotic watercolors by D'Auger, French text, Athens, 1949.

CATULLUS, GAIUS VALERIUS
Born 84 B.C. Died 59 B.C.

A native of Verona, Catullus was one of the outstanding Roman poets who influenced such writers as Byron and Swinburne. He lived a wild and extravagant life in Rome in his early years as a result of which he accompanied the praetor Memnius to Bithynia to restore his fortunes. His poems consist of 116 pieces, mostly of short length. Some are rather like imitations of Greek verse, but the main theme is love—extremely passionate and fiery love:

> My tongue is palsied. Subtly hid
> Fire creeps through me from limb to limb:

My loud ears tingle all unbid:
Twin clouds of night mine eyes bedim.

Among his longer works are *Epithalamium Pelei et Thetidos, Coma Berenices,* and *Attis.* In his coarser and more licentious works he can be compared to some of the unpublished poems of the Scotsman, Robert Burns.

CERVANTES-SAAVERDRA, MIGUEL DE
Born 1547. Died 1616.

This Spanish novelist, dramatist, and poet was born at Alcalá de Henarea and his first major appointment was to an office in the papal nuncio's household in Madrid, after which he accompanied his master to Rome. He left this service in 1570 and for five years served as a soldier. In 1575 while sailing from Naples to Spain he was captured by Algerian pirates and, with his brother, Rodrigo, was held in captivity as a slave for five years. It was in this period that he turned to writing verse and when he returned to Madrid in 1582 to serve under the duke of Alva he continued with his writing.

Life was not easy for him, however, even after this: in 1597 he was imprisoned for debt and in 1605, when a neighbor was wounded by some unknown person, Cervantes, attracted by his cries for help, went to his aid. As a result he and his family were thrown into prison on suspicion of having been the attackers. To make matters worse the neighbor died shortly thereafter. The last ten years of Cervantes' life were spent in dire poverty.

Yet despite all this he was a prolific writer throughout his life. His best poetic work was *La Galatea* (1585), but it has been his prose, and especially his novels, that have been most appreciated down the ages. His master work, *Don Quixote,* about the adventure-seeking gentleman on his horse, Rosinante, not only provided a lively story but a superb satire on the age of chivalry. His keen appreciation of the erotic in a variety of amatory situations shows itself best in his twelve *Novelas Exemplares* (1613). Of these amatory novellas in this work the three best are *The Generous Lover, The Jealous Estramaduran,* and *The Little Gypsy.* All three are witty, lively, and pleasantly erotic. Much of his writing, of course, was done in jail. *Novelas Exemplares* was translated into English by MacColl in 1902. As a playwright Cervantes was not so successful: *La Confusa* and *El Bosque Amaroso* were his best plays. Worth consulting is the *Life of Cervantes* by H. E. Watts (1894).

CHAUCER, GEOFFREY
Born circa 1340. Died 1400.

The exact date of Chaucer's birth is not known, but it is generally considered by his biographers to have been sometime around 1340–41. At the age of seventeen he was appointed page to Elizabeth de Burgh, the wife of Lionel, third son of King Edward III. Later he served in King Edward's army in France during the campaign of 1359. Taken prisoner at Retiers in Brittany, he was released the following year under the Treaty of Bretigny, and in 1367 awarded a modest life pension of twenty marks (about fifteen dollars) on the understanding that he served as one of the valets in the king's chambers.

His career thereafter was a varied one. It involved a good deal of travel overseas, covering France, Italy, and Flanders. Some of his work might well be designated as that of a secret agent; on more than one occasion he helped to negotiate various trade deals. In this period, despite his meager life pension, he acquired money of his own and seems to have done well for himself by handling the controllership of leather, skin, and woollen goods in the Port of London. In 1386 he reached what was probably the peak of his career when he sat as knight of the shire for Kent in the Parliament held at Westminster. Later that same year misfortune hit him: he seems to have acquired enemies for he was suddenly deprived of all his offices. However, Chaucer was a resilient character and he staged a recovery in 1389 when he asked for and secured the post of clerk of king's works at Westminster. In 1390 he was given a similar position at Windsor as well as being appointed member of a commission charged with the repair of a bank of the River Thames. In 1394 he was granted a slightly larger annual pension, but despite this he still had financial problems, often borrowing on the strength of his pension to save himself from being arrested for debt. When Henry IV came to the throne—the king was the son of Chaucer's former protector, John of Gaunt—Chaucer was granted an increased pension of forty marks.

Chaucer's literary genius in both prose and verse has been the subject of much discussion down the centuries and resulted in the creation of a Chaucer Society. He was a conscious and deliberate artist who tried to find a correct measure for his verse not only to present his thoughts and feelings, but to satisfy himself on grounds of assonance and scansion. Above all he owed much to his travels and his wide experience of life, as is amply demonstrated in his *Canterbury Tales*, a collection of stories said to have been gathered from various people making the pilgrimage to Canterbury to pay their devotions to the shrine of St. Thomas à Becket. Chaucer's tales represented that a company of pilgrims assembled at the Tabard Inn in Southwark, London, agreed to tell one tale each both in going to and returning from Canterbury. The one who told the best story was to be treated to a supper on the homeward journey. The work is, however, incomplete, and there is no record of any tales told on the way home. Some are distinctly erotic, most notably "The Wife of Bath's Tale," "The Merchant's Tale," and "The Miller's Tale." The Wife of Bath in particular goes into great detail about her cravings for amatory adventures.

In "The Miller's Tale" Chaucer tells of an aged carpenter married to a young girl who seeks gratification of her lusts through affairs with a lodger, Nicholas, and one Absolom.

> This carpenter had wedded newe a wyf
> Which that he lovede more than his lyf;
> Of eighteene yeer she was of age.
> Jalous he was, and heeld hir narwe in cage,
> For she was wilde and yong, and he was old,
> And demed himself ben lyk a cokewold.

As to the development of these affairs, they can perhaps be summed up briefly in this verse:

> Thus swyved was the carpenter's wyf,
> For al his keping and his jalousye;
> And Absolon hath kist hir nether ye;
> And Nicholas is scalded in the toute.
> This tale is doon, and god save al the route.

The earliest of Chaucer's works was the *Book of the Duchess*, following the death of Blanche, wife of John of Gaunt, and about this time Chaucer also did a translation of the classical work, *The Romance of the Rose*. It is clear that Chaucer was strongly influenced by the Italians and that he always managed to keep a balance between romantic conceptions of love and the way things are in everyday life. Tyrwhitt's edition of *The Canterbury Tales* (1775–78) is worth consulting if only for its "introductory discourse."

CHEVALLIER, GABRIEL
Born 1895. Died 1969.

This French novelist was born in Lyons where he spent the greater part of his life. Educated in various schools in that area and later at the École des Beaux Arts, he served in the French Army in World War I. His service in this war led to his being awarded both the Croix de Guerre and the distinction of Chevalier de la Légion d'Honneur. On his return to civilian life he earned his living in various ways for some years, ranging from commercial traveler to art teacher. He married and had one son and then seriously devoted his time to writing. His first book was a psychological novel, *La Peur* (Fear), Paris, 1930. This was followed by *Clarisse Vernon* (1933) and *Durand* (1934). Success came to him somewhat belatedly when he produced *Clochemerle* in 1936. It was translated into English and became a best-seller on two continents, with the result that the next six of Chevallier's novels were also published in London and elsewhere. They were *Sainte Colline, The Affairs of Flavie, Mascarade, Cherry,* and, finally, *Clochemerle Babylon.*

In writing *Clochemerle* Chevallier switched from the psychological novel to humorous fiction, at the same time making full use of his own perceptive psychological insight to make that book more effective. *Clochemerle* proved to be an original and brilliant picture of French village life and in a hilarious manner a subtly erotic book. The story of *Clochemerle* is set in a village situated in a district famed for its Beaujolais wine. The mayor of Clochemerle suddenly has the idea of building a urinal in the very center of the village, not one of those discreet small buildings one usually sees, but the kind of open *pissoir* in which the males of the town can be seen peeping over the iron railings while relieving themselves. The effect of the mayor's project on the small population is considerable: some of the men using the urinal wave over the railings and make flirtatious comments to girls nearby, while one grande dame of the village is angered when she sees a group of schoolgirls dancing arm-in-arm around the urinal. At once she protests to both the priest and the mayor. The narrative is effectively maintained from episode to episode, superbly presented as a result of Chevallier's grasp and understanding of the psychological peculiarities of various types of villages in the Beaujolais region in the 1920s.

CHOU, ERIC
Born 1916. Died 1980.

This highly skilled, versatile, and candid writer on Chinese love customs was born at Mukden in Manchuria. He had a classical education under private tutors from the age of seven and took his BA degree at Peking Normal University in 1938. From 1939–42 he lectured at the South-West Associated University and Tsing Hua University in China, and from then until the end of World War II he was a war correspondent in the China theater of operations. After a spell as Nanking correspondent for the *Ta Kung Pao*, a newspaper in Hong Kong, he became its editor from 1949–52. Disaster struck in 1953 when, on a return to China, he was arrested and held as a political prisoner from 1953–56 in both Shanghai and Peking. His wife, Virginia Chou, states that "in 1961 he came to London as a political refugee so that he could write *A Man Must Choose*, the story of his imprisonment by the Chinese Communist Government." This book was published in London and New York in 1964.

From then on Chou concentrated on writing, acting until the end of his life as a consultant editor for Forum World Features in London and as a research fellow for the Institute for the Study of Conflict. He was elected a fellow of the Chinese Academy of the Republic of China in Taiwan in 1968. The work that established him internationally as a writer was *The Dragon and the Phoenix* (1971), which won him the Playboy Book Club's monthly choice and was published in both London and New York, with translations in French, Dutch, and Japanese. This book was a frank and splendidly phrased description of Chinese customs and attitudes in lovemaking both past and present. It also contained a bibliography on the subject.

His other books included *Tales of the Forbidden Palace*, London, 1974; *The Man Who Lost China*, London and New York, 1976; and *Mao Tse-tung*, London, 1980. But apart from these works in the English language Chou wrote some twenty books published in Chinese between 1951 and 1976, including the best-seller political novel, *Memoirs of an A-D-C*, Hong Kong, 1953.

CHURCHILL, CHARLES
Born 1731. Died 1764.

There have been many descriptions of Charles Churchill and his character, but a gangling, awkward rake and rebel, a dissolute renegade clergyman, yet a warmhearted man with a strong streak of idealism probably sums him up most fairly. Born in Westminster, London, he was almost literally forced into the church by his father. When his father died he severed all links with religion, including a curacy in his father's old parish. He then turned to writing and in 1761 published anonymously *The Rosciad*, a satire on the leading actors of the day. He was a member of the notorious Hell-Fire Club that functioned in West Wycombe Caves and a close friend of members such as John Wilkes and Robert Lloyd, the poet. It was for his association with this strange society, officially called the Knights of St. Francis after its founder, Sir Francis Dashwood, and for the poems and letters he wrote about it that he gained a reputation as a recorder of erotic affairs both in verse and prose. A great deal of the details of the Hell-Fire Club have come down to posterity through Churchill. Female members of this society were known as the "Nuns of Medmenham" and the secret of their identity has been closely kept, except for a few. Churchill recorded that "London prostitutes dressed as nuns" took part in the orgies in the caves at West Wycombe that was the society's headquarters.

Churchill is regarded as a prime source of material about the secret society contained in the book, *Nocturnal Revels*, published anonymously in London in 1779. This refers to the "nuns" of St. Francis as follows: "In case the Ladies want to retreat temporarily from the world," medical aid was provided for them. Apparently there were births arising out of members' club-time activities, for the writer states that "offspring are styled 'The Sons and Daughters of Saint Francis,'" and that they become "officers and domestics in the seminary."

Churchill seems to have reveled in the orgies in the caves on some occasions and then on reflection to have condemned them as his poem *The Duellist* (1764) indicates:

> Under the temple [the West Wycombe caves were built beneath
>   the church on the hill] lay a cave;
> Made by some guilty, coward slave,
> Whose actions fear'd rebuke, a maze
> Of intricate and winding ways,
> Not to be found without a clue;

One passage only, known to few,
In paths direct led to a cell,
Where Fraud in secret lov'd to dwell,
With all her tools and slaves about her,
Not fear'd lest honesty should rout her.

A collective edition of Churchill's works was printed in 1763 and *Additional Poems* in 1964. Worn out by his dissipated life, Churchill died at Boulogne. A fifth edition of his *Works* was published in London in four volumes in 1774. See also: *Chrysal: The Adventures of a Guinea*, Charles Johnston, London, 1760 and 1761 (this is supposed to be based on Churchill's firsthand account of life inside the Hell-Fire Club).

CLELAND, JOHN
Born 1709. Died 1789.

Educated at Westminster School, London, John Cleland joined the British Consular Service in which he served for several years. Later he started to practice journalism, but made little headway and in 1748 was imprisoned for debt in the Fleet Prison, London. While in jail Cleland was encouraged to write an erotic novel by a publisher who specialized in such works. The news that this is what he had decided to try his hand at was received with disgust by members of his family, who suspended all relations with him. Between 1748 and 1750, while still in prison, Cleland wrote *Memoirs of a Woman of Pleasure*, known also as simply *Fanny Hill*. He was released from prison in 1752.

Fanny Hill was an instant success when it appeared in 1750, and since then it has been published several times in a number of languages, including French and German. It should, however, be noted that many versions of this book are bowdlerized and edited with drastic cuts, and some modern editions are merely copies of such versions. Publishers did very well indeed with *Fanny Hill*, but poor John Cleland is reputed to have made a mere twenty pounds out of his book, while at the same time he was attacked by many people for having written it. In addition to all his other troubles Cleland was summoned to appear before the privy council to answer charges in connection with this. Fortunately for Cleland, just as he seemed to be facing severe trouble, the earl of Granville, president of the privy council, took his side and he was let off with a caution and warned to avoid writing such material in the future. When the case was ended Lord Granville gave Cleland a modest pension to continue for the rest of his life. Cleland kept his promise and never again repeated work of the *Fanny Hill* type.

The popularity of Cleland's work can be attributed to the simplicity and lucidity of its style and the way in which the story of Fanny is told to make it sound like a genuine personal memoir. In contrast to many erotic works it makes no attempt to exaggerate or gild sexual behavior with improbabilities. It is the straightforward story of a young girl who leaves home in the country for life in London, as told in a series of first-person letters. Fanny, aged fifteen, is engaged by a Mrs. Brown, who operates a brothel in her well-furnished house. An elderly man has offered to pay fifty guineas for the privilege of going to bed with a virgin and Fanny is chosen as his victim. However, he fails to fulfill his wish.

Just as the aged roué is repulsive to Fanny ("great goggling eyes," she called him), so another client shortly afterwards is "an all-perfect manly beauty in full view." This is Charles, who rescues her from the brothel. All is well until Charles's parents find out and he is dispatched to run a factory that his family owns in the South Seas. Fanny is left to fend for herself, and, not unnaturally in those days, she enters a brothel once again. John Cleland was well acquainted with London brothels and made full use of this knowledge in writing his story of Fanny. On the whole the story is never pornographic, certainly far less so than, say, Frank Harris's *My Life*, but one suspects that it was the firsthand, accurate details of life inside London brothels that caused it to be condemned. Cleland gave away too much of what went on there—devices for posing as virgins, various fetishes, and flagellation. The author had used as his real-life model a brothel operated by a Mrs. Douglas of Covent Garden.

Cleland even gave the story a happy ending—the reunion by a happy chance of Fanny and her beloved Charles, which they celebrate by getting married. *Fanny Hill* found its way to the USA in the latter part of the eighteenth century, but in 1821 two Massachusetts book salesmen were imprisoned for trying to sell the book. Many editions have been published since, some of them titled differently (presumably to get around any risk of being banned), others either expurgated or forged. One such title was *Memoirs of a Man of Pleasure*, another was *Memoirs of a Woman of Pleasure*, while yet another title used under the name of Cleland was *Memoirs of a Coxcomb*.

CLEMO, JACK
Born 1916.

This English—or rather Cornish as he would probably prefer to be described—poet was the son of a Cornish clay worker. He finished his education at the age of thirteen, but soon showed his talent as a poet. Most of his life has been spent in Cornwall and his poetry is a mixture of Calvinist religious beliefs and erotic mysticism. All his life he has suffered from poor eyesight and hearing and this to some extent is a factor in his verse that often reveals his attraction to sexual themes and the curious ways in which religious dogma induces such thoughts in him and then seems to hold him back. A clue to his character is contained in his poem, "The Executioner," in which he writes:

> I fondle and understand
> In lonely worship this malicious tool.

His works include *The Clay Verge* (1951) and *The Map of Clay* (1961).

COCTEAU, JEAN
Born 1889. Died 1963.

Cocteau used to insist that filmmaking was not his true profession. Nevertheless this French poet discovered that this medium could often express what his poems, novels, and plays could not. It must be admitted that sometimes Cocteau's films were an improvement on his literature. As with other authors touching on erotic themes, it is not always possible to be sure what is and what is not Cocteau's work. There was, for example, *Le Livre Blanc* (The white paper), published by the Olympia Press in Paris in 1957. This is an anonymous work, but all the evidence and especially the illustrations suggest this was Cocteau's book. It must be remembered that a great deal of Cocteau's erotic work lay in his sketches. A New York publication of this book in 1958, subtitled *The Autobiography of a Homosexual* states that it is "attributed to Cocteau."

Born at Maisons-Lafitte, Cocteau revealed his versatility early on in his life with sketches, poems, plays, novels, and films. He was one of the earliest students of the arts of cinematography in its present form. Outstanding among his novels was *Les Enfants Terribles*, while *Les Parents Terribles* became one of his most popular plays. Another of his works, *Le Jeune Homme*, was performed to Bach's Passacaglia in C; it tells of a young poet, wracked with despondency, being visited by death in the form of a female figure: it is the most erotic scene in the performance.

Of his films those that most deserve special mention are *Le Sang d'un Poète*, *L'Eternal Retour*, and *Orphée*. An important book of Cocteau's is *The Art of the Cinema*, translated into English by Robin Buss and published in London in 1991. In this book Cocteau explains how he became passionately devoted to the cinema, seeing in its most visionary and dreamlike forms a glimpse of the phantoms that haunted the poet throughout his life. The last section of this book is particularly interesting in the insight it gives of the poet's mind in presenting previously unpublished synopses for unrealized film projects.

COLETTE, (SIDONIE-GABRIELLE COLETTE)
Born 1873. Died 1954.

Born in Burgundy, this much-loved French writer was married to an idle rogue named "Willy" Gauthier-Villars at the age of twenty. Knowing she had a talent to write, "Willy" exploited this by persuading her to turn some of the stories of her schoolgirl pranks and experiences into fiction. At the same time he urged her to "spice them up and attract the reader," which was exactly what she did with her highly erotic quartet, *Claudine*, (1900–1903). Eventually there was a divorce from "Willy," and Colette went on to the music halls where she mimed and danced. Her book, *La Vagabonde* (1910) was in part at least the result of this. This was a great improvement on *Claudine en ménage* and similar works in the quartet. In the opening to *La Vagabonde* Colette writes: "Three years in the music hall and the theater have not changed me; I am always ready too soon." This book contains the story of the eternal conflict between desire for passionate love and the equally intense desire for freedom; Renée (perhaps the first of the "new women of the age") weighs her career and loneliness against marriage to a rich suitor. Perhaps the letters of Renée—and there are many of them—constitute some of the best parts of this book: *Mon Dieu, comme je vous écris! Je passerais tout mon temps à vous écrire,—j'y ai moins d'effort, je crois, qu'à vous parler. Embrassez-moi! il fait presque nuit, c'est la mauvaise heure. Embrassez-moi bien serré, bien serré!"*

Chéri (1921) was, however, Colette's masterpiece, the story of initiation into the rites of civilized debauchery. It was followed by *La Fin de Chéri* (1926). Colette married again, this time to Henri de Jouvenal, but again there was a divorce, and later she married for the third time. Books still poured from her pen, the delightful *Gigi*, again touching on the theme of the elegant courtesan (1944), being followed by *L'Étoile Vesper* (1946), *Le Fanal Bleu* (1949), and *La Naissance du Jour* (1950). *Gigi* was made first into a play, produced in New York in 1951, and later into a film starring Maurice Chevalier. When she died at the age of eighty-one, Colette was given a state funeral, the only honor of its kind to be given to a French woman writer. Referring to her exceptionally sympathetic gift for exploring the problems of the human heart, the French Minister of Education, M. Jean Berthoin, said of her writing when speaking at the funeral: "She was pagan, sensuous, and Dionysiac."

CONNOLLY, CYRIL VERNON
Born 1903. Died 1974.

Essayist, critic, occasional novelist, dilettante, and gourmet, Cyril Connolly, had he lived until now, would have been amused to find himself included as a writer of any form of erotica. He is included in this section because of one single piece of fiction, a brilliant piece of spoofery debunking the Ian Fleming cult and James Bond, an article entitled "Bond Strikes Camp" in the *London Magazine* of April 1963.

Educated at Eton and Balliol College, Oxford, Connolly is reported to have had a novel published by the Obelisk Press through Jack Kahane in Paris many years ago. Perhaps this work was done under another name, since so far it has not been possible to detect it. His first venture into fiction was *The Rock Pool* (1935), a first edition of which is rare and valuable. In 1939 Connolly founded the magazine *Horizon* and edited it until 1950. In 1952 he published *The Missing Diplomats*, the story of Burgess and Maclean, two defectors to the USSR. He had been a close friend of both men and their disappearance behind the Iron Curtain fascinated him. Peter Quennell in his introduction to this book said of Connolly: "For the young he became a sort of legendary arbiter of avant-garde writing."

In "Bond Strikes Camp" Connolly satirized the Bond cult with some lively dialogue. In this story "M" (the spymaster) sends for Bond and orders him to disguise himself as a woman in order to trap a visiting KGB general. The general, explains "M," "likes drag. That's-er-men dressed up as women."

Bond, who has not dressed up in "drag" since he played Katisha in *The Mikado* at his prep school, sets off to receive the full treatment in disguise— "the fitting of an elaborate chestnut wig . . . the very latest in falsies—foam rubber, with electronic self-erecting nipples . . . slinky black lace panties . . . black shoes with red stilettos." When Bond eventually meets the KGB man in this remarkable getup, the latter asks: "Who is your best friend?" Bond remembers the gambit pawn and replies "Guy Burgess." The general guffaws: "I'll tell him. He'll be delighted. He doesn't often get a message from such a pretty girl."

But in the end the general turns out to be none other than "M" in disguise. "I'm sorry, James," he says. "It was the only way I could get you . . . Don't think I haven't fought against it."

Bond cuts him short with: "Have you got a gun, sir?" "M" nods. Bond looks at his watch. "It's a quarter past two. You may employ what means you prefer, but if I find you are still alive by nine o'clock I shall alert every newspaper here."

CRANE, STEPHEN
Born 1871. Died 1900.

A brief mention should be made of this American author, so well known for his vivid imaginative gifts in such works as *The Red Badge of Courage* (1895), his very first book. The reason for citing him in this section is for his work,

Maggie: A Girl of the Streets, privately published in 1893. The dialogue in this work is realistically like that of the characters of a true slum environment. Crane tries to show how environment conditions the lives of slum inhabitants and how one of the victims is Maggie. Few copies of this book are now available. Crane was born at Newark, New Jersey, and was a war correspondent in the Spanish-American war in 1898 and the Greek-Turkish war of 1897–98. His last book, *Wounds in the Rain,* was published in the year he died.

CRÉBILLON (PROSPER JOLYOT)
Born 1707. Died 1777.

The son of the French dramatist, Prosper Jolyot de Crébillon, Claude was born in Paris. Like his father he also wrote for the stage, though most of his work was fiction. In 1748 he married an Englishwoman, Lady Stafford. His novels were lively and licentious and included such titles as *Le Sopha,* Paris, 1745, which was translated into English in 1781; *The Wanderings of the Heart and Mind* (1736), English edition 1851; *Letters from the Marchioness of M——* (1732, English edition 1737); *Les Egarements du Coeur;* and *L'Ecumoire.* Some of the English translations of his work went into several editions and were still selling a hundred years after his death.

CROWLEY, ALEISTER (EDWARD ALEXANDER)
Born 1875. Died 1947.

This extraordinary dabbler in all kinds of magic—the head of two magical organizations and of several minor ones—came from a family whose religion was that of Plymouth Brethren. It was out of this somewhat contradictory background that the man emerged who became known as the Beast 666 (see Revelation 13:18). Asked once why he called himself "the Beast," he replied: "My mother called me the Beast." He was educated at two public schools, Malvern and Tonbridge, and then went to Trinity College, Cambridge. After extensive traveling all around the world, during which he spent much time studying the occult in various forms, he married Rose Kelly, daughter of Sir Gerald Kelly. He liked to regard himself as being in the same tradition as the great magicians of the past—Madame Blavatsky, John Dee, Cagliostro, and Eliphas Lévi.

His first book was published when he was an undergraduate at Cambridge—a book of verse entitled *Aceldama: A Place to Bury Strangers In.* This was followed by several volumes of poetry, some prose, and a certain amount of erotica. In 1904 he claimed that his "Holy Guardian Angel, Aiwass" had appeared to him to dictate a work he called *The Book of the Law,* this being an exposition of his creed of magic. In it he wrote: "The word Sin is Restriction. . . . There is no law beyond Do what thou wilt," a precept he took fairly literally throughout his life. In World War I he was mixed up in certain espionage activities, indulging in pro-German propaganda for Vierveck in *The Fatherland* and *The International*, which he edited for about a year. However, Crowley always claimed that he did this merely to ingratiate himself with the Germans so that he could spy on them. The American Intelligence Service in World War I seemed to have believed Crowley's story, though the British Naval Intelligence Service rejected him and his occult temple in London was closed down by the police. Eventually it was proved that he was genuinely trying to help the Allies when he revealed that the international head of the hermetic sect he had joined was a highly dangerous German agent, information he passed on to the Americans. Between World Wars I and II he spent a great deal of time in Berlin and gathered considerable information for MI5.

His erotic books included *Alice in Adultery* (1903); *Snowdrops from the Curate's Garden*, a reprint of which was published as recently as 1988; *The Lover's Alphabet*, a set of twenty-six poems associating a girl's name with a flower of the same initial from A to Z; and a lengthy poem, *La Gitana*. The last-named is perhaps the most typical of Crowley's mixture of the erotic and the occult:

> Your hair is full of roses in the dewfall as we danced,
> The sorceress enchanting and the paladin entranced,
> In the starlight as we wove us in a web of silk and steel
> Immemorial as the marble in the halls of Boabadil,
>
> . . . .
>
> In the starlight as we trembled from a laugh to a caress,
> And the God came warm upon us in our pagan alegresse.
> Was the Baile de la Bona too seductive? Did you feel
> Through the silence and the softness all the tension of the steel?
> For your hair was full of roses and my flesh was full of thorns
> And the midnight came upon us worth a million crazy morns.
>
> . . . .
>
> My Gitana, my Saliya, more delicious than a dove!
> With your hair aflame with roses and your lips alight with love!
> Shall I see you, shall I kiss you once again?
>
> . . . .
>
> I shall find you, I shall have you, in the summer and the south
> With our passion in your body and our love upon your mouth,
> With our wonder and our worship be the world aflame anew!
> My Gitana, my Saliya! I am coming back to you.

See *White Stains*, London, 1973, a reissue of privately printed poems of Crowley, with an introduction by John Symonds.

CUMMING, ANNE
Born 1917.

Anne Cumming spent her early years on a farm in South Africa, returning to Europe when her parents divorced. She was presented at the court of King George V and later trained as a stage designer and actress. In 1938 she married her first husband, a young playwright and member of the Bowes-Lyon family, and went to live with him in New York. When World War II broke out she was recruited by British Intelligence. In 1944 she returned to London and was then employed as an interpreter and courier by the British Council. After the breakup of her second marriage to a well-known novelist, she went to live in Rome where she entered into Italian literary circles. There she taught English and worked in the film industry. In 1977 she published her first volume of what was termed as her "erotic autobiography," *The Love Habit.* Then in 1991 she published *The Love Quest: A Sexual Odyssey,* which looked back on her travels and love affairs between the years 1952 and 1965. Anne Cumming has been twice divorced, has two daughters and four grandchildren, and now lives in London.

Her book *The Love Quest* looks back on her travels and her love affairs, detailing these from a Parisian orgy attended by two Very Important Persons to a passionate romance with a ruthless Tunisian gangster. One critic of Anne Cumming's work said of her last book: "The tone is set on her first night in Rabat which she spends with a professional cyclist: 'All I remember about him was his remarkable muscle tone and his beautiful strong thighs. . . . I like a man from the waist down.'" This critic said that "there are so many lovers in the book that we lose our bearings," adding that "throughout this book if we sometimes blush on her behalf, there is a salutary reminder on almost every page that lust is blind—to its own heroic absurdity and the prudery of others. However it appears to have kept the author well preserved in later life. Perhaps her book should be put on the Personal Fitness shelves . . . as evidence that a voracious appetite and the will to indulge it are fair guarantees of a ripe old age."

DAFYDD AP GWILYM
Born circa 1330–60.

Dafydd was a native of the parish of Llanbadarn Fawr in Ceredigion, West Wales. Some 150 poems by him have survived, many of them addressed to a girl called Morfydd, who is known to have been married to a merchant in

Aberystwyth. A large number of his poems were highly erotic, so much so that until quite recently they have been hidden away from the most diligent researchers. The best available English-language introduction to his work is Rachel Bromwich's *Aspects of the Poetry of Dafydd ap Gwilym*, University of Wales, 1986, but she does not discuss his erotic poems such as "The Penis," "Deer Coupling," and "The Poet Sends His Genitals as a Love Messenger." He is regarded as the greatest of all Welsh poets, yet until recently few had heard of his poem addressed to the penis: "You are a trouserful of wantonness, your neck is leather, image of a goose's neck bone; nature of complete falsity, pod of lewdness, door nail which causes a lawsuit and trouble." All his poems of this nature suggest that in those days eroticism was an accepted genre.

D'ANNUNZIO, GABRIELE
Born 1863. Died 1938.

The original name of this Italian writer was Rapagnetta and he was born aboard a yacht in the Adriatic Sea. He was only fourteen when he published a collection of lyrics, *Primavera*. These were full of eroticism, admittedly a juvenile eroticism, but they showed him to be a genius in the making. He delivered an improved version of this work in 1880. Following this early success came more poems, plays, and novels, some works being highly erotic such as *Il Piacere* (1889) and *Il Fuoco* (1900), the last-named being praised for its psychological insight but denounced by some critics for expressing immoral views. Perhaps one of the most attractive of his works was the epic *La Canzone di Garibaldi* (1901), which contains some remarkably beautiful passages. It was shortly before the turn of the century that D'Annunzio turned to drama with his *Sogno d'un Matino di Primavera* (1897), *Sogno d'un Tramonto d'Autunno* (1898), and *La Città Morta* (1898). His novels are notable for their powers of description and character analysis: most of them have been translated into English. He was one of the most vigorous partisans of intervention by the Italians in World War I.

DAUDET, ALPHONSE
Born 1840. Died 1897.

The Daudet family specialized in writing. Alphonse was one of the ablest novelists of his generation, his brother Ernest wrote political tracts and novels, his son Léon published a number of books of his own, while his wife, Julia, not only collaborated with her husband, but was herself the author of *Impressions de Nature et d'Art* and *Les Enfants et les Mères* among other works. Alphonse Daudet was born at Nîmes and produced his first volume of poems, *Les Amoureuses*, at the age of eighteen. Soon after this he contributed to *Figaro* and other journals and for five years was private secretary to the Duc de Morny. He took advantage of this experience when in 1877 he wrote *Le Nabab,* a study of Parisian manners in which the private life of the Duc de Morny was described in some detail.

One of a number of his erotic works was the novel, *Sapho* (1884), in which he told of the infatuation of a youth for an artist's model. Possibly his best work was *Fromont Jeune et Risler Aîné* (1874), for which the French Academy awarded him the Jouy prize. This, however, did not prevent him from writing a somewhat stringent satire on the French Academy, *L'Immortel,* in 1888. Daudet, like Balzac, drew very much from his environment and experiences for his novels, though not so intensely as the latter. His short stories were as splendid as his novels. His *Oeuvres Complètes* were published in Paris in 1899 and there was an English translation in 1902.

DEFOE, DANIEL
Born 1660. Died 1731.

Son of a London butcher, Defoe wrote his first known pamphlet, "A New Discovery of an Old Intrigue" on the Jacobite plot against King William III— drawing the attention of the public to him for the first time. From then on he devoted much of his time to various political campaigns and intrigues, as well as occasionally acting as a spy for government ministers. He was an ardent pamphleteer and after Queen Anne's accession to the throne for a time he upheld the Whig cause. It was one of his pamphlets, "The Shortest Way with Dissenters," that caused him to be convicted of seditious libel, fined, stood three times in the pillory, and imprisoned. When Lord Harley released him he became a government pensioner and so for a long time played a double game in politics, attacking the Tories while secretly helping their government, using his weekly paper *Review* as a cover for his activities.

Though Defoe is remembered most for his book, *Robinson Crusoe,* he was also the author of the amatory story of Moll Flanders, or, to give the book its full title: *The Fortunes and Misfortunes of the Famous Moll Flanders, Who Was Born in Newgate and during a Life of Continued Variety, for Threescore Years, besides Her Childhood, Was Twelve Years a Whore, Five Times a Wife (whereof Once to Her Own Brother), Twelve Years a Thief, Eight Years a Transported Felon in Virginia, at Last Grew Rich, Lived Honest, and Died a Penitent.*

The lengthy title gives a very detailed outline of what the book is all about. It should be stressed that the novel is totally free from any obscene language and even the erotic passages are restrained, but its autobiographical style very cleverly increases the reader's interest in the amatory scenes. One such is when Moll meets a man who says he "could lie naked in the bed with me and not offer me the least injury," and proceeds to prove this possible for quite a long time. "This was a surprising thing to me," declares Moll, "and perhaps may be so to others who know how the laws of nature work, for he was a vigorous, brisk person." Then one night when they are in bed together warm and merry, and having drunk more than usual, Moll helps the man to break his pledge. "After some other follies which I cannot name, and being clasped close in his arms, I told him (I repeat it with shame and horror of soul) that I could find in my heart to discharge him of his engagement for one night and no more. He took me at my word immediately and after that there was no resisting him; neither, indeed had I any mind to resist him any more."

Other works by Defoe include *The History of Colonel Jack* (1722), *A Journal of the Plague Year* (1722), *Tour through The Whole Island of Great Britain* (1724), *A History of the Devil* (1727). One of the best of a number of biographies of Defoe is *Daniel Defoe: A Study in Conflict* by Brian Fitzgerald, London, 1954. Among his many minor publications were two amatory poems, "The Problem" and "The Lady's Dressing Room."

DEKKER, THOMAS
Born circa 1572. Died circa 1632.

Knowledge of the life of this lively British dramatist is scanty, but from all accounts he was born in London. He was frequently in prison for debt, and indeed the first mention of him on record was in 1598 when someone advanced the sum of forty shillings to discharge him from the "Counter in the Poultry" where he was confined for debt. He was again in prison for debt from 1613–18. At least some of his work must have been written in prison. Apart from his various plays Dekker wrote a number of lengthy pamphlets, which were chiefly about contemporary life in London, especially in the criminal community. He made much use of his wide knowledge of the criminal world in some of his plays. The publications include *The Seven Deadly Sins of London* and *The Gull's Hornbook*, a description of Elizabethan life about town.

His most appreciated play (it is still sometimes performed) was *The Shoemaker's Holiday*, a comedy, 1600. Equally popular in its day was his erotic play, *The Honest Whore*, (in two parts, 1604 and 1630). The latter work has been described as "the play that transcends and plays with, rather than grasps and exposes the vices and follies of men." It tells the story of how Bellafront, a practicing whore, eventually settles down to a chaste life. There is in the play a verse that sums up the strumpet's characteristics:

> As Juno's proud bird spreads the fairest tail,
> So does a Strumpet hoist the loftiest sail,
> She's no man's slave; (men are her slaves) her eye
> Moves not on wheels screwed up with jealousy
> She (Horst, or Coacht) does merry journeys make,
> Free as the Sun in his gilt Zodiac:

As bravely does she shine, as fast she's driven,
But stays not long in any house of Heaven,
But shifts from Sign to Sign; her amorous prizes
More rich being when she's down, than when she rises.

Dekker's work varied from some occasional splendid verse of the highest order to a great deal of mediocre writing. He was particularly clever in portraying female characters in his plays. In some of his work he collaborated with others, as for example with *The Sun's Darling*, a masque that he produced with John Ford. Four volumes of *The Plays of Thomas Dekker* were published in London in 1873.

DEKOBRA, MAURICE
Born 1885. Died 1973.

Born and educated in Paris, where he attended the College Rollin, Maurice Dekobra was for many years a leading Paris newspaper correspondent in America, Europe, and Africa. In World War I he acted as liaison officer with the British and American forces. His career as a novelist took off in the early 1920s and his novels became so popular that they were translated into more than thirty languages. Dekobra's work included much of what can be described as restrained, but nevertheless extremely effective eroticism, because of the lucid elegance of his prose. His recreations included riding, fencing, and, so he went on record as saying, "thought reading." He was made an Officer of the Legion of Honor and his other awards included the Grand Cross of St. John the Baptist and Grand Officer of the Nicholas Iftikar.

Novels of Dekobra's deserving of special mention for readers of this guide include *Tu Seras courtisane, Mon Coeur au Ralenti,* and *La Volupté éclairant le Monde* (Paris), and the following works published in English in New York and London: *Madonna of the Sleeping Cars, His Chinese Concubine, Written with Lipstick,* and *The Lady Is a Vamp.*

DONLEAVY, JAMES PATRICK
Born 1926.

Born in Brooklyn, the son of a New York civil servant, Donleavy served in the U.S. Navy in World War II. In 1946 he went to Trinity College, Dublin, where he spent three and a half years studying microbiology. It would seem that at that time he had not made up his mind exactly what he wanted to do in life, not an unusual attribute among young men who served in the armed forces in that war. He left Trinity without a degree and first considered taking up painting. Eventually, with the sound family background of an English wife and two children, he established himself as a writer. This he achieved first of all with his novel, *The Ginger Man*, published by the Olympia Press of Paris in 1955. Expurgated versions were later published in London and New York in 1956 and 1958 respectively.

This first novel was hailed by one enthusiastic critic as "comic, dirty, and delightful." Later it was made into a play that was produced in London in 1959, but banned in Dublin. Perhaps there was some resentment in Ireland that the hero of the book, Sebastian Dangerfield, an American, was depicted as living in Ireland. This impoverished character was presented as reading law in Dublin and battling against a hard world in which he contended with all manner of problems. The dialogue is often bawdy, but an erotic undercurrent is maintained throughout by the manner in which Dangerfield tells of his actual day-to-day life in the third person, while presenting his thoughts in the first person.

Donleavy, who lives in Westmeath, Ireland, has also written short stories and sketches and the novel *A Singular Man* (1964), and the play *Fairy Tales of New York* (1960).

DOUGLAS, (GEORGE) NORMAN
Born 1868. Died 1952.

This novelist and essayist was born at Tilquillie Castle in the Kincardine district of Scotland, about which he wrote in his reminiscences, *Looking Back*, 1933. Educated first at Uppingham School, he went to Karlsruhe in 1886, after which he joined the foreign service. When he left the service he lived in Capri, where he wrote his popular novel, *South Wind*, 1917. He collected salacious and naughty limericks, composing a number of them himself, and in 1928 printed them privately in Florence under the title *Some Limericks*. A reprint of this work was published in Boston in 1942. The author's comments on the limericks are often as amusing as the limericks themselves. A typical entry is:

> A niece of the late Queen of Sheba
> Was promiscuous with an amoeba.
> This queer blob of jelly
> Would lie in her belly
> And, quivering, murmur; *"Ich Liebe!"*

DUFFY, MAUREEN PATRICIA
Born 1933.

This English author, who lives in London, was educated at King's College, London, and was a teacher during the 1950s. Her first book was *That's How*

It Was (1962), followed by The Single Eye (1964); The Microcosm (1966); The Paradox Players (1967); Lyrics for the Dog Hour: Poems (1968); The Venus Touch, poetry (1971); Evensong (1976); The Passionate Shepherdess (1977); The Erotic World of Faery (1980); and Collected Poems: 1948–1984 (1985).

Maureen Duffy has played an active roll in the cause of the arts generally and writers in particular during her career. She was "chairman" (her description in Who's Who) of the Greater London Arts Literary Panel, 1979–81, president of the Writers' Guild of Great Britain from 1985 and cofounder of the Writers' Action Group.

Unquestionably her major contribution to the cause of erotic literature was The Erotic World of Faery. This work was researched in great detail, as its list of "books cited and consulted" reveals. It is an examination of the eroticism to be found tucked away in fairy stories and folk tales down the ages, ranging from St. Augustine, the Arthurian legends, Grimm, Wilde, Sir James Barrie, and many other more recent writers. What Maureen Duffy does in this book is to show how from the time that the Blessed Isidore of Seville condemned fairies, satyrs, and their ilk, the fairy story has been used to conceal eroticism in a kind of code. The Blessed Isidore claimed that "Satyrs are they who are called Pans in Greek and Incubi in Latin. . . . For they often lust lecherously after women and copulate with them." She cites the double-talk of the fairy-story writers in such works as The Maydes Metamorphosis: "Ioculo: I pray you, prettie little fellow, what's your name?" "My name is little, little Pricke." "Little, little Pricke? O, you are a dangerous Fayrie and fright all little wenches in the country out of their beds." She also cites Charles Kingsley's The Water Babies, London, 1863, dedicated to Kingsley's youngest son, Grenville Arthur. Beneath this fairy story, argues Duffy, is "the book's ethic . . . concerned with how a boy may resist temptation and grow up pure to marry." She cites Kingsley: "Oh, my little man, I am too old to sing that song, and you too young to understand it. But have patience, and keep your eye single, and your hands clean, and you will learn some day to sing it yourself, without needing any man to teach you." Duffy argues that "whether he realized it or not, Kingsley's main aim was to try to stop the little boy masturbating."

Duffy refers to Wilde's fairy tale, The House of the Pomegranates, mentioning that when it was criticized by a reviewer of the Pall Mall Gazette as being of doubtful suitability for children, Wilde answered: "I had about as much intention of pleasing the British child as I had of pleasing the British public." Peter Pan, claims Duffy, is "based on games which Barrie had played with the original Lost Boys, the children of the woman he was in love with. Quite simply it's about sex or more precisely about infantile sexuality and sexual curiosity." She also examines the hidden eroticism in Christina Rosetti's Goblin Market:

Did you miss me?
Come and kiss me.
Never mind my bruises.
Hug me, kiss me, suck my juices
Squeezed from goblin fruits for you
Goblin pulp and goblin dew.
Eat me, drink me, love me:
Laura make much of me.

In this poem Duffy detects that here is a hint of the "fruit forbidden," which is sexual experience before marriage. The final verdict of this writer is that fairy stories were not originally composed for children, but that when they are written as such they provide an excellent cover for erotic secret writing.

DURRELL, LAWRENCE GEORGE
Born 1912. Died 1990.

Educated at the College of St. Joseph, Darjeeling, India, and St. Edmund's School, Canterbury, England, Lawrence Durrell spent much of his early life in the eastern Mediterranean. He worked as a British Foreign Service press officer in Greece and Egypt during World War II, and later was a press attaché in Alexandria and Belgrade and director of public relations in the Dodecanese Islands. After a spell as director of British Council Institutes in Kalamata, Greece, and Córdoba, Argentina, he was director of public relations and editor of the *Cyprus Review* from 1954–56.

Between the ages of sixteen and nineteen he wrote some poems that were published under the title of *Ten Poems* in 1932. His *Collected Poems: 1931–1974* appeared in 1980. In 1937 he wrote a novel, *Panic Spring,* under the pseudonym of Charles Norden. This was followed by *The Black Book* (1938), published only in France; *A Private Country* (1943); *Prospero's Cell* (1945), and *Cefalu* (1947), republished as *The Dark Labyrinth* (1958). Undoubtedly the work that brought him most fame was *The Alexandria Quartet,* a group of four novels intended to be read as a single book—*Justine* (1957), *Balthazar* (1958), *Mountolive* (1958), and *Clea* (1960). They were all published in a single volume in 1962. Durrell, like some earlier writers on erotic themes, frequently equated love with death. In the story of Clea in *The Alexandria Quartet* he writes: "Kisses themselves became charged with the deliberate affirmation which can come only from the foreknowledge and presence of death. It would have been good to die at any moment then, for love and death had somewhere joined hands." He goes on to say that "death (not even at hand, but in the air) sharpens kisses." He was, of course, writing of a time when sirens wailed every night to warn of air attacks. Repeatedly, however, it is the oddities of the sexual game that intrigue Durrell, as for example when he makes Clea go into a man's room and say: "I have come to ask you to *dépuceler* me, please, because I cannot get any further with my work unless you do." [dépuceler = to unvirgin]

Occasionally Durrell uses the limerick to express erotic thoughts:

> A *dévot* of the Ophite sect
> With member more or less erect,
> Snake-worship is the creed I hold
> And shall do till I get too old.
> The saucy serpent symbolizes
> A hundred Freudian surprises;
> With mine, I do the Indian trick
> Though it's become a shade too thick
> To stand up like an actual rope—
> I leave that to the Band of Hope.

Durrell also indulged in exchanges with other writers out of which developed *Art and Outrage: A Correspondence about Henry Miller between Alfred Perles and Lawrence Durrell with an Intermission by Henry Miller* (1959). After Durrell's death Barbara Robson, the executor and friend of Durrell's daughter Sappho, who committed suicide in 1985, declared that Sappho had an incestuous relationship with her father. The journals of Sappho became the subject of a court action when Eve Durrell, the writer's second wife, sought an injunction against publication of edited versions of these journals. The injunction was refused. In 1991 *Granta,* a quarterly literary magazine, published some thirty edited pages of Sappho Durrell's writings, but they contained no suggestion of incest. One entry in *Granta* stated: "I used to write him [Lawrence] letters, but since Claude [his third wife] died his traditional pattern of *wife = whore/stupid/bitch* and *me = virgin/wise* has disintegrated."

EURIPIDES
Born circa 480 B.C. Died circa 400 B.C.

It seems probable that Euripides was born on the island of Salamis. Though not popular in artistic and scholarly circles, largely because of his religious skepticism, he was highly educated and advanced in his thinking both in philosophic and scientific matters. He was a friend of Socrates, but virulently criticized by Aristophanes. As a playwright he used the language of the day, including the vernacular, to make his characters sound realistic. His best plays were the *Hippolytus, Medea, Alcestis,* and *Chrysippus.* The last named took as its theme the love of King Laius for the boy Chrysippus. Yet it was in the creation and portrayal of his female characters that Euripides excelled: their nobility of character tends to rule out the view of some that Euripides was a misogynist. Having spent the last years of his life at the court of Archelaus, king of Macedonia, he died after being bitten by dogs that were said to have been set upon him by his enemies.

FARRELL, JAMES T.
Born 1904. Died 1979.

This American author is best known for his proletarian Studs Lonigan triology set in Chicago in the 1920s. These books brilliantly capture the spirit, the dialogue, and the racial clashes of Irish religious fanatics, blacks, Jews, and other Americans in that period. Farrell's first book was *Young Lonigan* (1932), of which the author, A. J. Cronin, wrote: "[*Young*] *Lonigan* strains after nothing. It is the real thing. It is great. Bunged up with work as I am I have not been able to leave this book alone. And now that I have finished it, it will not leave me alone." This was followed by *The Young Manhood of Studs Lonigan* (1934), concluding with *Judgment Day* (1935). His whole work, including *Fellow Countrymen*, a collection of stories, concentrated on what he learned through harsh experience, or what one of his critics described as "the fag ends of humanity."

A *World I Never Made* (1936), dedicated to Hortense Alden, again stressed this particular talent of his. It was the story of various Irish-American Roman Catholics, their confused sex lives, their obsession with sin and the Church. Farrell's dialogue is maintained at an astonishingly realistic pitch throughout. "Mother, where is Aunty Margaret? She promised me she would be home and help me learn to read today." "She's out somewhere with the Devil." "She's not with the real Devil, is she?" "Indeed, she is!" Farrell manages to develop his amatory episodes through seemingly innocuous dialogue. For example, in *A World I Never Made* Margie says: "You don't know how much I appreciate your kindness. And you don't know how nervous I've been." Back comes the reply: "Margie, I know just what the prescription is for nerves when the patient is as handsome and healthy a girl as you are." "Now, there you go, Dickie-dear, getting fresh again," she teases, wagging an index-finger at him. "How did you know but what I was going to recommend some iron or a nerve tonic? Are you a mind reader, or a fortune teller?" Religious inhibitions again and again thwart the best erotic intentions in this book.

FIELDING, HENRY
Born 1707. Died 1754.

This English novelist, born in Somersetshire, was a prolific writer all his relatively short life. He started out as a playwright, his first play, *Love in Several Masques*, being produced at Drury Lane Theatre in 1728. This was followed by *The Author's Farce* and *Tom Thumb* (1730) and *The Historical*

Register for the Year at the Haymarket in 1736. This last-named play was a satirical attack on corruption in government circles, especially referring to the then prime minister, Walpole. As a result of this Walpole introduced theatrical censorship in the form of an act that enabled the lord chamberlain to prohibit certain plays. This act had the effect of denying a number of excellent plays production for more than a hundred years, including many that were erotic. Not until 1968 was that anachronistic act abolished.

As a novelist Fielding rebelled against conventional morality and all forms of humbug and he possessed a vigorous, if sometimes coarse style. *The History of Tom Jones* (1749) was his best novel: its dialogues between characters are amusing and endearing in Fielding's exposition of amatory topics. He had odd turns of phrase that owed more perhaps to his native Somerset dialect than to anything else: "The poor woman had indeed been loading her heart with foul language for some time, and now it scoured out of her mouth, as filth doth from a mud cart when the board which confines it is removed." Other works by Fielding included *A Journal from This World to the Next, The History of Mr. Jonathan Wild the Great,* and last of all *Amelia* (1751). The first collected edition of his works was published in 1762, and another edition in ten volumes edited by W. E. Henley appeared in 1904. He died in Lisbon.

FLAUBERT, GUSTAVE
Born 1821. Died 1880.

A native of Rouen, Flaubert spent most of his life at his paternal property of Croisset on the River Seine, the first steamboat station below Rouen. Though he started writing at an early age, it was not until 1857, some eleven years later, that his first and greatest novel, *Madame Bovary,* was published. This work first appeared in the *Revue de Paris,* and led to the indictment of the author for an offense against the moral code. It must seem astonishing that France of all countries, usually much more broad-minded than others, should in the middle of the last century have taken such offense officially against one of the acknowledged masterpieces of literature. In fact the indictment gave Flaubert useful publicity, ultimately helping to pave the way for his success, as well as bringing him as friends such influential supporters as Gautier and the De Goncourts.

The truth is that *Madame Bovary* was probably the first novel in modern times to present a detailed history of an adultery, for that is the theme of the book; if there is a moral in it it is the suicide of Emma Bovary. Trite as such a theme may sound at the end of the twentieth century, the appeal and above all the splendor of this novel lies in Flaubert's supreme descriptive powers. His view was that even such trivialities of rural life as the secret adultery of a doctor's young and attractive wife can be transformed into what becomes a realistic romance, if such a phrase can be permitted. Flaubert had the talent to make what was vulgar, what was commonplace and trivial, a thing of unique beauty when put into his prose. This was partly owing to a certain aloofness in his style. Who but Flaubert could or would have dared to write the love scene between Emma Bovary and Rudolphe in the middle of a crowded cattle market? He captured the atmosphere superbly, despite the background he chose for it. That passage alone in the book suddenly makes one recall that some of the happiest moments in life occur in the least-romantic places.

The year following the publication of *Madame Bovary* Flaubert published a historical romance, *Salammbô*. This was followed by *L'Education sentimentale* (1869), a novel similar in some ways to *Madame Bovary*; *La Tentation de Saint-Antoine*, another historical romance; and *Trois Contes* (1877), three short stories of which the first is contemporary and the other two historical. All his novels have been translated into English. He also wrote two dramas, *Le Candidat* and *Le Château des Coeurs*, and *Par les Champs et par les Grèves*, based on a tour of Brittany that he made with Madame Maxime du Camp in 1847.

A less well-known work of Flaubert's was his *Dictionnaire des Idées Reçues* in which he provided some remarkably witty and original definitions of his own. The word clarinette he defined as *"en jouer rend aveugle,"* giving as an example *"Tous les aveugles jouent de la clarinette,"* suggesting at the very least that some men actually coveted blind women. An *Institutrice* Flaubert defined as one who had an extensive repertoire of sexual techniques that she was happy to pass on to her clients. A *femme de chambre* was one who played the traditional role of the French domestic servant of the day by sitting herself astride the seated male, or providing what was sometimes called "sex in the arm chair." *"Plus chaudes que les blanches"* (hotter than whites) was Flaubert's definition of a negress. One could hardly call that racist, or racialist that is the more recent version of the word that has so many dubious meanings. *La poupette* was a female who liked to dress like a little girl and to be treated as one.

FLEMING, PAUL
Born 1609. Died 1640.

A native of Hartenstein in Saxony, Paul Fleming spent much of his short life accompanying ambassadorial missions sent by the duke of Holstein to Russia and Persia. It was in the last-named country that he acquired an interest in the erotic, though in a strange, almost academic way. His poems were not published until two years after his death, *Teutsche Poemata*, Hamburg, 1642. Though described as "a seventeenth-century erotic poet," he wrote much of his verse on a much higher plane, revealing a devout and simple nature. For this reason one needs to find a reason for the erotic verse; it would seem that in many respects he was an imitator of the Greek poet Anacreon, as well as some of the ancient Persian poets. F. Straumer wrote a popular version of Fleming's life in his book *Paul Flemings Leben und Orientalische Reisen* (1892).

FLETCHER, JOHN
Born 1579. Died 1625.

Born at Rye in Sussex, England, John Fletcher is best known for his prolific play writing, some of it undertaken in collaboration with Francis Beaumont. The two lived together in London and Fletcher carried on writing for the stage after Beaumont's death. In conjunction with Beaumont, Fletcher wrote *Philaster, The Scornful Lady, The Maid's Tragedy, A King and No King,* and *The Knight of the Burning Pestle.*

Fletcher alone produced *The Faithful Shepherdess, Four Plays in One, Wit without Money, Bonduca, Valentinian, The Loyal Subject, The Mad Lover, The Humorous Lieutenant, Woman Pleased, The Island Princess, Pilgrim, The Wild Goose Chase, Monsieur Thomas, The Woman's Prize, A Wife for a Month,* and *The Chances.* The plays, as some of their titles suggest, are full of lively and witty dialogue in explicit language when amorous activities are being discussed. There are many other plays in which Fletcher undoubtedly played a part in the writing such as *Cupid's Revenge, Love's Cure, The Lover's Progress,* and *The Fair Maid of the Inn.*

As a poet Fletcher has often been underrated by critics. It is also suspected by some scholars that some of his verses were actually stolen by Shakespeare for his own use, notably "The Bridal Song," "Dirge of the Three Queens," and "Orpheus." One of his livelier poems, entitled "Love's Emblems," strikes a happily amorous note:

> Yet the lusty spring hath stay'd;
> Blushing red and purest white
> Daintily to love invite
> Every woman, every maid:
> Cherries kissing as they grow,
> And inviting men to taste,
> Apples even ripe below,
> Winding gently to the waist:
> All love's emblems, and all cry,
> "Ladies, if not pluck'd, we die."

FORD, JOHN
Born 1586. Died 1639.

Baptized at Ilsington in Devonshire, England, John Ford was educated at Exeter College, Oxford University, and studied for the law. He entered the

Middle Temple in 1602. As a dramatist he revealed himself as an astute psychologist and one who could probe the secrets of the human heart with sympathy. His best-known play was undoubtedly *'Tis Pity She's a Whore* (1633), condemned by many because of both its title and its subject matter— the story of an incestuous relationship of brother and sister. Ford sometimes collaborated with other dramatists such as Dekker and Rowley, but in his own plays the themes were invariably of love affairs, often coarse but frequently tender and romantic, especially *The Broken Heart* (1633). Other titles of his work are: *The Lover's Melancholy* (1629), *Love's Sacrifice* (1633), *The Fancies Chaste and Noble* (1638), *The Lady's Trial* (1638), and *Beauty in a Trance* (1653). This last work was entered on the Stationers' Books records, but destroyed. Some of his other plays performed at the Cockpit Theatre, London, were also destroyed.

FRANKLIN, BENJAMIN
Born 1706. Died 1790.

It is perhaps hard indeed to equate Benjamin Franklin—ambassador, American postmaster general and a statesman who took part in the talks that led to the Declaration of Independence—with erotic literature. Certainly it should be stressed that this was a very minor part of his activities. Yet, curiously enough, the one single item that has caused him to have this reputation is not, in this author's opinion, erotic as defined in this book. It is scatological, even excrementitious for want of a better word—but that is all. Franklin wrote a letter to the Royal Academy of Brussels in which he set out his views on a cure for the problem (as he put it) caused by "digesting our common food," when "there is created or produced in the bowels of human creatures a great quantity of wind." After making various suggestions he ended his letter thus: "This invention, if completed, would be . . . bringing philosophy home to men's business and bosoms. And I cannot but conclude that in comparison therewith for universal and continual utility, the science of philosophers . . . even with the addition, gentlemen, of your *figure quelconque*, and the figures inscribed in it, are all together scarcely worth a Fart-hing."

This letter is now to be found in the Franklin Papers in the Library of Congress. Nevertheless, there was a fondness for the erotic in some of Franklin's other writings. When he was in England he wrote these words of advice to a friend who was cogitating on whether or not to seek a mistress. While urging that matrimony was undoubtedly the ideal state, Franklin suggested that if his friend must take a mistress he should avoid young virgins, but seek "a discreet and older woman: . . . because in every animal that walks upright, the deficiency of the fluids that fill the muscles appears first in the highest part, the face. Covering all above with a basket and regarding only what is below the girdle, it is impossible of two women to know an old one from a young one. And as in the dark all cats are grey, the pleasure of corporal enjoyment with an old woman is at least equal, and frequently superior."

While in England Franklin became a member of Sir Francis Dashwood's secret society, the Knights of St. Francis of Wycombe (more generally known as the Hell-Fire Club). The two men came closer together because each had been postmaster general in his own country. Franklin, though a Presbyterian, in 1745 had spent a whole year of bawdy revelry in the taverns of Philadelphia, drinking rum and Madeira and even writing such verse as this:

> Fair Venus calls; her voice obey;
> In beauty's arms spend night and day.
> The joys of love all joys excel
> And loving's certainly doing well.

This would explain Franklin's liking for membership of the Hell-Fire Club, for their activities were mainly drinking and womanizing.

The standard edition of Franklin's works is that in ten volumes, edited by Bigelow in 1887–89. See also his *Autobiography*, also edited by Bigelow in 1868 and *Benjamin Franklin*, by Carl Van Doren, New York and London, 1939; finally, *Curious Letters*, Benjamin Franklin, published in 1898.

GAUTIER, THÉOPHILE
Born 1811. Died 1872.

One of the most influential of French prose writers in the nineteenth century, and a noted romanticist, Gautier was born at Tarbes and first made his name as a poet in 1833 with his work *Albertus*. Then in 1835 he turned his attention to prose by publishing *Mademoiselle de Maupin*. This caused quite a considerable scandal at the time because its theme was a heroine who was involved in fornication, adultery, and homosexuality. Its publication was hailed by Balzac as an outstanding novel, while in England when it was eventually translated the critic George Saintsbury denounced it as "unfit for general perusal." This, however, was by no means a general view either in France or England, and most critics eventually took the view that *Mademoiselle de Maupin* had a delightful prose style and that many of the passages in the book were extremely eloquent if not elegant. Later in life Gautier traveled extensively and made a number of archaeological studies. He also wrote various books on painting, such as *L'Histoire des Peintres*, *L'Art Moderne*, and *Les Dieux et les Demi-Dieux de la Peintre*.

GAY, JOHN
Born 1685. Died 1732.

Best known as the author of that superb light opera, *The Beggar's Opera*, John Gay was also a poet with a fondness for erotic verse in its milder forms. Born in Devonshire, England, he published his first poem, *Wine*, in 1708. Four years later he became secretary to the duchess of Monmouth and shortly after this he devoted himself to play writing. First of these was *The Wife of Bath*, a comedy that was produced at Drury Lane and a farce, *What D'ye Call It?* that was played at the same theater. *The Beggar's Opera* in 1728 was such a success that for two seasons it caused Italian opera almost to disappear from England. A sequel to *The Beggar's Opera* entitled *Polly* was refused a license by the lord chamberlain, but it was published in 1729. The duke and duchess of Queensberry were so upset at this treatment of Gay by the authorities that they took him into their own home. When he died he was given a burial in Westminster Abbey.

Some of Gay's verse was satirical and this undoubtedly offended some of the Establishment. His poem, *The Shepherd's Week* angered some because it set out to ridicule the pastorals of the day. His ballads were always lively and dispensed with a keen sense of humor such as he showed in his *Fables*, *Black-Eyed Susan*, and especially *The Fair Maid of the Inn*. This last-named was written to celebrate the charms of a girl named by Gay as "Sweet Molly Mogg of the Rose." She was, in fact, a barmaid at the Rose Inn at Wokingham in Berkshire, and she figures in Gay's *Miscellanies in Verse*, London, 1727. Two typical verses are:

> I feel I'm in love to distraction,
> My senses all lost in a fog;
> And nothing can give satisfaction
> But thinking of sweet Molly Mogg.

> Were Virgil alive with his Phillis,
> And writing another Eclogue;
> Both his Phillis and fair Amaryllis
> He'd give up for sweet Molly Mogg.

Collected works of Gay include *Plays* (1760), *Works* (4 volumes) (1770) and *Poems Never before Printed* (1820), all published in London.

GENET, JEAN
Born 1910. Died 1986.

Abandoned by his mother in Paris, brought up in various public institutions until he was seven, Jean Genet did not obtain his birth certificate until he was twenty-one and then he learned that he was the illegitimate son of Gabrielle Genet and an unknown father. His whole life story is one of crime and frequent imprisonment, yet despite all this he succeeded to be recognized as a remarkably talented writer, praised by many serious critics of literature. Jean-

Paul Sartre said of him that "no other writer brings us into such close physical contact with an author."

There is some evidence that after Genet was placed in a home with foster parents at the age of seven he behaved well and studied hard. Then, at the age of ten, he was accused of stealing and sent to a reformatory institution. It was then, he says, that "I decided to repudiate a world which had repudiated me." He was in and out of prison for many years, once escaping to join the Foreign Legion in 1929. But he deserted from the Legion and spent some time as a homosexual prostitute in Spain, a pickpocket in Italy, and a cattle thief in Albania. Even during World War II and the German occupation of France he was often in prison. His first novel, *Notre-Dame des Fleurs* (translated into English as *Our Lady of the Flowers* by Bernard Frechtman) was published in Paris in 1943. This book was written in Fresne Prison and the hero of the book was modeled on one of Genet's male lovers. Critics were astonished at the elegant French that Genet produced, despite his use of homosexual and underworld jargon. This was followed by *Miracle de la Rose* (1946), *Pompes Funèbres* (1947), *Journal du Voleur* (1949, 1954), which was largely autobiographical.

In many ways his poem, *Un Chant d'Amour* (Song of love), which was made into a film, is his outstanding work. Based on his own experiences in prison, it tells of the attempts of two male homosexual prisoners to establish contact with one another through the wall that divides their cells. The theme may not sound erotic, but the eroticism is created by Genet's talent for suggesting ecstasy in the strangest moments and telling a heartrending story. One such moment that he exploits has one of the men puffing smoke through a straw inserted in a hole in the wall. His comrade in the next cell inhales the smoke with ecstasy, not just content to inhale it, but in sheer delight—yes, even sexual delight—at having this very slight contact with his mate. This poem was perhaps a surprising choice for a film, but it resulted in an effective one nonetheless.

His 1947 play *The Maids* has been performed countless times and even as recently as 1991 at London's Etcetera Theatre. Solange and Claire are the maids of the title and Madame is their mistress, heroine, and victim. Genet shows the two maids playing out their erotic fantasies.

GOMBROWICZ, WITOLD
Born 1903. Died 1969.

This Polish author was born in Maloszyce and educated at the University of Warsaw. Today he is recognized as one of the most important of European writers in this century. Much of his work has been translated into English, chiefly by Alastair Hamilton. His first work, *Memorial* (1933) was a collection of tales in which he attempted to expose human decadence and spiritual contortions beneath a veneer of social facades. His works include *Operetta; Princess Ivone; Ferdydurke* (1937); *Possessed; A Kind of Testament;* a play, *Slub* (The marriage), 1947; a novel, *Trans-Atlantyk* (1955); *Pornografia* (1960); and *Kosmos* (1965).

Pornografia, which has only just been published in London, tells the story of two old men who are visiting a country estate in Poland and who observe with a bizarre obsession the actions and motives of a teenage girl and a sixteen-year-old boy. The two men plot all kinds of imagined relationships until finally they are themselves absorbed into the world and magic of the youngsters. Gombrowicz was the recipient of the International Publishers' Prize, and perhaps his most important work was *A Kind of Testament*, which gave an insight into the man himself, modern literature, his own plays and novels, and views on the theater of the absurd.

GONCOURT, EDMOND-LOUIS-ANTOINE HUOT DE
Born 1822. Died 1896.

GONCOURT, JULES-ALFRED HUOT DE
Born 1830. Died 1870.

These two inseparable brothers were born in Nancy and Paris respectively and together they made a formidable writing team. Coming from a distinguished family, they had a classical education after which they decided to make a prolonged walking tour in 1849 taking them across Burgundy and Provence and then over the water to Algeria, painting, sketch making, and taking notes all the time. Afterwards they traveled together in Europe until in 1851 together they produced the novel, *En 18*. This was followed by various historical works such as *Histoire de la Societé Française pendant la Révolution* (1854), *Histoire de Marie Antoinette* (1858), and several similar works. After this the brothers branched out into the field of the realistic school of novelists, having earlier on had some success with their *Lèpres Modernes*, a study of women who sold their bodies, which was published under the title of *La Lorette* in 1853.

Their novels, though often pessimistic in tone, were lively and often erotic, especially *Soeur Philomène* (1861), which was the tale of the love of a nun for a doctor, actually based on a true-life story. Other novels of the erotic genre were *Renée Mauperin* (1864), *Germinie Lacerteux* (1865), *Manette Salomon* (1867). The brothers were close friends with most of the leading French writers of the day from Flaubert to Zola. Zola claimed that Jules Goncourt wrote to him saying that the secret of their success as joint authors was that "Edmond is the passion and I am the will." But the will unfortunately was curtailed latterly by the ill health of Jules who died young as a result of paralysis of the brain, caused, according to his biographer André Billy, by having contracted syphilis.

Edmond Goncourt lived to found the Académie Goncourt in 1896, a literary society composed of ten members who each year awarded a prize of the best work in imaginative prose. After the death of Jules, Edmond wrote *La Fille Elisa* (1878) and *Journal des Goncourt* (1887–92). English translations of most of the Goncourt brothers' works exist.

HALL, (MARGUERITE) RADCLYFFE
Born 1883. Died 1943.

This English writer was born in Bournemouth and educated at King's College, London, and in Germany. A fellow of the Zoological Society and a member of the Council for Psychical Research, she bred dogs as a hobby. For many years she lived at Rye in Sussex where she was easily recognizable by her severely tailored, masculine-style clothes. Her earliest writings consisted of poetry, *Twixt Earth and Stars*, London, 1906, and *Poems Past and Present*, 1910. It was after her poem, "The Blind Plowman" (1924) had been set to music that Hall turned to novel writing. So intent was she on succeeding that she frequently worked for as long as twelve hours at a stretch. In 1924–25 two novels were printed, *The Forge* and *The Unlit Lamp*. This last work was one of the first modern English books to touch on the theme of inverted love.

In 1926 she won the Femina–Vie Hereuse Prize with *Adam's Breed*. Perhaps encouraged by the success of that book she decided to be bold and to follow up the theme of inverted love in more detail. At any rate it was against the advice of a few of her closest friends that in 1928 she published *The Well of Loneliness*. This work tells in explicit if elegant prose of the sexual attachment of a young girl to an older woman. The very mention of the word *lesbian* in public at that time was more or less taboo and the book was condemned by a number of prominent people. As a result the case against it was heard in a London magistrate's court. Despite the fact that both Virginia Woolf and E. M. Forster supported the cause of Radclyffe Hall, Sir Chartres Biron, the magistrate, ruled that, though the book was "dignified and restrained," it made out a case for recognizing sexual inversion. Therefore he declared it to be an obscene libel and ordered all copies destroyed. Though that ruling applied in Britain, the novel was published in the USA despite an attempt to stop it by John S. Sumner of the American Society for the Suppression of Vice.

From 1907–16 Radclyffe Hall lived with a Mrs. Mabel Batten. Through Batten she met Una Troubridge, the wife of Admiral Sir T. H. Troubridge; Lady Troubridge ultimately became her lover and companion for the rest of her life. They lived in Rye, London, and Paris, where they associated with

Colette and other members of Bohemian society. In 1930 Hall received the Gold Medal of the Eichelbergher Humane Award. Her later works were *The Master of the House* (1932) and *The Sixth Beatitude* (1936). In 1985 M. Baker wrote *Our Three Selves: A Life of Radclyffe Hall*, which is the definitive account of her career.

HARRIS, FRANK
Born 1856. Died 1931.

"Unquestionably obscene, lewd, lascivious and indecent," was how Mr. Justice Levy at the supreme court in New York described Frank Harris's book, *My Life*, volume 2, which had been privately printed in France, in 1925. As a result the judge gave police the power to raid private printing works without a search warrant and to arrest any others who might print the book. The first volume of Harris's autobiography had already been savagely condemned throughout the English-speaking world. The chief complaints against Harris concerned his somewhat crude and excessively detailed accounts of early sexual adventures. Sometimes what Harris had to say was trite rather than erotic, e.g., "This experience with E . . . had the most important and unlooked for results. The mere fact that girls could feel sex pleasure 'just like boys do' increased my liking for them and lifted the whole sexual intercourse to a higher plane in my thought."

Harris was born in Galway, Ireland. In 1881 he joined the staff of the *Spectator* in London and a year later became editor of the London *Evening News*. He edited the *Fortnightly Review* from 1886 to 1894 when he bought the *Saturday Review*, which he edited until 1898. He was an outspoken critic who practically courted notoriety all his life, and, apart from his autobiography, he was the author of *Elder Conklin and Other Stories* (1895), *Montes the Matador* (1900), and a play, *Mr. and Mrs. Daventry*. The first volume of his autobiography was printed and published in Germany, though written in English. Altogether there were four volumes, the last two being published in 1927. Criticism of his work centered on the fact that he gave the impression of having been on the closest of terms with King Edward VII when the latter was prince of Wales.

Unquestionably he was a constant womanizer in every country he visited. In volume 2 of *My Life and Loves* he wrote:

> I have been from Cape to Cairo, and from Vladikavkas to Vladivostock, but one girl has taught me more than I could find in two continents. There is more to learn and love in one woman's spirit than in all the oceans. And their bodies are so fascinating—thank God!—as their souls. And all the lessons they have taught me have been of gentleness and generosity, of loving kindness and tender

pity, of flower-soft palms and clinging lips and the perfume of their flesh is sweeter than all the scents of Araby and they are gracious-rich in giving as crowned queens. All that is amiable and sweet and good in life, all that ennobles and chastens I have won from women. Why should I not sing their praises, or at least show my gratitude by telling of the subtle intoxication of their love that has made my life an entrancing romance?

In 1980 a book entitled *Letters to Frank Harris and Other Friends* was published in London. Its author was Enid Bagnold, who wrote *The Chalk Garden* and *The Chinese Prime Minister* and married the late Sir Roderick Jones, chairman of Reuters News Agency. The book revealed a passionate affair she had had with Harris when she was twenty-two and he was thirty-four years her senior. It all started in an upstairs private room at the Café Royal in London. What attracted her to Harris? "It was his talk," said Lady Jones, then aged ninety. "His talk made you feel as though you were living in heaven."

Harris gave her a job working as his assistant. In 1914 he was sentenced to imprisonment in London for contempt of court, and when he came out he left the country for America where he wrote diatribes against both America and England for their attitude to Germany. Before he left England he gave Enid back her love letters, but they continued to keep in touch. On Harris's death his wife, Nellie, destroyed all the letters he had received from innumerable women, including those from Enid. However, she had kept copies of some of them in a scrapbook. One letter from Frank Harris to her is included in the book. It is dated January 20, 1916, and begins: "A superb letter! A woman's love at its best does include all other sorts of love; has at one and the same time the passion of sex, the loving tenderness of a mother, and a sort of amusing kindness found sometimes in an elder sister," and ends with the comment: "Wait! The man will come to you; you are superb, and more desirable through experience and beauty than nine out of ten."

HAWES, STEPHEN
Born circa 1480. Died circa 1523.

This English poet was probably a native of Suffolk and one of his earliest jobs was that of groom of the privy chamber to King Henry VII, where he gained an insight into life at court. He became a poet in praise of love, or, as he put it, he wished to revive the "floure of chyvalry which hath be longe decayed." His principal work was *Passetyme of Pleasure* or *The Historie of Graunde Amoure and La Bell Pucel* (1509), which was full of romance, ecstasy, and dreams of love. His other works were: *The Conversyion of Swerers* (1509), *The Exemple of Vertu* (1512), *The Comfort of Lovers,* and *The Temple of Glasse.*

HAZLITT, WILLIAM
Born 1778. Died 1830.

This English critic and essayist was born at Maidstone and moved to London in 1812, setting himself up as a literary critic for various periodicals. In 1818 he delivered his *Lectures on the English Poets* and in 1820 *Lectures on the Dramatic Literature of the Age of Elizabeth*. These were followed by two volumes of essays, *Table Talk*, in 1821–82 and a *Life of Napoleon* (1828–30). Partly because he was a great admirer of Napoleon and also because of some of his political views, Hazlitt was largely played down by many critics, but he was one of the most stimulating writers of his day.

Yet the one work that made him famous has nothing to do with literary criticism. It was *Liber Amoris; or, The New Pygmalion*, which was privately printed, with an introduction by Richard Le Gallienne, in 1894, long after Hazlitt's death. The book consists of eleven letters from Hazlitt to his friend, P. G. Patmore, including his manuscripts on the subject of *Liber Amoris*—a letter from his landlord's daughter, Sarah Walker, to Hazlitt, material from the diary of Mrs. Hazlitt and five letters from that lady to her son and sister-in-law written between 1824 and 1831. Thomas de Quincey said of the book that it greatly raised Hazlitt in his opinion because it showed him "to be capable of stronger and more agitating passions than believed to be within range of his nature."

Hazlitt married Sarah Stoddart, a notorious flirt of indecisive character, in 1808, and they had one son, William. The marriage was not a success, each party for various reasons being difficult to live with. Before the autumn of 1819 they were living apart. It was on August 16, 1820, that Hazlitt recorded that it was "the time I first saw the sweet apparition." The "sweet apparition" was Sarah Walker, daughter of a Mr. Walker, a tailor and lodging housekeeper in Southampton Buildings, Chancery Lane, London. Hazlitt idealized her: whatever her physical charms may have been, he certainly attributed to her mental, spiritual, and moral qualities that she was far from possessing. Undoubtedly this passion for Sarah Walker was partially responsible for Hazlitt's ultimate divorce from his wife. "To pretend to know Hazlitt and to ignore the *Liber Amoris* is, in a lesser degree, as though you should write a life of Coleridge and never even whisper 'opium,'" wrote Richard Le Gallienne, "but whereas Coleridge's weakness was disastrous, Hazlitt's was only silly."

Hazlitt was hopelessly infatuated with the young Sarah Walker, as his diary of conversations between them so clearly shows: "Stay and hear me a little," he tells her. "I shall soon be where I can no more hear thy voice, far distant from her I love. . . . The smallest share of thy tenderness would make me blest; but couldst thou ever love me as thou didst him, I should feel like a

God! . . . I am thy creature, thy slave—I only wish to live for your sake—I would gladly die for you." To which Sarah replies: "That would give me no pleasure. Indeed you greatly overrate my power."

Every little detail of the day-to-day talks between Hazlitt and Sarah are given in the book—their quarrels, his impassioned declarations of love, the way in which she plays him along, sometimes keeping him mollified by sitting on his knee and exchanging kisses and at others fending him off. Always she addresses him as "Sir."

It is, of course, a tale of futility and unrequited love in its worst form. Hazlitt made it worse by his constant nagging of the poor girl, despite her attempts to make him happy. "Am I to suppose, then, that you are acting a part, a vile part, all this time, and that you come up here [i.e., to his room] and stay as long as I like, that you sit on my knee and let me take other liberties with you, and this for a whole year together, and that you do all this not out of love or liking or regard, but go through your regular task, like some young witch, without one natural feeling, to show your cleverness, and get a few presents out of me, and go down into the kitchen to make a fine laugh of it?"

To which Sarah replies that she had never made a jest of him to anyone: "You have no ground for complaint in my conduct. . . . I told you my regard could amount to no more than friendship." In yet another of Hazlitt's recording of their talks he asks her, "Kiss me, thou little sorceress!" "Never," she replies. "Then go," answers Hazlitt, "but remember I cannot live without you—nor I will not."

HERODOTUS
Born 484 B.C. Died 432 B.C.

Described as the "father of history" and certainly the first Greek historian, Herodotus lived at the time of the war between Greece and Persia, and it was into the factors that helped create this war that he diligently probed. Much of his historical work has since been criticized and challenged, some of it on the grounds that it is based on legend and even fiction. While not attempting to deny that he wrote what he believed to be true, it must be admitted that some of it suggests a certain license toward a fictional style, not least when he touches on amatory matters. For example, he writes of "a certain King of Sardis, Candaules by name," who is so proud of his wife's beauty that he even encourages one of his friends, Gyges, to hide himself close to their bedroom so that he can see for himself how magnificent she is in the nude. Gyges at first resolutely declines the king's suggestion, but King Candaules continues to press him and insists that there would be no risk of his wife's seeing Gyges. Gyges then complies with his master's wishes and the queen, as he feared, happens to detect his presence. She says nothing, but the following morning she summons Gyges to her room. Then she tells him that she has seen him hiding in the bedroom the night before. Gyges is given two choices: to kill his master forthwith and thus become king, or to be killed himself that instant in her room. Gyges complies with her wishes.

HERRICK, ROBERT
Born 1591. Died 1674.

Son of a London goldsmith, Herrick was foremost among the young wits and poets who formed a court circle with Ben Jonson and it was no doubt through this association that he developed a remarkable talent for conjuring up terse, but amusing, and often amatory verses. At some early date, surprisingly enough for one of his temperament, he must have taken holy orders, since in 1627 he was appointed chaplain to an expedition to the Isle of Rhé, and in 1629 he became vicar of Dean Prior in Devonshire. It is a constant surprise to any biographer of erotic literature how often there are bishops, canons, priests, and monks in their ranks. Herrick's poetry is not without some religious feeling, but it is his erotic and secular work that sounds the more convincing. Typical of this are his verses on one "Julia": he describes her in one of them as "Fresh Cheese and Cream":

> Would ye have fresh cheese and cream?
> Julia's breast can give them:
> And if more, each nipple cries,
> To your cream, her strawberries.

Maybe such extravagant imagery made him enemies in the Church, or possibly he indulged too much in the amorous antics he wrote about, but he lost his living as a vicar in 1647. His complete works, edited by W. C. Hazlitt, were published in 1869.

HOMER
Lived circa ninth century B.C.

Homer still remains a mystery as a person and while some authorities suggest he lived in the twelfth century B.C., others claim he was alive around 800 B.C. Even his birthplace is doubtful and as many as seven cities have been suggested in this connection. All one can say is that he was born on the mainland of Greece and that he probably lived at Chloe or Smyrna. Even his authorship of the *Iliad* and the *Odyssey* is usually qualified by the word *reputed*. Many other works have, of course, also been ascribed to him—the Homeric Hymns, which are so markedly erotic that some Greek authorities have dropped the description of Hymns as being inappropriate. Other works attributed to Homer are the *Batrachomyomachia; or, Fight of the Frogs*, the *Margites*, the *Thebaid* and *Epigoni*, the *Epigrams*, and several so-called cyclic poems.

All one can honestly say is that certain Greek works of old are still attributed to Homer and that the first reference to either the *Iliad* or *Odyssey* being circulated was in 850 B.C. *Iliad* referred to the siege of Troy and *Odyssey* was the story of the adventures of Ulysses. The *Iliad* does not cover the whole history of the Trojan War, nor even of the major incidents at its climax and ending. Ulysses, or Odysseus (to give him his true Greek name), was one of the chief Greek leaders in the Trojan War, the man who entered Troy in the wooden horse and after the war wandered far and wide for about ten years.

What is most impressive about the Homeric works is the command of language, the harmonious vocabulary and the skill in telling the various stories. It has been said by some Greek scholars that the expressions of practical wisdom and morality in Homer's work caused some of his poems to be regarded as the Bible of Greece. On the other hand the great German scholar Friedrich August Wolf insisted that there was "no one Homer." Certainly the poems of Homer show the Greek language at a very early stage as compared with Attic Greek. In Homer's works one finds all the erotic deities on which ancient Greece built its civilization. This is particularly noticeable in book 14 of the *Iliad* in which he introduces Zeus's daughter, Aphrodite, and spins a tale of amatory enticement (see chapter 2).

Some of the best editions of the *Iliad* are those of Van Leenwen and Da Costa (1895–96) and Monro (1896), published in London. Of translations into English of the Homeric works there are Lord Derby's *Iliad* (1867) and Worsley's *Odyssey* (1895). Also worth consulting is William Morris's *Odyssey* in verse and prose (1901).

HORACE [QUINTUS HORATIUS FLACCUS]
Born 65 B.C. Died 8 B.C.

Horace, as he is more generally known, was born near Venusia in Apulia, but was educated in Rome and Athens. In 44 B.C. when Brutus visited Athens after the murder of Julius Caesar, Horace accompanied him as military tribune and took part in the battle of Philippi in 42 B.C. When he returned to Rome he was employed in the quaestor's office and later he acquired an estate in the Sabine country where he lived latterly. He spent the rest of his days writing lyrical poems on a variety of subjects, many of them on the agonies and ecstasies of love addressed to imaginary females. The following is an example of such poems:

> Horace speaking: "Say our first loves we should revoke,
> And severed, join in brazen yoke:
> Admit I Chloe put away,

And love again love-cast-off Lydia?"
To which Lydia replies: "Though mine be brighter than the Star;
Thou lighter than the cork by far;
Rough as the Adriatic Sea, yet I
Will live with thee or else for thee will die."

Much of Horace's work reveals the character and personality of Horace himself: he comes over as a genial, courteous, and kindly man, compassionate toward people who have committed errors in their lives, but a scourge against all forms of dishonesty. Translations of his work were made by Lord Lytton, London, 1872, and by F. W. Newman, London, 1876 (the latter being translations of the Odes of Horace alone).

HROTSVITHA OF GANDERSHEIM
Lived circa 933–1000

This German poetess came from a distinguished Saxony family and entered the Benedictine nunnery of Gandersheim in Brunswick where she remained until her death. She wrote what were then described as eight metrical legends, including *Theophilus*, the medieval Faust, as well as six comedies in prose, aiming at the transformation of what was then called heathen into Christian poetry. She is perhaps best known for her drama entitled *Paphnutius*, which tells the life story of a particularly outrageous harlot named Thais and how she ultimately redeemed herself. There is a complete edition of Hrotsvitha's works compiled by K. A. Barack in Berlin in 1858.

HUXLEY, ALDOUS LEONARD
Born 1894. Died 1963.

One hesitates to be unjust to any writer, whether alive or dead. As Aldous Huxley is dead and unable to defend himself, it should be mentioned that he is included in the section only after much thought and self-argument. It would be wrong to label him as an author of erotic literature, yet because of one single, brilliant novel, *Eyeless in Gaza*, he deserves a place if only because here is eroticism in an entirely new, almost revolutionary framework. But unless this novel is studied in the context of Huxley as not only novelist, but essayist, playwright, philosopher in his own original right, and literary critic, then many of the worthwhile points made in it may be totally missed. Though he is not often quoted today, Huxley was one of the perceptive geniuses of the 1920s and 1930s.

As a young man his intention was to become a doctor of medicine, but he was failed on account of bad eyesight, a defect he overcame in later life by adopting what is known as the Bates Method. His novels all tend to reveal something of Huxley himself, and one sometimes feels they were written as undercover portrayals of his own complex personality and deeply sentimental feelings. His works included *Crome Yellow* (1921), *Antic Hay* (1923), *Those Barren Leaves* (1925), *Point Counter Point* (1928), and the highly speculative and imaginative *Brave New World* (1932). In connection with the last-named title it should perhaps be said that Huxley, having seen the advent of both silent films and "the talkies," went so far as to suggest that the ultimate in such films would be "the feelies." This surely was a highly erotic suggestion even though Huxley covered it up to some extent by introducing "the smellies" by which appropriate perfumes and other smells were introduced to the audience during such films. Both in an amusing and erotic way Huxley in later life enjoyed exploiting this theme in conversation.

Eyeless in Gaza was first published in London in 1936. The title for the book was taken from a line in Milton's *Samson Agonistes:* "Eyeless in Gaza, at the mill, with slaves." It is in this context that the book needs to be read. It is the story of a weak-minded young man, Anthony Beavis, who spends his life making mistakes, especially amorous ones, in what he sees as being "a meaningless, valueless world." It is in his descriptions of his characters and their feelings that Huxley excels. For example, there is the occasion when Huxley allows Brian, one of the other young men in the story, to lapse into French when recalling his being lured back to her apartment by a woman who has sat at his table in a café at Grenoble when he and Anthony Beavis are learning French there: "The real temptations were not the worst, but the best. At Grenoble, it had been the best in literature. *Et son ventre, et ses seins, ces grappes de ma vigne. . . . Elle se coula à mon côté, m'appela des noms les plus tendres et des noms les plus effroyablement grossiers, qui glissaient sur ses lèvres en suaves murmures. Puis elle se tût et et commenca à me donner ces baisers qu'elle savait.*"

In similar fashion the author equally splendidly captures the thoughts of Helen:

> The second time she kissed him it was for fun; for fun and, at the same time, out of curiosity. It was an experiment, made in a spirit of hilarious scientific inquiry. She was a vivisector—licensed by perfection, justified by happiness. Besides, he had an extraordinarily nice mouth. She had never kissed such full soft lips before; the experience had been startlingly pleasurable. It was not only that she wanted to see, scientifically, what the absurd creature would do next; she also wanted to feel once more that cool resilience against her mouth, to experience that strange creeping of pleasure that tingled out from her lips and ran, quick and almost unbearable, like moths along the surface of her body.

It is in such descriptive passages that Huxley is at his best, making similar attempts to portray erotic thoughts in many other writers seem second-rate. At the end of the story the character Anthony Beavis is converted to Huxley's own mystical doctrines and to vegetarianism and Eastern mysticism. Educated at Eton and Balliol College, Oxford, Huxley started to specialize in studies of mysticism when he went to settle in California in 1937. He developed these themes in his later works such as *Time Must Have a Stop* (1944) and *The Perennial Philosophy* (1945).

HUYSMANS, JORIS-KARL
Born 1848. Died 1907.

Of Dutch extraction, this French novelist was born in Paris and was an early disciple of Emile Zola. His books attracted a wide readership, beginning with *Le Drageoir aux Epices* (1874) and *Marthe* (1876). His novel, *A Rebours* (Against nature), published in 1884, was typical of what was then called the Decadent Movement in literature and painting, as it not only introduced decadence in the character in Des Esseintes, but focused on the then-popular theme of Salome dancing. Of Salome he wrote: "She was no longer just the dancing girl who extorts a cry of lechery from an old man by the lascivious movements of her loins. . . . She had become the symbolic incarnation of undying Lust, the Goddess of Immortal Hysteria, the Beauty above all other Beauties."

Huysmans's decadent hero, Des Esseintes, develops an astonishing passion for a ventriloquist: "It was not so much the woman as the ventriloquist who appealed to him. . . . As he held the woman in his arms, a hoarse, drunken voice roared from behind the door. . . . He derived a remarkable pleasure from the panic-ridden hurry of a man running a risk and interrupted in his fornication." Other novels of Huysmans wre *Là-Bas* (1891), *En route* (1895), *La Cathédrale* (1898)—by this time he had suddenly become a devout Roman Catholic—*La Bièvre et St. Sévérin* (1898), *Sainte Lydwine de Schiedam* (1901), and *De Tout* (1902). In some ways he was a nineteenth-century version of Hrotsvitha.

JONG, ERICA
Born 1942.

This American author of more than sixteen books is the daughter of a painter mother and a musician father. "I almost became a painter myself at one time," she says. Her special subject originally was eighteenth-century English litera-ture and she was a lecturer in English at the City College of New York from 1964–66 and from 1967–68 a lecturer at the University of Maryland European Extension at Heidelberg. From 1971–73 she was instructor in English at Manhattan Community College. Her first book was *Fruits and Vegetables* (1971). Since then she has produced novels, poetry, and children's fiction, but it was the highly praised *Fear of Flying* (1973) that put her among the best-sellers: it sold ten-million copies in twenty-two languages. This book's theme was the quest for sexual fulfillment by one Isadora Wing.

Erica Jong has been married four times and now divides her time between New York and Connecticut. Her more recent books have included *At the Edge of the Body*, a poem (1979); *Parachute & Kisses* (1984), and *Any Woman's Blues* (1990). Because of this last book Erica Jong was described by one critic as "model for female sexual independence." *Any Woman's Blues* is at times almost autobiographical with a tendency toward purple prose, describing a passion "older than Pan and the dark gods and goddesses lurking in the shadows behind him." The book tells of a rich Jewish painter, Leila Sand, who is madly in love with a not very pleasant young man who indulges in drug taking. One sentence in the book stands out as typical of the kind of puzzles that Erica Jong sometimes sets her readers: "We lived that year in a tangle of thighs, art history, and extra-virgin olive oil."

JOYCE, JAMES (AUGUSTINE ALOYSIUS)
Born 1882. Died 1941.

This Irishman, who spent most of his life on the continent of Europe, was born in Dublin where he was educated. However, a sense of restlessness was induced in him early in life by his family's constant changes in residence. Joyce was a boarder at Clongowes Wood College, then Belvedere College for five years during which time he contemplated becoming a Roman Catholic priest. He made this latter school a feature of his book *A Portrait of the Artist as a Young Man* (1916). By the time he went to University College, Dublin, to study modern languages he had given up all idea of entering the priesthood. After graduation he went to Paris and it was here that he became influenced by the works of the symbolists and the "stream of consciousness" school of writers and those like Édouard Dujardin who spoke of "interior monologue" in order to express the mind's activity. His first published work was a volume of verse, *Chamber Music* (1907), London. This was followed by *Dubliners* (1914), *A Portrait* (1916), *Exiles* (1918), and *Ulysses*, which was first of all serialized in the *Little Review*, New York.

It is largely because of *Ulysses* that Joyce is included in this series of biographies, for controversy still rages as to whether this book is erotic or pornographic, or—among other things—a ridiculous and prolonged piece of pretentious writing. The work was originally published in Paris in 1922, then in London that same year, and later editions were printed in New York in 1934, Paris again in 1924, and Hamburg and Bologna in 1932. Five-hundred copies of the first London edition were burned by the New York post office authorities and a similar number were seized by customs at Folkestone, England. Alfred Noyes, the British poet and historiographer, described *Ulysses* as "the foulest book that has ever found its way into print."

One could say that *Ulysses* was Joyce's own odyssey, though it shows a day's life in Dublin through the eyes of three people. In his own peculiar way Joyce tried to make it a parallel of Homer's own work, and it is quite clear that it took him many years to write, rewrite, and sometimes even then change and write again. Indeed, a main criticism of *Ulysses* is that it was rewritten too often; even now the academic world debates this subject, resulting in a new and so-called improved version of the book by Professor Hans Walter Gabler, a textual scholar at Munich University. The ban of publishing the full, unexpurgated version of *Ulysses* in the United States was not lifted until the end of 1933. Prior to this the editors of the *Little Review* had been prosecuted in connection with their serialization of the work.

There is both eroticism and pornography in *Ulysses*, the former showing rather more of the French influence, the latter being typical of Irish crudity in its loudest form, sometimes Irish male chauvinism. One also gets the feeling that Joyce was perhaps inhibited by his religious upbringing and this frequently gets in the way of his narrative, interrupting his train of thought. To pick out almost any brief quotation from *Ulysses* is rash and misleading because the moods, the style, the language range from sometimes attractive prose to sheer crudity of dialogue. But to fail to make such a quotation would be remiss, so here is one of the happier ones:

> Pillowed on my coat she had her hair, earwigs in the heather scrub my hand under her nape, you'll toss me all. O wonder! Coolsoft with ointments her hand touched me, caressed: her eyes upon me did not turn away. Ravished over her I lay, full lips full open, kissed her mouth. Yum. Softly she gave me in my mouth the seedcake warm and chewed. Mawkish pulp her mouth had mumbled sweet and sour with spittle. Joy: I ate it: joy. Young life, her lips that gave me pouting. Soft, warm, sticky gum-jelly lips. Flowers her eyes were, take me, willing eyes. Pebbles fell. She lay still. A goat. No-one. High on Ben Howth rhododendrons a nannygoat walking sure-footed, dropping currants. . . . Wildly I lay on her, kissed her eyes, her lips, her stretched neck, beating, woman's breasts full in her blouse of nun's veiling, fat nipples upright. Hot I tongued her. She kissed me. I was kissed. All yielding she tossed my hair.

In 1939 Joyce published *Finnegans Wake* in which he tried to give a world history through the dream of a Dublin publican. It never lived up to the reputation of *Ulysses*, probably because of its publication on the eve of World

War II and also because it is even more difficult. But amid (or buried in) its profusion of puns in Joyce's unique "night language" are many erotic, not to mention pornographic, allusions and episodes.

Worth consulting is *The Scandal of Ulysses* by Bruce Arnold, London, 1991.

JUVENAL [DECIMUS JUNIUS JUVENALIS]
Born circa A.D. 55. Died circa A.D. 135.

If Juvenal touched on erotic themes, it was not so much that he took any delight in them, but more that he was one of the foremost public denunciators of the vices and immoralities of his day. He is reputed to have been the son of a rich man of Aquinum; he started to write his satires at an early age. His extant work consists of sixteen satires, which were published in five books. The first nine satires contain attacks in the most biting language against crime, vice, corruption, and especially on the licentiousness of women, the last-named theme being something about which he was obsessive. Probably it was this obsession and his constant reiteration on the need for moral crusading that caused his characters to be singularly unlifelike. English translations of his work were made by John Dryden in 1693 and William Gifford in 1802. See also *D. Junii Juvenalis Satyrae*, Houseman, London, 1905.

KAWABATA, YASUNARI
Born 1899. Died 1972.

This Japanese author, who won a Nobel Prize in 1968, was all his life obsessed by love and death, so his eventual death by suicide in 1972 came as no surprise. His books are filled not only with a death urge, but the subject of sexual neuroticism. Yet he dealt delicately and with distinct flair on the theme of the hopelessly erotic, something hard to define, but which Kawabata did with great skill and feeling. His *House of the Sleeping Beauty* (1969) was a collection of some of his best stories. *Izo no odoriko*, Tokyo, 1925, examined his own infatuation for an itinerant dancer with deep understanding. This work was published as *The Izu Dancer* in the *Atlantic Monthly* in 1925. His later works include *Yukiguni* (1937), another detailed description of a love affair, which was translated and published as *The Snow Country* (1957) and *Sembaruzu* (1949–51), which was translated into English as *Thousand Cranes* (1959), the last-named yet again concentrating on sexual neuroticism.

KIRKUP, JAMES
Born 1923.

This highly productive novelist, playwright, poet, and critic has most surprisingly combined his nonstop output of works with academic posts in various parts of the world. Educated at South Shields High School, England, where he was born, and Durham University, he received the Atlantic Award in Literature (Rockefeller Foundation) in 1950. From 1950–52 he was Gregory Fellow in Poetry at the University of Leeds and from 1953–56 he had the appointment of visiting poet and head of the English Department at the Bath Academy of Art. For some time after this Kirkup lectured in universities in Stockholm, Salamanca, Tokyo, and the USA, being poet in residence and visiting professor at Amherst College, Massachusetts, in 1968. In 1969 he was president of the Poets Society of Japan.

His first book was *The Drowned Sailor* (1948), published in London and followed by *The Creation* (1950), *The Submerged Village* (1951), *The Descent into the Cave* (1957), *A Journal of Japan* (1962), and *Heaven, Hell and Hari-kari* (1974). Plays included *Upon This Rock* (1955), *The True Mystery of the Nativity* (1957), and such television drama as *The Peach Garden* and *Two Pigeons Flying High*. Some of his poetic works, especially those touching on religious themes, have been savagely attacked by his critics, even accusing him of blasphemy. Notable poems of his are *Poems of the Prodigal Son* (1959) and *Poems from Japan* (1968). His autobiography *The Only Child* was published in 1957.

Whatever his most virulent critics may say there can be no doubting his talent and his originality, and if his verse is condemned by some, there is the indisputable fact that he received the Keats Prize for Poetry in 1974. Kirkup lived for many years in Japan and acquired a deep understanding of many unusual aspects of Japanese life even to the extent of examining Zen culture and philosophy. One result of this was a novel published in London in 1991 entitled *Gaijin on the Ginza*. In this work Kirkup most effectively told the improbable story of the misadventures of a homosexual army major and a nymphomaniac actress. This is a lively and hilarious novel that explores the seedier side of Tokyo life rarely seen by Westerners. Anyone who reads this book should bear in mind what Kirkup gives as his recreation in the English *Who's Who*: he describes it as "standing in shafts of moonlight."

His most recent book, yet another autobiography, is *A Poet Could Not but Be Gay*, London, 1991, which tells of his disaffection with England and subsequent experiences in Sweden and then in Spain, where he fell passionately in love with a young American man. The book is both enlightening and humorous while at the same time uninhibited in its homoerotic exposures.

KOCK, PAUL HENRI DE
Born 1819. Died 1892.

This lively French writer of the latter part of the nineteenth century owed an enormous debt to his father, Charles Paul de Kock, and in many respects he carried on the writing tradition learned from his father. Charles Paul de Kock was a Dutch banker who went to live in Paris and wrote in French. Altogether he produced about a hundred novels, many of which were translated into English. It is, however, suspected that as time went on a great deal of the work on these novels, if not the whole of some of them, was done by his son. Both father and son took as their subjects the low and middle-class life in Paris at that period, all of which is described in witty and bawdy prose.

Paul Henri de Kock wrote *L'Amoureuse de Pierrefonds, Les Cocus Célèbres, Les Courtisanses Celebres, Les Treize Nuits de Jane.*

LACLOS, PIERRE AMBROISE FRANÇOIS CHODERLOS DE
Born 1741. Died 1803.

Born in Amiens, this French artillery officer who eventually became a general, saw no active service until he was over sixty. A member of the Jacobin Club, he played a considerable part in the French Revolution, but ensured long-lasting fame for himself with his work, *Les Liaisons Dangereuses*, Paris, 1782. Not only has this novel been translated into a number of languages, but it has been made the subject of highly successful films and plays in recent years. One such translation into English was made by Richard Aldington in 1924, titled *Dangerous Acquaintances*. In a subtle yet realistic manner Laclos's novel tells of the corruption of innocence and virtue by Valmont, a libertine, and his equally vicious and immoral mistress, Madame de Merteuil. Corruption is their amusement, almost their recreation. The book is an astute study of the fascination that evil can have for some people and the power this fascination creates. It is not cynically told: indeed, the absence of cynicism or frivolity makes the message of *Les Liaisons Dangereuses* all the more effective.

LAUTRÉAMONT, COMTE DE [ISIDORE-LUCIEN DUCASSE]
Born 1846. Died 1870.

This French writer was born at Montevideo and was considered to be one of the forerunners of the surrealist school. Indeed, in his work, *Les Chants de Maldoror*, he seemed to many of his contemporaries to sum up the surrealist view of beauty when he suggested that lovemaking was "as beautiful as the chance meeting on a dissection table of an umbrella and a sewing-machine." At least this somewhat abstruse definition is no worse than the one contained in *The Abridged Dictionary of Surrealism* that claims eroticism to be "a sumptuous ceremony in a tunnel." *Les Chants de Maldoror* has been regarded by many French writers as an important guide to the erotic side of surrealism and its imagery is certainly as curious as the single quotation above. This book was first published in Paris and Brussels in the 1870s, and a translation by Alexis Lykiard was published in London in 1970.

A remarkably imaginative novel that re-creates the life of the Comte de Lautréamont was published in London in 1991. *Isidore*, by the poet Jeremy Reed, presents his own picture of this Frenchman as a forerunner of the surrealists.

LAWRENCE, DAVID HERBERT
Born 1885. Died 1930.

Novelist, poet, and essayist, D. H. Lawrence, as he is still best known, was born at Eastwood, a small mining town in Nottinghamshire, England, a neighborhood he used for many of the scenes in his novels. In *Sons and Lovers* (1913) he called Eastwood "Bestwood." He attended Beauvale School and in 1898 was the first pupil to win a scholarship to a grammar school. Lawrence and a group of friends were training to become teachers in 1902 at No. 97 Lyncroft in the same town. They called themselves "the Pagans" and No. 97 "Pagan Headquarters." For a while after this Lawrence taught in the Croydon area of Surrey and later, having made friends with Constance Garnett at nearby Limpsfield and other members of the Bohemian literary fraternity in London and elsewhere, he settled down in Hampstead. By 1918 he was on the move again, this time living in the Derbyshire village of Middleton-by-Wirksworth were he started to write his "never-to-be-finished" *Studies in Classic American Literature.*

Lawrence was dogged by ill health for a great deal of his life and many of the various moves he made were in the hope that a new location might make him feel better. With his wife, Frieda, he lived at Zennor in Cornwall at one time and tried to establish what he called "a tiny literary settlement" with John Middleton Murray and Katherine Mansfield. Because his wife was German and he himself had been dubbed an "antiwar fanatic" they both became victims of the hysteria on this subject that was so much more marked in World War I than World War II. On October 12, 1917, the police searched their cottage and they were told to leave. Lawrence later recalled something of the unpleasantness of this situation in his semiautobiographical novel *Kangaroo.*

He was a writer of many talents, a novelist with a supreme gift for characterization, a competent poet, a serious critic, and an essayist who held one's attention all the time whether one agreed with him or not. *Women in Love* (1921), *England, My England* (1922), and his historical short story, "A Fragment of Stained Glass," based on Beauvale Priory near to his original home, are all splendid in their different ways. Though of working-class origin he moved with ease in company with some of the Garsington community as they were known because it was at Garsington Manor that Lady Ottoline and Philip Morrell held court with such people as Middleton Murray, Lytton Strachey, Clive Bell, and others.

Nevertheless, as has been the case with so many writers, Lawrence became far more famous after his death than ever he was in his lifetime. This was almost entirely the result of his banned book, *Lady Chatterley's Lover,* which in 1960 was the subject of a highly publicized legal action in London that resulted in Lawrence's book being published in the United Kingdom for the first time. This work was originally produced in 1928 and even then the unexpurgated version of the book could only be published on the Continent. Various notable people in the literary world and even a bishop (the late Right Reverend John Robinson, himself author of *The Honest to God Debate*), testified in favor of Lawrence's book in the legal case that resulted in the publication of a work described by Ralph Ginzburg as "not only the finest erotic novel ever written in the English language, but probably the best ever written in any language." This may be a somewhat extravagantly favorable judgment, but nevertheless the descriptive writing of the love scenes, even where he used words that were certainly taboo in most circles in Lawrence's time, is a particularly good example of the author at his best.

The story of the book is a of a woman, Constance, married to Sir Clifford Chatterley who is paralyzed "from the hips down." Denied the normal pleasures of married life, Lady Constance has an affair with her husband's gamekeeper. The affair becomes serious and she asks her husband for a divorce. He refuses and she goes to live with the gamekeeper. In an introduction to his book in its first privately printed Paris edition Lawrence wrote that the real point of his story was that he wanted "men and women to be able to *think* sex, fully, completely, honestly, and cleanly. Even if we can't *act* sexually to our complete satisfaction, let us at least think sexually, complete and clear." Perhaps the following example of his prose shows how he tried to make this possible in *Lady Chatterley's Lover:*

> She . . . ran out with a wild little laugh, holding up her breasts to the heavy rain and spreading her arms and running blurred in the rain with the eurhythmic dance-movements she had learned so long ago in Dresden. It was a strange pallid figure lifting and falling, bending so the rain beat and glistened on the full haunches swaying up again and coming belly-forward through the rain, then stopping again so that only the full loins and buttocks were offered in a kind of homage towards him, repeating a wild obeisance. . . . He jumped out, naked and white, with a little shiver, into the hard, slanting rain. . . . Connie, her hair all wet and sticking to her head, turned her hot face and saw him.

There was an article in *Encounter*, London, February 1962, by John Sparrow, warden of All Souls College, Oxford, entitled "Regina v. Penguin Books, an Undisclosed Element in the Case," in which the theory was put forward that in *Lady Chatterley's Lover* Lawrence advocated a perverted form of inter-course with Connie.

Another interesting book by Lawrence is that published in German in 1971 entitled *Pornographie und Obszonitat und Anders Essays uber Liebe. The Rainbow* (1915) was yet a further example of his skillful handling of amatory themes and his vivid and realistic appreciation of the beauty of the natural world as well as something of the sacramental quality of life itself. A new biography of Lawrence was published in 1991—*D. H. Lawrence: The Early Years,* by John Worthen, Cambridge.

VARGAS LLOSA, MARIO
Born 1936.

This native of Peru has established an international reputation for himself as one of Latin America's most important novelists and his work has been widely translated. He has lived and worked in Paris and is at present living in London. A man of many interests, he has been novelist, playwright, and literary critic, and was president of PEN (Poets, Playwrights, Editors, Essayists, and Novel-ists, International) from 1976–79. During the last decade he has shown his versatility by producing and hosting the Peruvian equivalent of Britain's South Bank Show. Having declined the prime ministership of Peru in 1984, he stood as a candidate in the 1990 presidential elections.

Most of his works have been translated into English. They include *Aunt Julia and the Scriptwriter* (1983); *The War at the End of the World* (1985); *The Real Life of Alejandro Mayta* (1986); *Captain Pantoja and the Special Service* (1987); *The Perpetual Orgy* (1987); *Who Killed Palomino Molero?* (1988); *The Storyteller* (1990); *In Praise of the Stepmother* (1991), and *Cubs and Other Stories* (1991). Llosa is a brilliant writer of modern erotic literature and indeed the *Publishers Weekly* of London hailed *In Praise of the Stepmother* as "an unre-servedly brilliant work." It was the story of Dona Lucrecia, the sensual step-mother; Don Rigoberto, the father; and Alfonso, his son; told in a witty and lively manner as a meditation on the mysterious nature of human happiness and the corrupting power of innocence. The setting for the story is Lima and, needless to say, the boy Alfonso makes love with his stepmother, and what the author cleverly focuses on is the cherubic innocence of the boy and its contrast to the elaborate sexuality of the adults and a father who lives in a world of sexual fantasy.

The Cubs and other Stories was mainly written between 1953 and 1957 when Vargas Llosa was a student in Lima. One of the stories, *The Challenge,* won him a trip to Paris at the expense of *La Revue Française.* "The Cubs," the best of all these stories, was, however, written in Paris and there is a hint in it that the author was homesick at the time. It tells how a tightly knit group of male friends comes under strain and then breaks up as the friends start going out with girls.

Aunt Julia and the Scriptwriter has been made into a film by Columbia Pictures. It is the story of a love affair between a college student and his aunt in Peru, interwoven with a number of bizarre plots and ploys. Once again there is an autobiographical quality about it, as Llosa himself made his first marriage to his aunt who was named Julia. The scriptwriter in the story, Pedro Camacho, sees Mario the student as a kind of protégé and undertakes to help him in the wooing of his aunt with sometimes hilarious, sometimes disastrous results. The whole book is filled with that almost wild mixture of the exotic, the erotic, the horrific, and the amusing that Vargas Llosa portrays so well.

LONGUS
Lived circa third century A.D.

Hardly anything is known about Longus and what there is seems largely speculative except that he was the originator and author of the pastoral romance, *Daphnis and Chloe*, which ever since has been the source of inspiration for countless authors down the ages. How much modern translations or adaptations of this work have been embellished or added to is also somewhat of a poser. A reprint of the 1657 translation of *Daphnis and Chloe* by George Thornley, was published in 1931 by the Rarity Press of New York; this should be consulted by students of this subject. In this work there are not merely the traditional pastoral scenes of the shepherd Daphnis, but adventure, war, and the agonies and rivalries of love. Daphnis, as the lover of Chloe was the model for Allan Ramsay's *Gentle Shepherd* (1725) and the story is also the basis of *Paul et Virginie* by Bernardin de St.-Pierre (1787) as well as George Moore's *The Pastoral Loves of Daphnis and Chloe*, London, 1924. See MOORE, GEORGE, in the A–Z section.

LOUŸS, PIERRE
Born 1870. Died 1925.

This French poet and novelist, born in Paris, after education at the Lycée de Sailly and the Sorbonne took degrees in science and literature. At an early stage of his life he joined the circle of Parnassian poets, which included Gautier, Verlaine, and José-Marie de Heredia, whose daughter, Louise, Louÿs married. His first volume of verse *Astarte* appeared in 1894, followed in the same year by *Chansons de Bilitis*, which was about Sapphic love. This was followed in 1895 by *Aphrodite: Amours Antiques*, the story told in what can only be described as voluptuous prose about a courtesan who requires her lover to commit theft, murder, and sacrilege to win her affections. This book was refused by many publishers before it was accepted and then it was denounced in harsh terms by Senator Béranger. Nevertheless it sold 150,000 copies and a stage spectacle based on it was produced at the Century Theatre in New York. A version of this erotic tale of ancient pagan love was also published in English by Frances Keene.

Most of Louÿs' themes and his exploitation of them were concerned with sensual gratification and even to this day some of his works such as *La Maison sur le Nil*, Paris, 1894, and *Lêda ou la Lounage des Bienheureuses Ténèbres* (1898) are set aside in many libraries with the notice "not suitable for general circulation." *La Maison sur le Nil* tells of the man entertaining a male visitor and saying to him after their meal together: "It is time for bed. I know the duties of hospitality. Here are my two daughters. The younger hasn't had a man before, but she is of age to be approached. Go and take your pleasure with them."

Louÿs exploits very cleverly the situation of the younger sister who is always kept in the background by the older one. She, jealous of her sister, tells the visitor: *"Après toi je me serais prêtée a un autre, et a un autre, et ainsi jusqu'à mon mariage. Sais-tu que ma soeur a déja connu plus d'étrangers que je ne dirais en ouvrant sept fois mes deux mains? Et moi aussi, j'aurais fais cela . . . O je sens si bien que toute ma vie j'appartiendrai au même homme, au premier qui m'aura saisie. Et c'est toi celui-là'! Emmène-moi, garde-moi toujours! Je veux être ta femme et te suivre."*

Lêda was, of course, Louÿs' version of the story of Greek mythology concerning the wife of Tyndarus to whom the god Jupiter came in the guise of an amorous swan when she was bathing. Louÿs, who sported rather a splendid beard, was sometimes compared to a Vandyke portrait. He had the habit of sleeping all day and working all night and is said to have smoked more than eighty cigarettes a day. *Psyche*, a romance, was published three years after his death, as was *Satyrs and Women*. Indeed, it was in the 1930s and afterwards that his work came to be published in English as well as French, James Cleugh being one of his chief translators. A dramatized recording of one of his most explicit works was made in the 1970s: this was *Manuel de Civilité pour les Petites Filles a L'Usage des Maisons D'Education*. This was a long-playing record and is today a rare piece of Louÿs ephemera. Well worth reading is *A Friendship of the Nineties: Letters between John Gray and Pierre Louÿs*, produced in a limited edition by the Tragara Press in 1984.

MAP, WALTER
Born circa 1140. Died circa 1209.

Sometimes incorrectly called Mapes, Walter Map was of Welsh descent and probably a native of Hereford. He was appointed a clerk at the court of King Henry II of England and in 1179 was present at the Lateran Council in Rome.

He was an archdeacon at Oxford and eventually rose from canon to the chancellorship of Lincoln Cathedral. An author of Latin verse of a satirical character, he also delved into legendary folklore, at the same time collecting court gossip that he put into some of his prose. His outstanding work was *De Nugis Curialium* (Courtiers' triflings). This included a somewhat salacious story concerning a merchant named Olla. This work was edited for the Camden Society in 1850, and translated by the author, M. R. James.

MARGUERITE D'ANGOULÊME, QUEEN OF NAVARRE
Born 1492. Died 1549.

The daughter of Charles of Orleans, Marguerite was born in Angoulême and was first of all married to the duke of Alençon in 1509. As a very young woman she was extremely studious and applied herself to the sciences as well as the arts, of which she was a lifelong patroness. On the death of the duke she married again, this time Henri d'Albert, king of Navarre (1525). At court and in Navarre generally she used her influence in favor of tolerance of a variety of opinions. Generally speaking, she was a liberal with a strong sense of humor long before that term crept into politics. Toward the end of her life she devoted a great deal of time to writing and it was as a result of this that she produced the work for which she became famous, *Heptaméron des Nouvelles*, also known as *Histoire des Amantes Fortunes*.

This book was modeled on the *Decameron* of Boccaccio and was quite an extraordinary mixture of religious mysticism and lively eroticism that included some daringly novel expressions on questions of morals. The tales in the *Heptaméron*, seventy-two altogether, covered all manner of amatory adventures, as the titles of the stories suggest. These ranged from "The Wicked Monk, Brought to Shame by His Lusts," and "The Young Man Who Assailed the Honour of a Princess," to "The Lustful King of Naples," and "The Man Who Married His Own Sister." The whole book is remarkable in that it is written by a woman, and a queen no less, but with the ribald sense of humor and a delight in sheer bawdiness that is masculine in tone. For a medieval queen Marguerite had an astonishing knowledge of the naughtier ways and manners of the world she lived in. In the first full French edition of the *Heptaméron* in 1559 there is a very short but typical story of a Franciscan priest preaching a sermon in which he mentions how scandalized the ladies of the congregation have been by the news that a friar had made the daughter of his hostess pregnant. "But wouldn't you have been even more scandalized if the daughter had gotten the friar with child?" Some sermon!

One cannot help wondering whether Queen Marguerite did not owe something to the Seigneur and Abbé Pierre de Bourdeille Brantôme (1540–1614) who was at one time attached to her court. Brantôme had traveled widely and served in Africa in the Spanish army and had made a collection of anecdotes of amorous adventures. It is quite possible that he passed on to her some of his stories that mainly concerned the erotic customs of ladies of sixteenth-century France. Certainly he wrote stories himself and they nearly all suggested that there was a remarkable laxity of morals among the married ladies at court at that time.

MARIVAUX, PIERRE CARLET DE CHAMBLAIN DE
Born 1688. Died 1763.

A native of Paris, Marivaux produced for his first book, surprisingly enough, a parody of the *Iliad,* but it was as a writer of light comedy that he showed his real talent. His romance, *La Vie de Marianne,* was highly regarded, as also was his *L'Amour et la Verité* (1720). His style was somewhat precious and fastidious—rather that of the dilettante—and Voltaire said of him: "Marivaux knows all the bypaths of the human heart, but not the highway." His *Oeuvres Complètes* were published in ten volumes between 1827–30.

One of his most elegant comedies was *La Dispute,* which has a typically sophisticated Marivaux theme. It poses the question, Which of the two sexes is the first to be unfaithful? To try to find the answer a somewhat bizarre experiment is conducted. Four babies, two female and two male, are reared in isolation by two servants. When they finally reach maturity they are introduced to each other and their behavior and actions are carefully monitored. The eighteenth-century original play is an elegant look at eroticism in a new way altogether. Unfortunately, all this was changed in 1991 when the play was produced in English in London. The answer to the question of the play in the original version is that both man and woman are equally unfaithful; in the English production the women were presented as far more calculating characters. A critic wrote of the London version:

> In the original play there is a lot of elegant talk but a minimum of physical passion. Here, however, the actors set about each other like alley cats, sniffing, biting, stroking, splashing around in a pond, and rolling all over the stage together in transports of ecstasy. . . . The riotous sexuality becomes increasingly disturbing. . . . By the end the four main characters are driven almost mad by the inconstancy of the human heart, neurotically changing partners in the pursuit of an illusory happiness, unable to break free of their prison and those who manipulated them."

MARLOWE, CHRISTOPHER
Born 1564. Died 1593.

A native of Canterbury, England, and educated at Corpus Christi College, Cambridge, Marlowe went overseas quite early in his life and, while it has been suggested that he may have served as a soldier in the Netherlands for a time, the evidence is that this could have been little more than a cover for his real work. His career as a spy began at Cambridge where he was recruited by Sir Francis Walsingham, Queen Elizabeth's intelligence chief. In 1587, while still a secret agent and posing as a Catholic sympathizer, he started work as a dramatist and he wrote *Tamburlaine*, the first great blank-verse tragedy. This was followed by *The Tragical History of Doctor Faustus* (c. 1592) and *The Jew of Malta* (1588). In 1592 the controversial historical tragedy of *Edward II* was produced: for many years this play was not performed because of its homosexual undertones. In 1969 the play was presented in Britain including the scene in which the king hugged and kissed his homosexual lover. Marlowe's only other surviving play, *The Tragedie of Dido, Queen of Carthage*, was finished off by Thomas Nash. His poems include "Amores" in *Epigrams and Elegies*, "Hero and Leander," and "The Passionate Shepherd to His Love" in *The Passionate Pilgrim* (1599). This pleasantly erotic poem begins with the oft-quoted verse:

> Come live with me and be my Love,
> And we will all the pleasures prove
> That hills and valleys, dales and fields,
> Or woods or steepy mountain yields.

Marlowe was much criticized in his lifetime, partly because of what was supposed to have been his immoral life-style, but mainly because he was a virulent atheist, despite his posing as a Catholic sympathizer. Certainly he made enemies, as double agents inevitably do, and in 1593 he was summoned before the privy council to answer a charge of heresy. But before his case could be heard Marlowe was dead, slain in a brawl at a tavern in Deptford, London. His death still remains a mystery. His killer was given a free pardon for some mysterious reason and it was never explained what Robert Poley, a known spy for the English Secret Service, was doing in an upstairs room at the tavern where Marlowe was stabbed to death.

MAROT, CLÉMENT
Born 1496. Died 1544.

Le style Marotique, which takes its name from this French poet, has had a considerable influence on the French literary language down the ages. Born at Cahors, Marot became a page to Marguerite d'Alençon, afterwards queen of Navarre. He participated in a French expedition into Italy and was wounded and taken prisoner at the Battle of Pavia. He returned to France when he was released and made a number of enemies because of the anti-Catholic views he expressed. As a result he was frequently imprisoned. He became very popular with the Huguenots, however, and his poems won him many friends at the French court. His complete works were published in 1538 (*Oeuvres Complètes*) and a new edition of them was printed in 1881.

MARTIAL [MARCUS VALERIUS MARTIALIS]
Born A.D. 40. Died A.D. 103.

A master of the epigram—some filled with uplifting homilies, others obscene and lascivious—Martial was born at Bilbilis in Spain and went to Rome about A.D. 63. He worked his epigrams into short poems in a variety of meters and covered a wide range of subjects. He flattered the Emperor Domitian and largely held his own as a poet by doing so. While some of his poems were genuinely erotic, far too many of them were not merely pornographic but disgusting. One book of his epigrams is full of descriptions of almost every form of sexual perversion. Consequently, there have not been many modern translations of his work. There was a complete, but not very good English translation by Elphinston in 1782.

MAUPASSANT (Henri-René-Albert), GUY DE
Born 1850. Died 1893.

Almost certainly one of the best short-story writers of all time, Guy de Maupassant was born at the castle of Miromesnil in Seine-Inférieure. Early in life he came under the influence of Flaubert and his style to some extent was based on what he learned from that masterly writer. From his earliest days Maupassant was desperately anxious to study and learn from other writers and he was one of a number of young men who wrote stories to be read in company at Émile Zola's home at Médan. Some of these stories were later published as *Soirées de Médan* (1880). Of these perhaps the best known today is "Boule de Suif."

Maupassant's novels were not as outstanding as his short stories, possibly because his chief strength as a writer was in building a story very subtly out of a single, small but very definite situation or event. A splendid technique in writing, rather than inspiration, was the key to Maupassant's work. His sense of the erotic was acute and realistic, so much so that one senses that Maupassant wrote a great deal from personal experience. Ten years after his death his mistress, using the name "Madame X," wrote an article in *La Grande Revue* (cited by Frank Harris in volume 2 of *My Life*) in which she told how Maupassant wrote to her saying, "How I love you! How I wished to throw myself on my knees before you, there in the dust of the sidewalk, and kiss your lovely hands and your little feet, the hem of your dress—kiss them all with hot tears."

Madame X said that Maupassant once confessed to her that he was "a romance writer even in his embracings," and she added: "I would rather say that he remained a lover even in his romances . . . and what a wonderful lover he was."

Of his erotic stories the one that always comes to mind for a variety of reasons is "La Maison Tellier" (1882). The story opens in a bordello in Normandy and cleverly tells how consternation surfaces when the prostitutes one day all go to a country church for Holy Communion. There they become deeply affected by the atmosphere of incense and candles and church music and begin to feel a sense of living lives of sin. They return to the bordello at midnight where the customers are tense and angry, awaiting their return. In the end the habits of a lifetime restore all to normality: drinks are poured out, customers are cheered up, and life goes on as usual.

In 1892 Maupassant suddenly developed a strange kind of madness. He made an attempt on his life, failed, but was sent to an asylum at Auteuil where he died a year later. His other works include *Mademoiselle Fifi* (1882), *Contes de la Bécasse* (1883), *Clair de la Lune* (1883), *Les Soeurs Rondoli* (1884), *Yvette* (1885), *Contes de Jour at de la Nuit* (1885), and *Le Rosier de Madame Husson* (1888). All his works have been translated into English.

MECHAIN, GWERFUL
Lived circa 1450–1500.

Gwerful's cognomen indicates that she was a native of the region of Mechain in Montgomeryshire in Wales. She is known to have been the daughter of Hywel Fychan ap Hywel of Llanfechain. Some forty poems are ascribed to her in existing manuscripts, all of them in Welsh. One poem is addressed to the female pudenda. Two of her verse titles are "Sexual Intercourse" and "The Cleric and the Virgin." See *Medieval Welsh Erotic Poetry*, Dafydd Johnston, Cardiff, 1991.

MEDICI, DE', LORENZO
Born 1449. Died 1492.

Son of the founder of the Platonic Academy in Florence, Lorenzo de' Medici was one of the most distinguished scholars of his time as well as a poet who wrote in Latin and in the vernacular. Known as "Lorenzo the Magnificent," he ruled Florence for twenty-three years with great skill and imagination. His policy, which proved effective, was to ally Florence with Milan against Venice. He was said to have had one of the finest collections of books and manuscripts in the whole of Europe.

Many of his poems were erotic and some of these have been translated into English, notably by J. A. Symonds, *Italian Renaissance* (1875–86) and Oliphant Smeaton's *Medici and the Italian Renaissance* (1901). There was a jubilant, elated touch about Medici's verse, as the following example shows:

Youths and maids, enjoy today;
Nought ye know about tomorrow.
These blithe satyrs, wanton-eyed,
Of the nymphs are paramours:
Through the caves and forests wide
They have snared them mid the flowers;
Warmed with Bacchus in his bowers,
Now they dance and leap away.

And Lorenzo goes on to say:

Let sweet love your bosoms fire
In the future come what may!
Youths and maids, enjoy today!
Nought we know about tomorrow.
Fair is youth and void of sorrow;
But it hourly flies away.

MILLER, HENRY
Born 1891. Died 1980.

A strange query has been raised concerning Henry Miller since his death: some of his critics ask whether he was basically religious or just "a sex-obsessed bum." It is a fair question, but to try to answer it one must remember that for the greater part of his life he lived in an atmosphere in which (at least outside Paris) there was a relentless taboo on all forthright talk on the subject of sex, especially when such talk was put into print. *The Tropic of Cancer,* his best-known work (1934), was not published in the USA or Britain until the 1960s. Born in New York, with madness in the family, a hopeless mother, a homosexual father, and a backward sister, Miller had an unsatisfactory start to life. At the age of thirty-nine he went to Paris where his life as a writer really began to take off with *Whoroscope* (1930), *Tropic of Capricorn* (1939), *Black Spring,* and *The Rosy Crucifixion,* a triology including *Sexus* (1949), *Plexus* (1953) and *Nexus* (1960). After nine years in Paris he returned to America.

His novels have been condemned by some, banned in many countries and yet always regarded seriously by some discerning critics. Altogether he wrote some thirty volumes under various titles, most of them indirectly or directly attacking organized society, exposing what he regarded as the irrational nature of life itself and always seemingly obsessed with sex. Yet one of his critics, Professor John Weightman of London University, says of him: "Miller's basic stance was religious, however foul his language and however vapid the mystic nonsense he sometimes wrote. He had a core of existential genuineness, which makes itself felt every now and again." While some of his writing frequently seems more pornographic than erotic, there are flashes of what one might call poetic-erotic comic meditations. In *The Tropic of Cancer*, for example, he writes:

> There was something about her eloquence at that moment and the way she thrust that rosebush under my nose which remains unforgettable; she spoke of it as if it were some extraneous object which she had acquired at great cost, an object whose value had increased with time and which now she prized above everything in the world. Her words imbued it with a peculiar fragrance; it was no longer just her private organ, but a treasure, a magic, potent treasure, a God-given thing—and none the less so because she traded it day in and day out for a few pieces of silver.

Miller was married twice and his second wife, June, became the character "Mona" in his books. Yet another woman in his life was Anaïs Nin, an eccentric who helped him in his early days in Paris. It is interesting to note the semiautobiographical comment that Miller made in *Tropic of Cancer* about the women in his life: "Going back in a flash over the women I've known. It's like a chain which I've forged out of my own misery. Each one bound to the other." There is an excellent biography of Miller published in 1991: *The Happiest Man Alive: A Biography of Henry Miller*, by Mary V. Dearborn, New York.

Sometimes the sheer crudity of Miller's prose spoils the intended erotic effect. Nonetheless in *Opus Pistorum*, New York, 1983, his most explicit novel, one is carried away to some extent by his tales of Marcelle and Tania, Alexandra and Anna in his quest for the perfect woman and the perfect experience.

MOORE, GEORGE
Born 1852. Died 1933.

Born at Carra Lough in Ireland, where he was educated early on, George Moore described himself in those early days as "a boy no schoolmaster wants. . . . I was expelled when I was sixteen for idleness and general worthlessness." He returned to a country home, but when his father was elected a member of the British Parliament he moved to London. After a spell at Kensington Museum, studying art, Moore fulfilled his greatest wish—to live in Paris. Here he came under the influence of Flaubert, Maupassant, and Zola and started to write seriously as a result. His novels nearly all showed the French influence for they were strongly realistic: *A Mummer's Wife* (1884),

A Drama in Muslin (1886), Esther Waters (1894), Evelyn Innes (1898), The Untilled Field (1903), The Lake (1905).

Something of the happiness of his stay in Paris became apparent when in 1886 he published in London his Confessions of a Young Man. This book was annotated and edited by Moore in later editions in 1904 and 1916. Walter Pater praised this work for its "Aristophanic joy" and "unfailing liveliness." From 1901–11 Moore lived in Dublin and from then onwards he made his home in Ebury Street, London, where in 1924 he produced Conversations in Ebury Street. He made a habit of searching for inspiration in the distant past for many of his books. "I go to the Middle Ages for Héloise and Abélard," he once said. "I go to the beginning of our era for The Brook Kerith (1916). This passion for the distant past showed itself most in Moore's one great erotic theme, that of The Pastoral Loves of Daphnis and Chloe, London, 1924. In his introduction to this book, based partly on translation from the Greek and partly on Moore's vivid imagination, Moore writes: "It recounts the fortunes of two foundlings, a boy and a girl, one of whom was suckled by a ewe and the other by a she-goat, and how these twain strove to assuage their love with kisses."

Moore also mentions the uncertainty of the actual author of the original story of Daphnis and Chloe, Longus (see LONGUS in A–Z section). He comments that "the name of the reputed author, Longus, is not mentioned by Photius or Suidas, and the name Longus is Latin and not Greek." Yet he admitted that the name Longus appears on all original manuscripts. In the most elegant and musical prose Moore tells the love story that has attracted so many people down the ages:

> For he [Daphnis], being now lusty and well filled out, having spent the whole winter within doors doing nothing, thrilled after the kiss and was big, as the phrase runs, for embraces, more curious in every one, more hardy than he ever was before, pressing Chloe to grant him all he asked for and to lie with him in flesh longer than was their custom. For, said he, that is the one thing of Philetas's counsels that remains untried, the one and only medicine that soothes the pain of love. Chloe asked what else they could do but kiss and lie together as they were in their clothes, and what he thought he might do if they were to lie together naked. That which the rams do to the ewes and the bucks to the she-goats. Thou hast seen that after the jump the ewe runs no longer from the ram; they graze together, assuaged and content, so there is of a certainty a sweetness unknown to us, a sweetness that surpasses the bitterness of love. But hast not seen, said she, that the rams and the ewes and the bucks and the she-goats whilst tasting of the sweetness do not

lie together, but taste whilst standing up, the rams leaping on the ewes, the ewes receiving them on their backs? Yet thou wouldst have me lie on the ground with thee, and naked. Are our beasties not clothed in wool and hair more closely than I am in these garments? He believed her and lay beside her, and for a long time he lay doing nothing, for he was without knowledge how to do that which he ardently desired to do. He lifted her up and endeavored to imitate the goats, but failing from behind as he had done in front, he sat down beside her and began to weep, for it was sad to find that he knew less about the ways of love than a tup.

Eventually, of course, it is left to another and more knowledgeable female to show Daphnis how to make love.

And Lycoenium, seeing him even more simple and natural than she had imagined, began to instruct him and in this manner. She ordered him to sit close to her and to kiss her as he and Chloe were accustomed to kiss each other, and whilst kissing her to embrace her and to lie on the ground beside her. And as he was sitting by her, kissing her and lying beside her, she, finding him ready, raised him up, slipped beneath him, and put him in the way that he had long sought; and then nature coming to his aid, the natural was accomplished. No more was done; so finished the amorous lesson.

The book is an example of achieving eroticism in writing without straining for effect, and in this sense it is a model of its kind. It ends on this delightful note: "Meanwhile Daphnis and Chloe lay naked in bed, where they exchanged kisses and embraces without closing an eye all the night, wakeful as the nightjars, Daphnis practicing with Chloe all that Lycoenium had taught him, and Chloe coming to understand that all they had done hitherto in the woods was but the play of children."

MORAVIA, ALBERTO [FALBERTO PINCHERLE]
Born 1907.

"Unsophisticated eroticism" is how one critic has described the writings of Moravia, a man of many talents who at the age of seventy-seven became a member of the European Parliament. This Italian journalist and novelist started his writing life with some bitter attacks on fascism and, when war came, lent strong support to the Resistance movement in the 1939–45 period. This certainly enhanced his standing in Italy after the war and he received various decorations for his service. He married Elsa Morante, a writer like himself. His first work was *Gli Indifferenti* (The time of indifference, 1929), followed by *Agostino* (1944), the story of a young boy who becomes aware of the sexual facts of life while on holiday. *La Romana* (The woman of Rome) in 1947 was based to some extent on his wartime experience and again sexual relationships played a key part in the narrative. This was about a young girl, Adriana, who, having failed to make a career for herself, becomes a prostitute. *La Ciociara* (Two women, 1957) was again based on wartime experiences. This novel tells of a shopkeeper who when Rome is threatened with war moves with her daughter to what she hopes is a safer area. The daughter is raped by Occupation troops and mother and daughter both turn to theft and prostitution. Some of Moravia's work has been translated into English. Especially interesting of his later work are *Bitter Honeymoon and Other Stories*, *La Noia* (Empty canvas, 1960) and *L'attenzione* (The lie, 1965). He has also written for the theater.

MURASKI, SHIKIBU
Born circa 987. Died circa 1026.

Often referred to as "Lady Murasaki," this Japanese lady of the Imperial Court was one of the world's earliest novelists in the modern sense of the word. Her *Genji Monogatari* (The tale of Genji) has been superbly translated into English by Edward Seidensticker and was published in 1976. There were earlier translations, notably one by Arthur Waley in 1925–33. Anthony Thwaite, a distinguished British academic who has lived and taught in Japan, refers to *The Tale of Genji* as "this huge prose fiction . . . an amazing experience. Some people compare it with Proust's masterpiece. Reading it most recently, I found myself sometimes muttering Jane Austen and sometimes Iris Murdoch." Perhaps it should be stressed that this work is not just another piece of oriental eroticism, but an admirable background to other such works of that period, as well as being a witty and lively work. Murasaki served in the court of Akiko, as is mentioned in her diaries of the period 980–1011.

MUSSET, ALFRED DE
Born 1810. Died 1857.

"The wayward, idle apprentice of the Romantic movement," is the way St. John Lucas described de Musset, but the early careless irresponsibility of this poet eventually grew into what was a new classical spirit. Born in Paris, he began to write poetry at the age of seventeen, as a result of which Victor Hugo invited him to join his *Cénacle* (coterie). When he was only twenty he produced *Contes d'Espagne et d'Italie*, Paris, 1830, which greatly impressed literary circles there. The same year he wrote a play, *La Nuit Vénitienne*, but this was not so successful. Such poetic works as *Namouna*, *La Coupe et les Lèvres* and *A Quoi rèvent les Jeunes Filles* quickly made him join the ranks of the great lyrical poets of France, and his four *Nuits* made him one of the immortals. De Musset had a remarkable talent for plumbing the depths of amatory passion with ease and grace, while at the same time creating erotic effects in his verse. A translation of one such work, *Gamiani; or, Two Nights of Excess*, was published in unexpurgated form in London and New York in 1968, with an introduction by Paul J. Gillette.

The great tragedy of de Musset's life was his love affair with Armadine Dudevant, or "George Sand" as she was known. She had separated from her husband and started writing when she met de Musset in Paris. Together they traveled to Italy in 1834, but they soon separated. De Musset returned to Paris, an embittered and unhappy man. From that moment onwards his health deteriorated and it became worse as alcohol took its toll on him. Armandine Dudevant's correspondence with de Musset was published in 1897, some years after her death. She also told the story of her affair with de Musset in her work *Elle et Lui.* De Musset's own autobiographical *Confession d'un Enfant du Siècle* (1835) was a sad expression of cynicism and disbelief in the higher moral values of life. For a while he became a librarian while writing such popular comedies as *Il ne faut Jurer de rien* (1836), which was performed on the Parisian stage for many years. Something of the lyrical spirit of de Musset at his best can be seen in his poem, "A la Malibran," written as a tribute to Maria Felicia Garcia Malibran, the singer who died so young in 1836. The last verse of this is:

> *Meurs donc! ta mort est douce et ta tache est remplie.*
> *Ce que l'homme ici-bas appelle la génie,*
> *C'est le besoin d'aimer; hors de là tout est vain.*
> *Et, puisque tôt ou tard l'amour humain s'oublie,*
> *Ll est d'une grande âme et d'un heureux destin*
> *D'expirer comme toi pour un amour divin!*

NABOKOV, VLADIMIR
Born 1889. Died 1977.

This Russian-born novelist and poet was educated in England and lived in Europe until 1940 when he moved to live permanently in the United States. Originally he wrote in Russian, using the pen name of Vladimir Sirin, but after 1940 his work was entirely in English. Much of his early life was spent in France and Germany. Always intensely anxious to ensure that his own prose was maintained at the high standards he set for himself, Nabokov was sometimes almost virulently critical of other distinguished writers. There seems to be no doubt that he thought his own writing was very good indeed and it was the care he took with it that made him disparage others: T. S. Eliot he condemned as "a big fake" with a "vulgar mind." His life, judging from his letters, seems to have been a happy one, shared intensely with his wife Vera, and his passion for hunting butterflies in her company.

Unquestionably the one book that made him world famous was *Lolita*, which he actually started in Paris late in 1939, prompted, oddly enough (or so he said) by "a newspaper story about an ape in the Jardin des Plantes." He started to write the work in Russian. Then, when he had settled in America, he decided not only to write the book in English, but to turn his central character (Humbert Humbert) from a Central European into an American and the nymphet Lolita, whom Humbert seduced, from French to American. *Lolita* was eventually finished in 1954 and was turned down by four shocked American publishers before it was eventually published in 1958 in New York. In an appendix to the book Nabokov wrote: "There are gentle souls who would pronounce *Lolita* meaningless because it does not teach them anything. I am neither a reader nor a writer of didactic fiction. . . . *Lolita* has no moral in tow. For me a work of fiction exists only insofar as it affords me what I shall bluntly call aesthetic bliss."

During the writing of this book the backgrounds of the characters were changed more than once. Instead of making Humbert an American, Nabokov first made him "a foreigner and an anarchist" living in America. The setting of the story was still the United States. Sordid though the theme sounds— that of a man who marries a woman in order to have the opportunity of seducing her juvenile daughter—the elegant writing, the subtle touches of humor, and the sheer skill with words raise the work to a classic of its kind. It was such a remarkable success when first published by Olympia Press in Paris that its publication in America was practically guaranteed. The reader's attention is superbly captured in the very first paragraph:

> Lolita, light of my life, fire of my loins. My sin, my soul. Lo-lee-ta: the tip of the tongue taking a trip of three steps down the palate to tap, at three, on the teeth. Lo. Lee. Ta. She was Lo, plain Lo, in the morning, standing four feet ten in one sock. She was Lola in slacks. She was Dolly at school. She was Dolores on the dotted line. But in my arms she was always Lolita.

Of course Nabokov had many harsh critics after his work was published. "Why did he have to write it?" asked one. "Why should I read about maniacs?" said another. It seems certain that Nabokov anticipated a great deal of the criticism when he was writing the book. It was probably because of this that he gave *Lolita* that remarkable foreword by the fictitious "John Ray, Jr., Ph.D." In the appendix to the book in the New York edition the author stated, "After doing my impersonation of suave John Ray, the character in *Lolita* who pens the Foreword, any comments coming straight from me may strike one—may strike me, in fact—as an impersonation of Vladimir Nabokov talking about his own book." The fictitious foreword does in fact give the work a buildup: "As a case history," says fictitious Dr. Ray, *"Lolita* will become no doubt, a classic in psychiatric circles."

Other works of Nabokov that can be recommended are *Invitation to a Beheading* (1959); *Laughter in the Dark* (1938); and *Nabokov's Dozen* (a collection of short stories), New York, 1958. Posthumously published in London in 1991 were Nabokov's *Selected Letters: 1940–1977.* The material herein gives a fascinating insight into Nabokov's character and personality. The letters contain a great deal about butterflies (his great hobby), exchanges of views with fellow writers and family and much about his love of the Rocky Mountains. The progress of his work, *Lolita,* from its conception right up to publication is carefully charted, and Kenneth Tynan (see TYNAN, KENNETH, A–Z section) is told that Nabokov had no interest in pornography and would certainly not contribute to an anthology of erotica "written for the express purpose of arousing the author's own sexual impulses," which Tynan was hoping to publish. These letters are a sheer delight to read and should be compulsory reading for anyone wishing to study Nabokov and his works.

NEFZAWI, SHAYKH SIDI MOHAMMED EL
Born circa 1370. Died circa 1440.

Very little is known about the life of this man other than his work, *Al-Raud Al-Atir,* or, by its modern title, *The Perfumed Garden.* Some sources suggest this work did not appear until the sixteenth century, but the view taken by the late Professor C. F. Seybold of Tubingen University in Germany is that after considerable research he believed the book was written sometime between 1394 and 1433. It was not brought to the attention of Western scholars, however, until the late 1840s when a French army officer, serving in Algeria, came across a manuscript copy of an Arabic work entitled *Al Raud al atir wa nuzhat al Khatir.* He was so fascinated by what he read that he decided to translate it into French. The work appeared in Algiers in 1876, entitled *Le Jardin Parfumé,* and he gave the author as "Sidi Mohammed el-Nafzaoui" and his own name simply as "Monsieur le Baron R——, Capitaine d'Etat major." This edition of Nefzawi's work contained some forty-three erotic illustrations and some blank pages. The identity of the translator has never been established for certain.

The Perfumed Garden is in many ways similar to the Hindu work, the *Kama Sutra,* in that it sets out to describe in detail various techniques for the better enjoyment of sexual intercourse, and in addition also makes suggestions regarding the use of aphrodisiacs and the choosing of partners according to temperament (see chapter 2). Not unnaturally Nefzawi's work is addressed to Mohammedans and Islamic marriage customs. In 1886 an English edition of

The Perfumed Garden was published under the auspices of the Kama Shastra Society for its subscribers only, this time with a translation by Sir Richard Burton. The society took its name from *Kama*, which in Sanskrit means love or pleasure, and *Shastra* (doctrines). Originally there were only two members of the society, Burton and a friend of his, Forster Fitzgerald Arbuthnot.

In setting out what Nefzawi calls "the manners" of performing the act of coitus he sometimes uses his own terms—e.g., *el asemeud* (the stopperage), *el modefeda* (frog fashion), *el mokefa* (with the toes cramped), *el mokeurmeutt* (with legs in the air), *el setouri* (he-goat fashion), *el loulabi* (the screw of Archimedes) and *el kelouci* (the somersault). Regarding the translation of *el loulabi* it should perhaps be mentioned that the Archimedes Screw was a spiral screw for raising well water, developed by Archimedes. Bearing this in mind readers will have to use their own imagination to understand the implications! Nefzawi cites altogether some twenty-seven manners of which the most forceful is *dok el outed* (driving the peg home) and the most relaxed is *el khouariki* (the one who stops in the house).

Some of Nefzawi's work is expressed in the form of stories such as "The History of Djoaidi and Fadehat el Djemil," and "The Story of the Man Who Was an Expert in Stratagems and Was Duped by a Woman." There are appendices on such subjects as "medicines which provoke abortion," "the causes of impotence in men," and "prescriptions for increasing the dimensions of small members and for making them splendid." An excellent English edition of *The Perfumed Garden* was also published in London in 1963, entitled *The Perfumed Garden of the Shaykh Nefzawi*. It was as translated by Sir Richard Burton, but edited with an introduction and additional notes by Alan Hull Walton. This is an invaluable book if only for the detailed introduction and notes, and it is worth noting this comment of Walton's: "The work is certainly encumbered with a quantity of matter which cannot but appear ridiculous in the eyes of the civilized modern reader, but we should not have been justified in weeding it out. . . . Those oddities are moreover instructive as they make us acquainted with the manner and character of the Arab under a peculiar aspect . . . also with the Arab of our own day."

OAKLEY, ANN
Born 1944.

Ann Oakley started life as a sociologist and became a director of the Research Unit on this very subject. This resulted in a few books connected with this theme—*Sex, Gender, and Society*, London, 1972, *Housewife* (1974), *Women Confined* (1980), and *Subject Women* (1981). In 1991 she was made professor of sociology and social policy at London University. Yet this serious-minded academic produced in 1988 a novel entitled *The Men's Room*, which was not only a great success, but, when made into a film by the BBC in London in 1991 attracted some five million viewers each week while it lasted.

The daughter of a professor of sociology, Ann Oakley decided to make this her own subject when she finished reading politics, philosophy, and economics at Oxford University. When her first novel was published reviewers largely ignored her sociological approach to her theme but concentrated on the sexual antics. This, she has since declared, convinced her that the British were "an oddly repressed bunch" on sexual matters, especially as reviewers outside of Britain dealt mainly with her sociological theme, most notably male-dominated society. The chief male in *The Men's Room* is one Mark Carleton who always has sex on his terms, thereby making a series of women unhappy by his inability to be faithful. Says Ann Oakley: "Yet he goes on making the same mistake. Women are never going to be willing to share. He should go away on his own and work out why he is like that. Then he might be able to have a more adult relationship."

In an interview with Cassandra Jardine in the *Daily Telegraph* of London (October 23, 1991) Ann Oakley made clear her own views on her sociological approach to sexual problems. "People should concentrate on the relationship they are in and not look for something better. No one person will ever provide everything. The perfect partner doesn't exist and, except for sex, you can never make up for the other person's deficiencies." As for infidelity, she believes in confession: "Secrets do harm. I know other people don't agree with me and say I am too straightforward. But if you are lying, you don't any longer know what the truth is yourself."

Certainly *The Men's Room* is an odd story of a weak-willed, insecure, and emotionally immature Professor Mark Carleton and his lover, Charity. Because of his inability to accept responsibility for his actions Mark ends up by not only making a mess of his own life but of everyone with whom he comes in close contact. Ann Oakley ended her book with the couple reunited in an Amsterdam hotel bedroom on a summer night in the year 2000. While Mark is ecstatic, Charity realizes that she could well do without this situation, but feels that she can never altogether eradicate Mark from her inner self. In the televised film one sees the lovers keeping a rendezvous on a bridge in Amsterdam in the year 2000, but it is not made clear whether this is one of Charity's dreams, or actuality.

Clive Hirschorn, television critic of the London *Sunday Express*, posed the question: "Was it prurience that kept us glued to the box, or the shock of recognition?" referring to the fact that some of the sexual positions portrayed in it were "new, even to the *Kama Sutra.*" This critic may well have had a real point and not have been exaggerating. Dr. Malcolm Read, an orthopedic physician from the London Bridge Clinic, warned those tempted to emulate these positions: "If it hurts, stop it." Dr. Elizabeth Stanley, founding member of the British Association for Sex and Marital Therapy, wondered whether the explicit sex on screen as shown in this film was good for viewers' mental health. "Some couples would have been encouraged to talk about their own relationship. It can lead to shedding inhibition. But the others, seeing sex on screen can reinforce existing doubts. They may think they have to behave like the lovers on television."

Very soon Ann Oakley's second novel, *Matilda's Mistake*, will be televised and this time Ann Oakley is anxious to keep a tighter control of the adaptation.

OVID [PUBLIUS OVIDIUS NASO]
Born 43 B.C. Died A.D. 17.

One of the outstanding Roman poets of his day as well as an active political administrator, Ovid was born at Sulmo in the Appennines. He was appointed as one of the *centumviri* (judges who adjudicated on civil and criminal law cases) and later one of the *decemviri* (a body of ten presidents). He knew both Horace and Virgil and for a time enjoyed the confidence of Emperor Augustus Caesar (originally Octavian). This confidence was abruptly ended when in A.D. 9 he was suddenly banished to Tomi on the Black Sea, close to the mouth of the Danube. The reason why has never been altogether satisfactorily explained, but it is almost certainly on account of a poem of his that angered the emperor. His work, the *Ars Amatoria*, had something to do with this, and it is interesting that Julia, the emperor's daughter, was banished at the same time. Ovid remained at Tomi until his death.

He was by far the most productive of all Roman poets. His works extended to thirty-three thousand hexameter or elegiac lines. These included, apart from the *Ars Amatoria* (a book of guidance on love affairs) and *Amores* (brief erotic poems), *Heroides*, a series of letters purporting to be sent from and to famous pairs of lovers in the Greek tradition and history; *Metamorphoses*, recounting mythological tales; *Tristia* and *Epistulae ex Ponto*, which tells of his unhappy life in exile and includes appeals to the emperor for his freedom to return to Rome. His works greatly influenced writers of the Middle Ages, especially his concept of love on a romantic plane.

See *Ovid*, by J. Church, London, 1876, and *Thesaurus Eroticus Linguae Latinae*, Stuttgart, 1883. Also *Corpus Poetarum Latinorum*, Postgate, London, 1894.

PAINTER, WILLIAM
Born circa 1525. Died circa 1595.

This English author was appointed headmaster of Sevenoaks School in Kent in 1560 when he would have been just out of his teens, and a year later he was made clerk of the ordinance in the Tower of London, a post he held until his death. He specialized in translating works from Greek, Latin, Italian, and French originals, and as a result of this created his own erotic book, *The Palace of Pleasure* published in 1566, 1567, and 1575. This was reprinted in 1813 and 1890, and an entirely new edition in four volumes was published in London in 1929.

PEPYS, SAMUEL
Born 1633. Died 1703.

Pepys had only one book of his published in his lifetime, his *Memoirs of the Navy* (1690). His most popular work by far was his *Diary*, which, together with his library, he left to Magdalene College, Cambridge. There it remained, a day-to-day record of his life written in a shorthand code of his own invention until it was eventually deciphered by an undergraduate named John Smith in the early part of the last century. It was eventually published in 1825, duly edited by Lord Braybrooke, and entitled *Memoirs of Samuel Pepys*. A further edition, edited by H. B. Wheatley, including far more of the material of the diaries, this time entitled *Diary of Samuel Pepys* in nine volumes and supplements was published in London between 1893–99. A great deal of the diaries is taken up with accounts of Pepys's various amatory adventures that contain much erotic detail.

Born in London, Pepys started his career in 1659 as a clerk in the Exchequer, but after the Restoration and the accession of King Charles II he became clerk of the privy seal and then clerk of the acts of the navy. In 1673 he was appointed secretary for the affairs of the navy and in the same year entered Parliament as member for Castle Rising. In 1679 he became Parliamentary member for Harwich until he became highly unpopular because of his association with the duke of York. He was accused of selling information to the French and sent to the Tower. However, the charges against him did not succeed and he was released. Then in 1684 he was again appointed secretary to the navy and at the same time made president of the Royal Society. The following year he became master of Trinity House and once again sat as MP for Harwich. In 1689 he was once again accused of having secret relations with the French and as a result he retired from office.

One of the reasons for using a code for his diaries was to keep them protected from the prying eyes of his wife, an extremely jealous woman. For nearly two centuries they baffled all attempts to decipher them and it was eventually an inquisitive clergyman who found the key to Pepys's special brand of what he called "tachygraphy." It was this clergyman, the Reverend Honorable George Neville, master of Magdalene College, together with Lord Braybrooke, the hereditary visitor to the college, who decided to tackle the problem, employing an undergraduate, John Smith, to help them. Pepys confided to his diary both his own promiscuities and his doubts about his wife's fidelity. He wrote of persuading one Doll Lane into a winehouse where he ordered her a lobster. Then, when he had plied her with sufficient wine, he "toused her all over. . . . She had a very white thigh and leg, but monstrous fat." Pepys was so determined an amorist that he practiced his intrigues in church. On one occasion he mentioned standing beside a pretty maid and trying to take her hand in his. She must have objected strongly, for he recorded that "at last I could perceive her to take pins out of her pocket to prick me if I should touch her again, which seeing I did forbear and was glad to spy her design."

On another occasion he noted seeing some other young girl in church "and I did go about to take her by the hand, which she suffered a little and then withdrew. So the sermon ended and the church broke up and my amours ended also."

Yet, later, Pepys, who indulged in fornication or flirtation at the slightest pretext, expressed the suspicion in his diary that his wife went twice to church on a Sunday to catch a glimpse of a man named Pembleton: "I am loth to think the worst, still . . . it makes me curse the time I consented to her dancing. . . . I am ashamed to think what a course I did take by trying to see whether my wife did wear drawers today as she used to do, and other things to raise my suspicion of her, but I found no true cause of doing it."

Clearly, Pepys's diaries were never intended for publication for much of them comprised confessions and details of his behavior that would have aroused even greater suspicions in his already jealous wife. For example: "I was sorry to hear that Sir. W. Pen's maid Betty was gone away yesterday, for I was in hopes to have a bout with her before she had gone, she being very pretty. I had also a mind to my own wench, but I dare not for fear she would prove honest and refuse and then tell my wife."

Sometimes Pepys would roam the streets in quest of amorous adventure. He described one walk toward Westminster in his diary:

> Being in an idle and wanton humor, walked through Fleet Alley, and there stood a most prettie wench at one of the doors, so I took a turn or two, but what by sense of honor and conscience I would not go in, but much against my will took coach and got away to Westminster Hall, and there 'light of Mrs. Lane, and plotted with her to go over the water. So met at White's Stairs in Chanel Row, and over to the Old House at Lambeth Marsh, and there ate and drank, and had my pleasure of her twice, she being the strangest woman in talk of love of her husband sometimes, and sometimes again she do not care for him, and yet willing to allow me a liberty of doing what I would with her. So spending five shillings or six

shillings upon her, I could do what I would, and after an hour's stay and more back again and set her ashore there again.

In his diary Pepys frequently mixed French and sometimes Spanish with English that he normally used: "And so to the Swan, and thither come Doll Lane, and *je* did *toucher* her, and drank and so away." And on another occasion he wrote: "I led her into a little blind alehouse within the walls, and there she and I alone fell to talk and *baiser la* and *toker su mammailles*, but she mighty coy." Poor Pepys, he most honestly recorded his amorous failures, as is shown in this entry: "Here did I endeavor to see my prettie woman that I did *baiser* in *las tenebras* a little while *depuis*. And did find her *sola* in the bookshop. But had not *la confidence para aller à elle*. So lost my pains. But will another time."

PETRONIUS, GAIUS
Died circa A.D. 66.

Petronius had the misfortune to be a leading figure at the court in the time of the despot Emperor Nero. He governed Bithynia with firmness and sound judgment, but his writings, especially those critical of the vicious practices and corruption of the period, made him a number of enemies. Chief among these was one Tigellinus, who denounced him to Nero as a conspirator. There are two versions of his death, which was undoubtedly brought about by Tigellinus's accusations: one was that he was executed, another that he committed suicide. What is certain is that his veins were opened and he bled to death. The works that helped to bring about his downfall were the *Satyricon*, a mixture of prose and verse of which the principal item was known as *Trimalchio's Banquet*, or, in Latin, *Cena Trimalchionis*. This told of the escapades and amatory adventures of three men, Encolpius (the narrator), Giton, and Ascyltus. It is believed that the following passage was so near to the truth about certain contemporary persons that it caused his downfall: "By this time Gito had been worn out with his repeated onslaughts in the lists of love, and was trying to get back his strength, when Tryphoena came back to me . . . and all on fire with coming to me with nothing gained, managed to intrigue with both Lycas and his wife. As soon as I discovered the treachery of Tryphoena and the thanklessness of Lycas I went away."

PIRON, ALEXIS
Born 1689. Died 1773.

This French poet was born at Dijon and is best known as the author of the comedy, *La Metromanie*. He wrote many satires and songs as well as verse, some of which were almost spiritual in essence and a great deal more markedly licentious. He was an archenemy of Voltaire and is thought to have had his election to the French Academy blocked by King Louis XV because of his allegedly obscene poem, "Ode à Priape," though the supporters of Piron claimed that this poem was no more than "a youthful indiscretion." This highly erotic work is included in a nineteenth-century edition of Piron's *Oeuvres Badines*.

PLATO
Born circa 428 B.C. Died 347 B.C.

Plato belonged to an aristocratic Greek family of Athens and early on in his life he came under the influence of Socrates. It was an interesting association because Plato was an aristocrat, while Socrates came from a humble background. On the other hand Socrates was opposed to the democratic regime that then existed in Athens. Socrates' view was that it was a question of principle, not party that was important. In this Greek state leaders and generals were chosen by lot and the large assembly tended to be swayed by the passions and expectations of the masses. Socrates was convinced that this kind of politics ruled out any genuine increase in knowledge and gave no insight into the true aims of life. When Socrates was condemned to death by his opponents in 399 B.C., Plato along with other of his disciples fled to Megara. Afterwards, for about ten years, he traveled to Egypt and the Greek colonies in Italy. Later, when he visited Syracuse, he very nearly became forced into slavery by the tyrant Dionysius.

Plato's career really took off on his return to Athens when he founded his school of philosophy that later became known as the Academy. His writings have been preserved far better than many other ancient writers and both in the original and in translations have been faithfully and accurately published all over the world. Many of these writings take the form of dialogues, often using this method for refuting the ideas of Socrates. This mode of writing was later effectively employed in many of Oscar Wilde's essays. However, for the purpose of this book, it is not his philosophical ideas that concern us as much as his development of the idea of Platonic love and love as a theme in such works as *Phaedo* and *Symposium*. With Plato love was frequently equated with friendship. Nevertheless, whatever his modern supporters may say, one gets the impression that Plato remained somewhat undecided on what he really believed about amatory affairs. In the *Protagoras* one finds Plato seeming to identify all that is good with pleasure. Later he abandons this idea and in the *Gorgias* appears to suggest that a good life and a life of pleasure are totally different. One must not expect to gain much firm guidance from Plato either on eroticism or love, but he provides plenty of suggestions that can be accepted or rejected, according to one's taste.

In the *Symposium* there is the suggestion that in life there is a ladder one can climb to rise above mere human love to divine love. It is an admirable idea, no doubt, but Plato implies that it involves abandoning the normal concepts of human love. Those who studied Plato and his ideas in later life on the whole rejected such an extreme view, the Medievalists turning Platonism into Courtly Love and later poets and writers developing the theme of romanticism—in other words, the romanticization of ordinary human love.

PLAUTUS, TITUS MACCIUS
Born circa 254 B.C. Died circa 184 B.C.

A native of Sarsina in Umbria, Plautus spent his early life as a servant to actors and working a handmill in a baker's shop. From the actors whom he served he learned a great deal so that even in these periods of work he was able to write comedies and other plays, some twenty-three of them in all. The rest of his life he devoted to the career of playwright. Much of his inspiration came from earlier Greek works. He combined this with a comic touch of his own. His characters were exceptionally lifelike. Included among his works were the *Menaechmi*, on which to some extent Shakespeare's *Comedy of Errors* was based; *Truculentus*, and *Aulularia*, from which Molière borrowed parts for his *L'Avare*.

POLIZIANO, ANGELO [ANGELO AMBROGINI]
Born 1454. Died 1494.

This Italian poet and humanist was born at Montepulciano and his real family name was Ambrogini. He was appointed tutor to Lorenzo de' Medici's sons and in 1480 became professor of Greek and Latin literature at Florence. He wrote exquisitely in Latin, but his outstanding works in Italian were *Stanze per la Giostra* (1476–8), to celebrate a tournament in which one Giuliano had taken part, and *Orfeo* (1480), a lyrical drama on the subject of Orpheus and Eurydice. The *Stanze* contains some exquisite verse relating to Simonetta, Giuliano's mistress. In A *Ballata*, Poliziano indulges in amorous imagery as is shown in this English translation of his work by J. A. Symonds:

> I gazed and gazed. Hard task it were to tell
> How lovely were the roses in that hour:
> One was but peeping from her verdant shell,
> And some were faded, some were scarce in flower:
> Then Love said: Go pluck from the blooming bower
> Those that thou seest ripe upon the spray.
>
> . . . .
>
> For when the full rose quits her tender sheath,

When she is sweetest and most fair to see,
Then is the time to place her in thy wreath,
Before her beauty and her freshness flee.

PRÉVOST D'EXILES [ANTOINE-FFRANÇOIS]
Born 1697. Died 1763.

This French abbé was born at Hesdin in Artois. He joined the Benedictine
order at St. Maur and wrote *Gallia Christiana* in 1715. A somewhat restless
character, Prévost tired of the Benedictine order and went first to Holland
and then to England in 1734. Two years later he became chaplain to the
prince de Conti. During his lifetime he produced a number of books ranging
from *Memoires d'un Homme de Qualité* (1728), *Fils Natural de Cromwell* (1732),
Le Pour et le Contre (20 volumes, 1733–40) and his *Ouevrres Choisies*, published after his death. But his most popular masterpiece (and the main reason
for including his biography in this guide) was undoubtedly the novel, *Manon
Lescaut* (1731). His original work was not only extremely elegant in the writing, but markedly more erotic than the various editions and translations passed
on to later generations. It was the story of the chevalier des Grieux, a seventeen-year-old student of philosophy who seduces Manon, an even younger
girl, as she is on her way to the convent to which her parents have consigned
her. This love affair is deeply passionate at first, but gradually leads to disaster
for the chevalier and Manon, whose other passion is for money. There are
occasionally reconciliations, but Manon remains faithless and in the end is
deported to America on the grounds that she is a prostitute. There she meets
a sad end.

This work inspired two operatic versions of the theme, Massenet's *Manon*,
which expertly captures Prévost's narrative and atmosphere, and Puccini's
Manon Lescaut.

RABELAIS, FRANÇOIS
Born circa 1494. Died 1553.

No fewer than three different dates have been given by various authorities for
the birth of Rabelais, but at least it is generally agreed that his birthplace was
at La Devinière, near Chinon in Touraine. At the convent school of La
Baumette, near Angers, where he received his early education, he made
friends with the brothers du Bellay who later became his protectors. In 1519,
having become a monk, he held some position in the Franciscan convent of
Fontenay-le-Comte in Poitou. However, he did not find himself happy in this
order and in 1524 received permission to join the Benedictines. For anyone
as individualistic and boisterous in his life-style as Rabelais no order could

really have been congenial and about 1530 he quit the monastic life and entered the faculty of medicine at Montpellier where he started to produce his work, *Pantagruéline Prognostications* under the pseudonym of Alconfribas Nasier, a series that unfortunately has not been passed on to our age, at least not in full. Later he developed these themes in *The Great and Inestimable Chronicles of the Grand and Enormous Giant Gargantua* (1532). The earliest dated edition of *Pantagruel* is 1533 and of *Gargantua* 1535. Mr. W. F. Smith produced a translation of *The Five Books of Gargantua* and *Pantagruel* for the Rabelais Club, London, 1893. An earlier translator of his works in English was Sir Thomas Urquhart in 1653.

It may well be asked why Rabelais should be included in a study of erotic literature. True, his work was mainly of outrageous buffoonery, much of the language distinctly coarse and vulgar (hence the phrase "Rabelaisian language" even today), yet despite this he is still regarded in many countries as one of the greatest of French humorists. A certain amount of his humor is genuinely erotic and, above all, it is in his choice of words and, perhaps even more important, in his quite extraordinary gift for actually creating new words that this tendency is most evident. Sometimes the words he creates are obvious as to their meaning, at others they present puzzles for the reader. The following about the youthful age of Gargantua will illustrate these points:

> This little lecher was always groping his nurses and governesses upside down, arsy versy, topsy-turvy, *Harribourrquet*, with a *Yacco haic, hyck gio*, handling them very rudely in jumbling and tumbling them to keep them going; for he had already begun to exercise the tools, and put his codpiece in practice; which codpiece his governesses did every day deck up and adorn with fair nosegays, curious ribbons, sweet flowers, and fine silken tufts, and very pleasantly would pass their time in taking you know what between their fingers, and dandling it like a little baby; then did they burst out in laughing when they saw it lift up its ears, as if the sport had liked them. One of them would call it her pillicock, her fiddlediddle, her staff of love, her tickle-gizzard, her gentle titler. Another, her sugarplum, her kingo. . . . Another again her branch of coral, her placket-racket, her Cyprian sceptre, her tit-bit, her bib-lady . . . my lusty live sausage, my crimson chitterlin . . . my pretty rogue.

Yet beneath all this fun making with words, Rabelais was a profound philosopher and a man of great learning. Despite the fact that he had many enemies, that sometimes the sale of his work was stopped, he was strongly supported by Cardinal du Bellay and from 1550–52 held the curé of Meudon.

RESTIF DE LA BRETONNE [NICOLAS EDMÉ RESTIF]
Born 1734. Died 1806.

A native of Sacy, near Auxerre, Restif (sometimes Rétif) was a prolific writer all his life. When he arrived in Paris as a young man he was so fascinated by the varied sexual habits, practices and fetishes that he observed that he compiled an exhaustive study of them, taking notes in hieroglyphics that only he could understand. In the 1760s he roamed the streets of Paris by night, noting other people's amorous adventures while indulging himself in similar activities. He used his statistics and observations as source material for a series of tales of an amatory character such as *Les Nuits de Paris*, *Le Paysan Perverti*, and *La Fille Naturelle*. Restif recorded all manner of oddities from encounters with prostitutes to his own peculiar fetish for women's shoes—the sight of a high-heeled shoe once caused him to follow a girl from Paris to Lyons.

His work, *Pornographe*, intended as a crusade for social reforms in the brothels of Paris, was taken seriously by some of the revolutionary leaders of the period. Yet he was much more of a romantic than has sometimes been represented. He developed his own concept of the ideal bordello where prostitution was to be invested with a romantic ambiance. The girls of these establishments would each be addressed by the name of a flower that indicated their appearance and talents. Restif declared: "Here we shall have at least one Orchid, but no Daisies. Perhaps one Lily, certainly a delightfully exquisite Rose." He wrote: "The Controlling Sisters will receive each client and refuse entry to any who are not in a sound state of health and free from disease. Clients found to be suffering from such will be fined. . . . Money raised from the fines will be used for house repairs and decorations. . . . The Favorites will wear a distinctive uniform, also a pink taffeta bonnet embroidered with a bow and arrow and two numbers indicating category and rank." The "categories" referred to were what Restif called "Young Favorites," "Joyous Courtesans," and "Mature Women."

Restif's most formidable and lengthy work was *Monsieur Nicolas* (fourteen volumes on all), published in Paris between 1794–97: there was a new edition of fourteen volumes in 1883–84. A full English translation of his *L'Anti-Justine*, which he wrote in response to some of Sade's work, was published in London in 1990 under the title of *Pleasures and Follies of a Good-Natured Libertine*.

RONSARD, PIERRE DE
Born 1524. Died 1585.

This French poet born at Vendôme started life as a page, first at the French court and then at that of James V of Scotland. In 1541 he decided to devote his life to studying the classics and to impart something of the romanticism and classic polish of ancient Rome and Greece to French culture. He linked up with Joachim du Bellay (see BELLAY, JOACHIM DU in this section) to form the Pléiade society for this very purpose. This literary group attracted poets from all over France. He called some of his poems *amours* and it is surprising how many of these have an impact on modern readers, as for example "A sa Maitresse" and "A son ame," the latter starting off:

> *Amelette, Ronsardelette,*
> *Mignonnelette, doucelette,*
> *Tres-chère hôtesse de mon corps.*

It was Sainte-Beuve who resurrected the work of Ronsard in the early nineteenth century and restored his reputation after he had been allowed to sink into obscurity for many years. See the *Oeuvres Choisies de Ronsard,* edited by Chalandou and published in 1875.

ROSSETTI, DANTE GABRIEL
Born 1828. Died 1882.

This English poet and painter was the son of Gabriele Rossetti, the Italian poet-patriot. Born in London, he became a pupil of Ford Madox Ford as a painter and his first poem, "Damozel," was written before he was twenty. While he is perhaps still best known for his paintings, especially those in which Elizabeth Siddall (later his wife) was the model, such as *Beata Beatrix,* he was a musical and romantic poet. However, his verse sometimes led to acute and bitter controversy on the part of his critics. Much of this criticism concerned the way in which Rossetti managed to combine aesthetic and spiritual appeal with sensuality, notably in such poems as "Jenny," "Blessed Damozel," and "Nuptial Sleep," which last named was omitted from some editions of his poems in the early days. "Jenny" was attacked because its subject was a prostitute, despite the fact that some of it could be said to be moralizing. It was, however, distinctly erotic as this verse suggests:

> Your silk ungirdled and unlaced
> And warm sweets open to the waist
> All golden in the lamplights gleam.

So much did Rossetti idolize his wife that when she died he had his *Poems* buried with her. Later they were disinterred and published in 1870, to be followed by an article in *Contemporary Review* entitled "The Fleshly School of Poetry" by Thomas Maitland (he called himself "Robert Buchanan" in this magazine). "Full of coarseness from the first line to the last," he wrote of "Jenny," a surprisingly extravagant comment.

The Rossetti Papers, London (1903), and A. C. Benson's *Rossetti* (1904) are useful sources for a study of this poet.

ROTH, PHILIP
Born 1933.

Perhaps this American author is more comic than erotic, but sometimes eroticism requires comic treatment if only to maintain the right balance. Born in Newark, New Jersey, Roth was educated at Newark College of Rutgers University and Bucknell University in Pennsylvania where he took his degree. After spending one year in the U.S. Army, he went to Chicago University as an instructor in English. Having written a certain amount for magazines while teaching, in 1958 he gave up the latter profession and started writing full-time. His first book, *Goodbye Columbus* (1959), resulted in his receiving the Guggenheim Fellowship and an award from the National Institute of Arts and Letters. He used the money from this to travel to Europe, spending some time in Rome before returning to the USA in 1960 to teach at the University of Iowa. *Letting Go*, another novel, was published in 1962. It told the story of a young university teacher and his amusing and bawdy girlfriend. This was followed by *When She Was Good* (1967) and the best-known and most controversial of all Roth's works, *Portnoy's Complaint* (1969).

This book so outraged some critics that it was somewhat unfairly dubbed "a masturbation novel." This, however, is a gross exaggeration: autoeroticism is simply expressed by the book's main character, Alexander Portnoy, from the psychiatrist's couch. "Portnoy is so violently obscene," says Philip Roth of his own book, "because he wants to be saved from taboos which, rightly or wrongly, he experiences as unmanning." In many ways *Portnoy's Complaint* is a well-argued book dealing with the kind of psychological problems hardly touched on in a novel previously. It is saved from any suggestion of pornography by the comic touch that Roth brings to bear on his narrative.

Roth married Margaret Martinson in 1959. They separated in 1963 and she died in 1968. In 1972 Roth wrote *The Breast*, which was praised by some critics but which in no sense equals the much more powerful *Portnoy's Complaint*.

SAIKAKU, IHARA
Born 1642. Died 1693.

Saikaku is what is known in Japan as a "literary name" and this poet and writer of popular fiction adopted it when in his early thirties. Prior to that his name was Ihara Kakuei, though his original name is said to have been Hirayama Togo. He was born in Osaka and is believed to have worked for a family merchant's business until the death of his young wife in 1675. He then shaved his head after the fashion of retired gentlemen and devoted himself to his career as a writer, traveling widely and visiting theaters everywhere he went. His first work of prose fiction was *Kōshoku ichidai otoko* (The life of an amorous man, London, 1964).

Saikaku had begun writing *haikai* (comic verse) in his teens, but few of his early verses survive. In 1673 he took part in a twelve-day gathering of poets at the Ikudama Shrine in Osaka and out of some ten thousand verses produced by the two hundred poets present he edited a selection of three hundred, and outlined his objections to some of the poetry then being produced while advocating a new style of verse, later called the New Danrin School. Meanwhile his various stories told as much about the amorous man as the amorous woman—"tales of the floating world" he called them. In *Kōshoku ichidai otoko* he almost burlesques another Japanese classic, *Genji monogatari* (The tale of Genji), making his hero Yonosuke almost a caricature of Prince Genji. When only seven years old Yonosuke tries to make love to a maidservant and two years later by a clever ruse gets his calligraphy teacher to write a love letter for him. Each chapter of this work is brief, telling one episode in the hero's life, but the style is a combination of the comic and the rhetorical. After a life spent in chasing bath girls, shrine maidens, top-ranking courtesans, and even, occasionally, boy actors, Yonosuke ends his career at the age of sixty by sailing off to the fabulous *Nyogo no Shima* (The island of women).

Saikaku's other works included *Shoen okagami* (The great mirror of the beauties), subtitled *Kōshoku nidai otoko* (Son of the amorous man); *Saikaku shokokubanashi* (Saikaku's stories from the provinces); and *Kōshoku ichidai onna* (The life of an amorous woman), this latter also being published in translation in London in 1963. In this work Saikaku's heroine very much resembles Yonosuke in her constant pursuit of sexual activity. He makes her tell of her escapades while staying in a monastery, and goes on to portray her gradual decline from elite circles to the company of streetwalkers, while suggesting that at the end of her life she goes into pious retirement.

Saikaku had a great love of the theater and occasionally he composed dramatic works, a notable one being *Kōshoku gonin onna* (translated in 1956 as *Five Women Who Loved Love*). This was actually produced in Japan in 1686. It tells the story of two women who are eventually executed, one who commits suicide, another who becomes insane, and a fifth who seduces a homosexual samurai. One of Saikaku's themes in some of his other works was the homosexual loves of the samurai military heroes of the Japanese upper classes, while at the same time presenting his samurai as men of honor and renown. His final work, published the year after his death, was *Saikaku oridome* (Saikaku's last weaving), though some suggest that *aikaku okimiyage* (Saikaku's parting gift) was his last effort.

Modern works or translations worth consulting in any study of Saikaku are: *The Japanese Family Storehouse*, a translation by G. W. Sargent, London and New York, 1959, and (a work about Saikaku) *Saikaku nempu kosho*, Noma Koshin, Tokyo, 1952.

SARTRE, JEAN-PAUL
Born 1905. Died 1980.

It may seem strange to include an author who both in his personal philosophy and in his books dwelt so much on pessimism and all that was most depressing in life. However, included he should be if only for his admittedly unusual eroticism in his collection of stories, *Intimacy* (1949). This was one of his most compelling works of fiction.

This French philosopher, playwright, and novelist was born in Paris and educated at the Lycée de la Rochelle and the Lycée Louis-le-Grand, after which he graduated in philosophy at the Ecole Normale Supérieure in 1925. For a while he taught in Havre and other palces in France; then he traveled widely in Italy, Germany, Egypt, and elsewhere before becoming one of the foremost supporters of the existentialist movement. Sartre committed himself to this abstruse form of philosophy by being what he described as "an atheist Existentialist" and rather suggested in some of his works that "hell was other people." His first novel was *La Nausée* (Nausea), 1938. He joined the French Army as a private in World War II, was taken prisoner by the Germans in 1940, and directed plays for his fellow prisoners to take part in during the nine months before he was released. Returning to Paris, he secretly joined the Resistance and his first play, *La Mouche* (translated as *The Flies*) was produced in 1943. An example of one of his most depressing novels was *Huis Clos (No Exit)*, 1944. In this book he pictures hell as a fourth-class hotel where two women and a man were condemned to living in each other's company. In the same year he wrote another play, *The Respectful Prostitute*.

SCHNITZLER, ARTHUR
Born 1862. Died 1931.

This playwright and novelist was born in Vienna of upper middle-class Jewish parents and showed a talent for writing at an early age. At nine he wrote a five-act tragedy. However, his parents were anxious for him to follow the profession of his father, who was a doctor. Having done his medical studies, he practiced in various hospitals in Austria, but still maintained his interest in writing. In 1891 he founded the Young Vienna Group, a literary and artistic society, and gradually turned away from the medical profession. By the age of thirty-three he was devoting all of his time to writing, first with plays and later with novels. His first great success was *Change Partners*, performed in

1900. In this play he described the erotic experiences of a count with a prostitute, a son with his family's maid, and a poet and a young girl. The dialogue is extremely effective as in the scene in which the count wakes up and tries to recall what has happened:

> "Where am I? [He looks around and sees the woman in bed] . . .
> Oh, there she is. . . . Strange how things like that can happen at
> my age. . . . I knew that something had to happen . . . what has
> happened? Nothing, or did I? Let's be honest, I was drunk." He
> turns and looks at the sleeping girl and says: "I must get out of here.
> I don't remember anything, but I'll put the money on the table just
> the same."

Other works by Schnitzler: *Beatrice* (1913), *Casanova's Homecoming* (1918), *Flight into Darkness* (1926), and *The Festival of Bacchus,* another play.

SECUNDUS, IOANNES
Born 1511. Died 1535.

Ioannes Secundus was an enthusiastic imitator of the Roman poet Catullus. Born at The Hague, the son of a highly respected writer and authority on the law, his original Dutch name was Jan Everaerts. Though his life was short, he managed to produce an enormous output of both prose and verse, nearly all of it highly erotic. Much of it was an adaptation of the themes of Catullus, exuberant and voluptuous. He wrote in Latin with facility and assurance and soon established a reputation for himself as an orator as well.

His outstanding work was *The Basia,* which became so widely popular that it was translated into English, French, Spanish, Italian, Dutch, and German from the original Latin text. Among his poetic works are *Love Poems* (three books), and "Epithalamium" and "Wedding Chant." The *Love Poems* are dedicated to Julia Monobiblos, whereas *The Basia* (kisses) is addressed to a Spanish female, Neaera, whom he met when for a short while he became secretary to the Archbishop of Toledo. He was highly regarded in Spain and would probably have been promoted to a post at the court of Charles V but ill health caused him to return to Holland. He then secured an appointment as secretary to the bishop of Utrecht, which he held until he died.

SEDLEY, SIR CHARLES
Born circa 1639. Died 1701.

A native of Aylesford in Kent, England, Sedley came into his own after the Restoration and was a favorite of King Charles II at his court, where he was noted for his wit and amusing limericks, not to mention his reputation as an incorrigible rake. He was, however, also a poet of some repute: "the Tibullus of our age," Dryden called him. Apart from his amusing verses, mainly composed for the king's enjoyment, Sedley was the author of three tragedies, and three rather better comedies, *Mulberry Garden* (1668), *Bellamira* (1687), and *The Grumbler* (published in 1719, some time after his death). His reputation today, however, rests chiefly on his poem, "Phillis Is My Only Joy," in which come a series of verses all ending in the line, "And something else, but what I dare not name." A typical verse is:

> A thousand times he kiss'd her,
> Laying her on the Green;
> But as he farther press'd her,
> Her pretty leg was seen:
> And something else, but what I dare not name.

SEI SHONAGON
Born circa 965. Died circa 1015.

Sei Shonagon undoubtedly provided herself with a place among the immortals in literature when she wrote *Makura no soshi*, or, as it was translated into English in London in 1960, *The Pillow Book*. This was in effect a tenth-century diary of impressions of life in general, many of them distinctly erotic in the most delightful manner. Here was a natural, spontaneous writer whose very elegance comes over in the most unpretentious way. Her book starts off with an account of the four seasons and the time of day most suited to each of them. As to the origin of the title, the story is that in 994 Empress Sadako's brother came to court with a large quantity of paper. The empress inquired of her ladies-in-waiting as to what she should do with it. Sei Shonagon is reported to have replied that it would be "perfect for a pillow." But did she mean a pillow in the sense of something one can lie down on and contemplate, or as a notebook to record her dreams? A student of Sei Shonagon's work, Edwin A. Cranston, has commented that "Shonagon's natural bent is to be amused and her anecdotes sparkle always on the verge of laughter. . . . Her relations with courtiers combined intellectual and social camaraderie with a tingle of sexual excitement that provides a certain breathlessness to her anecdotes. . . . The world of the Heian court was one that prized the arts of love."

Some of the best passages in *The Pillow Book* tell of the meetings of lovers for the first time and also descriptions of how they part. It is clear that she drew most of her pictures of amorous activities from what went on in court circles and for this reason *The Pillow Book* not only seems realistic, but comic and satirical as well. Sei Shonogan was quick to pick up mistaken tactics in lovemaking just as she also reveled in what was splendid.

The name by which she was known, Sei Shonogan, was actually the name bestowed upon her while she served at the Imperial Court. She was a Kiyohara and Sei is the Sino-Japanese reading of the first character used in writing this family name. The word *Sonogan* means "lesser counsellor." Her father was Moto-suke, a scholar and poet. Details of her early life are few, but at some time in the late tenth century she became a lady-in-waiting at the court of Sadako, and she was known to Murasaki Shikibu, the author of *The Tale of Genji*, who mentioned Sei Shonogan in her own diaries, though not in a complimentary fashion: "Any-one who takes such pleasure in making herself different from others will inevi-tably fall in their regards" was one of her comments.

Sei Shonogan said very little about her own love life. She is supposed to have had a liaison with Fujiwara no Tadanobu, and she may at some time have been married to Tachibana no Norimitsu. Norimitsu and Sei were referred to at court as "elder brother" and "younger sister." There is also a suggestion of a second marriage to one Fujiwara no Muneyo, and it is a fact that marriage relations at the Heian courts were regarded as being merely temporary in many cases. There are also hints that she spent her last days in relative solitude and even a degree of poverty.

For further information see *The Pillow Book of Sei Shonogan*, translated by Ivan Morris, two vols, New York, 1967; and *Sei Shonogan's Poetic Catalogues*, Mark Morris, *Harvard Journal of Asiatic Studies*, June 1980.

SHAKESPEARE, WILLIAM
Born 1564. Died 1616.

Descended from a family of English yeomen, Shakespeare was born at Strat-ford-on-Avon, though the actual day and month is uncertain. Far less is known about Shakespeare's early life than of some other famous figures of the period, which is perhaps one reason why some still claim that he had little education and that his plays were written for him by Marlowe, among other candidates. (See MARLOWE, CHRISTOPHER in this section).

Shakespeare married Anne Hathaway, of the neighboring hamlet of Shot-tery in 1582 when he was still only eighteen years old, yet there is no record of this marriage in any of the parish registers. About 1585 he moved to London as a result, it is said, of a poaching expedition. This story is supposed to be substantiated to some extent by the character of Mr. Justice Shallow in *The Merry Wives of Windsor*. In London Shakespeare immediately associated himself with theaters, first, according to Sir William Davenport, with the job of tending to playgoers' horses. Then in 1594 he was an actor member of the Lord Chamberlain's Company. His reputation as a dramatist really began after Marlowe's death and in 1597 the first printed copies of his plays began to appear.

Shakespeare has not been regarded as a writer on erotic themes either in his plays or his verse for more than two hundred years. This is largely the result of the work of Dr. Thomas Bowdler (1754–1825), the man who gave the word *bowdlerism* to the English language. It was Bowdler who "sanitized" Shakespeare's work, or as he somewhat priggishly put it: "Those words or expressions are omitted which cannot with propriety be read aloud in a family."

In fact, there is a wealth and variety of erotic expressions, themes, and presentations in all Shakespeare's work. There is the detailed suggestion for winning one's love "with a French brawl" in *Love's Labour Lost*, when Moth tells Armado that this means: "Jig off a tune at the tongue's end, canary to it with your feet, humor it with turning up your eyelids, sigh a note and sing a note, sometime through the throat, as if you swallowed love by smelling love; with your hat pen-house-like o'er the shop of your eyes. . . . These are complements . . . these betray nice wenches."

Hamlet has in parts been ruined by the ridiculous rewriting of Dr. Bowdler, but it is possible for a discerning modern reader to guess where distortions have been made. There is the scene in which Hamlet talks to Ophelia:

> HAMLET: Lady, shall I lie in your lap?
> OPHELIA: No, my lord.
> HAMLET: I mean my head upon your lap.
> OPHELIA: Ay, my lord.
> HAMLET: Do you think I meant country matters?
> OPHELIA: I think nothing, my lord.
> HAMLET: That's a fair thought to lie between maids' legs.

Despite Dr. Bowdler it was in Victorian times that the question was once raised as to who was "Mr. W. H." to whom Shakespeare devoted his sonnets, and at the same time indirectly suggesting that Shakespeare may have been a homosexual. This was done first by Oscar Wilde in his essay, *The Portrait of Mr. W. H.* and somewhat later by Frank Harris. Today the argument continues (see chapter 4). Perhaps Matthew Arnold's comment is still the fairest: "The true identities of young 'Mr. W. H. and the dark lady' may never be known. But it is beyond doubt that William Shakespeare loved both the good-looking young man and the dark beauty to whom he addressed these sonnets . . . and that probably his love was more constant than theirs." The puzzle, of course, arises in the very second line of Shakespeare's sonnet:

> A woman's face with Nature's own hand painted
> Hast thou, the master-mistress of my passion.

Shakespeare was not noted for his originality: most of his plots and ideas, even his themes, are borrowed from other writers. But in the end product of his works by his own skill in the use of words and his sense of the dramatic he made himself the outstanding playwright of his era and probably all time.

The most recent recommended reading on the life and works of the Bard of Stratford are: *Shakespeare the Man*, A. L. Rowse, London, 1973; *Study of Shakespeare*, Algernon Charles Swinburne, London, 1880; *Shakespeare Lexicon*, Schmidt, London, 1874. Shakespeare spent his last days in Stratford-on-Avon, where he is commemorated by the Royal Shakespeare Memorial Theatre.

SHIH-CHENG, WANG
Born circa 1540. Died 1593.

Though the identity of the author who wrote *Chin P'ing Mei* (Metal vase plum-blossom) has not been absolutely confirmed, it is practically certain according to most reliable authorities that he was Shih-Cheng. The book deals with life during the Sung dynasty in the reign of Hui Tsung (1101–26), but it was actually written toward the end of the Ming dynasty. It is generally understood that Wang Shih-Cheng's aim was to give an account of life in an earlier era while at the same time introducing a subtle satire directed at one of his contemporaries. It is a lengthy work extending to approximately 340,000 words and it is filled with a variety of erotic tales dealing with the life and adventures of Hsi Men and his six wives, chief of whom is the fascinating Golden Lotus. Indeed, it is because of her prominent role in this vast novel that translations of *Chin P'ing Mei* have been entitled *The Golden Lotus*. Undoubtedly the best of the English translations is that, under this title, done by Clement Egerton, London, 1939, which runs to four volumes.

Mr. Egerton, who researched deeply at the School of Oriental Studies in London when translating this work, has this to say about the elusive character of Shih-Cheng:

> A popular tradition says that he [Shih-Cheng] poisoned the pages of his manuscript and then offered it to his enemy, the Prime Minister, Yen Shih-fan, in the hope that he would become engrossed in the reading of it and absorbed the poison as he turned the pages. The book existed only in manuscript for many years and, when it was first printed nearly a hundred years after its assumed author's death, the fifty-third and fifty-seventh chapters had been lost and were supplied by another unknown hand.

The book was almost immediately placed on the list of prohibited books by the Emperor K'ang Hsi, when it was first printed. Later there was a translation of the work into Manchu by a brother of the emperor who banned it, and this was highly popular. The names of some of the characters in the book are fascinating: e.g., Beauty of the Snow, a maid in the household of Hsi-men; Heart's Delight, a nurse; Moon Lady, Hsi-men's chief wife; Plum Blossom, a maid to one Moon Lady; and Welcome Spring, a maid to Moon Lady. The names of the servants seem to be more exotic than those of their mistresses! There is also quite a lot of verse worked into the novel, as for example when Hsi-men sat on the bed and made the Lady of the Vase place herself upon the cushions and play the flute for him:

> The red lips open wide; the slender fingers
> Play their part daintily.
> Deep in, deep out. Their hearts are wild with passion.
> There are no words to tell the ecstasy that thrills their souls.

The novel is packed with all a reader could desire in the erotic descriptions of life around Hsi-men's menage, sometimes the work is interspersed with philosophical reflections and the variety of characters alone lends a special charm to this writer's talent. *Chin P'ing Mei* has even resulted in the formation of a society known as the Golden Lotus (see Glossary). See also chapter 2.

SKELTON, JOHN
Born 1460. Died 1529.

A prolific writer of verse and some satirical prose, this English poet was born in Norfolk and early in life appointed tutor to Prince Henry, later King Henry VIII. He had entered the Church, but was suspended for alleged immorality, after which he took up writing in earnest. Like many poets of his period he wrote about and appealed especially to simple. humble people, using the kind of language they spoke, as is so very apparent in this poem of his about Elynor the "ale-wife" in connubial bliss after clients had left her premises:

> Ich am not cast away,
> That can my husband say.
> When we kisse and play
> In lust and liking,
> He calls me his whiting,
> His mulling and his mittine,
> His nobes and his conny,
> His sweeting and honny,
> With basse, my pretty bonny,
> Thou are worth good and mony;
> This make I my falyre Fanny,
> Till he be dreame and dromy:
> For, after all our sport,
> Then will be rout and snort;
> Then sweetly together we lye
> As two pigges in a stye.

A main target of Skelton's satire was Cardinal Wolsey, whose subservience to the king, his greed, and tyrannical attitude he attacked in his "Why Come Ye Nat to Courte?" and "Collyn Cloute." Skelton gave an amusing picture of low life in London in the long poem just quoted, which was entitled "The Tunnyng of Elynor Rummyng," yet he was capable of compassion and sheer lyrical beauty in such a work as "Phyllyp Sparowe," a girl's lament for her dead bird. While sheltering from the wrath of Wolsey, Skelton took sanctuary at Westminster until the cardinal's death. His collected works first appeared in 1568 and a selection, *Poetical Works of John Skelton*, was published in London in 1903.

SMOLLETT, TOBIAS GEORGE
Born 1721. Died 1771.

This Scottish novelist who rejoiced in producing in his work some of the most scatological prose of his day was born at Dalquhurn near Dumbarton and was originally apprenticed to a doctor. In 1739 he set out for London. There he accepted the post of surgeon's mate in the Royal Navy and he took part in the Carthagena expedition of 1740–41. On his return he left the navy and set up as a surgeon on his own account, but, finding this did not provide him with much money, he turned to writing. In 1746 he published a poem entitled "Advice," satirical in style like another poem "Reproof" that appeared the following year. However, in 1748 his novel *Roderick Random* met with instant success. The forthright, coarse language appealed to the general public and his revelations of some aspects of life inside the navy led to such an outcry that it was followed by drastic reforms of the service.

His next novel, *Peregrine Pickle*, was even livelier, touching in part on his experience during a visit to Paris while including in the original text the "Memoirs of a Lady of Quality," which were in fact concerned with the real-life escapades of Viscountess Vane. Between 1750 and 1752 Smollett tried once again to make a living as a surgeon, this time at Bath, but once again this proved to be a failure. He moved back to London, living in Chelsea, and threw himself wholeheartedly and finally into writing, not only books but articles for two papers which he edited, the *British Magazine* and the *Briton*. In 1759 he was sentenced to three months' imprisonment for a libel on one Admiral Knowles, and on his release he traveled widely for some time in France and Italy, thereby furnishing himself with material for his *Travels in France and Italy* (1766).

Other works by Smollett were: *Ferdinand, Count Fathom*, the story of a villain (1753); *A History of England* (1757–65); *The Reprisal*, a comedy (1757); *The Adventures of an Atom*, a work that attacked almost everybody and everything about England (1769); *Humphrey Clinker* (1771).

SOUTHERN, TERRY
Born 1924.

This American novelist and screenwriter was born in Alvarado, Texas, and began to write when he was only eleven though it was many years after this that he had his work published. He first of all wanted to be a doctor, but found himself disillusioned with what he regarded as the cynicism of the medical profession. From 1943–45 he served in the United States Army in Europe, after which he went first to the University of Chicago and then lived in Paris for four years, studying at the Sorbonne. On his return to the USA he married Carol Kauffman in 1952.

He and his wife lived in Geneva for a while and in 1958 *Flash and Filigree*, his first work, was published in London. This was a satire directed against the medical profession and what he regarded as many of their false values. This was followed by *Magic Christian* in 1960 and then about the same time his masterpiece, *Candy*, was written in cooperation with Mason Hoffenberg. It was first published as by "Maxwell Kenton." Banned by the French government somewhat surprisingly, it was reissued as *Lollipop* and published in the USA in 1964.

Candy, as the name partially suggests, was to some extent a modern version of *Candide*. It is the story of a lovely but innocent young girl who cannot because of her sweet nature refuse the amorous requests of various men. "It is not an obscene book," said William Styron, defending it from the attacks of some reviewers: "In its best scenes it is wildly funny to read."

The language of *Candy* may be erotic, but it has a pleasant, almost endearing choice of phrase. Southern writes of "a sweetening damp," "a pulsing jellybox," and a "little sugar-scoop," all suggestive of adolescent appreciation of sex. "Candy lay back again with a sigh, closed-eyed, hands behind her head, and Grindle resumed his fondling of her sweet-dripping little fur-pie. 'Do you experience feelings of creamy warmth and a great yielding sensation?' demands Grindle. 'Yes,' said Candy, thinking he was surely psychic."

Southern also wrote *End of the Road* (1970), which was made into a film by Aram Avakian. Later he went to Hollywood and worked on a number of pictures. Other books are *Red Dirt Marijuana and Other Tastes*, a collection of stories (1967) and *Blue Movie* (1970).

SPENSER, EDMUND
Born 1552. Died 1599.

Born in London and related to the Spensers of Althorp (ancestors of Princess Diana of Wales), Spenser left the capital in 1576 and settled down at Hurstwood in Lancashire. It was here that he started to write lyrical verse, much of it in honor of his "Rosalind" of whom in his work, *The Shepherd's Calendar*, he speaks of his unrequited love. "Rosalind," it is now established was a certain Rose Dyneley, the daughter of a Clitheroe (Lancashire) yeoman.

In 1578 he returned to London and became a member of the earl of Leicester's household and joined the literary coterie that was known as the "Areopagus." It was *The Shepherd's Calendar*, published in 1579, which brought him fame. The following year he was appointed secretary to the lord deputy of Ireland, Lord Grey de Wilton, and in 1581 he was made clerk to the Irish Court of Chancery and given grants of land in various parts of Ireland, including Kilcolman Castle, County Cork. During a visit to England in 1589–91 he published the first part of *The Faerie Queene* and other poems. This work owed much to the influence of Italian poets, thus making it a romantic epic. Spenser's creation of Amoret in *The Faerie Queene* gave a new word to the English language (see glossary), suggesting the perfect type of female loveliness—"witty and good, soft as a rose, sweet as a violet, chaste as a lilly, gentle as a dove." All this led to Spenser being considered the leading figure in English verse of his period. As a result of his courtship and marriage to Elizabeth Boyle he wrote his *Sonnets* and *Epithalamion*.

The eroticism of Spenser is never blatant, and often it is disguised by his own verse. To understand Spenser one needs to realize that for him it is the intensity with which one feels passion or love that purifies and that anything less than real intensity is unworthy, even revolting. There is the picture of Venus and Adonis in the Garden with Venus being portrayed as one who "possesseth him and of his sweetnesse takes her fill," and again in another verse, "And whilst he bath'd, with her two crafty spyes, She secretly would search each dainty limb." One of the tragedies of Spenser's life was that the existing *Faerie Queene* was never finished and it terminated just as Spenser was writing some of his best and most musical verse. In 1597 he had returned to Ireland and the following year was appointed sheriff of Cork. Then, during the rising of the earl of Tyrone, Kilcolman Castle was burnt down and Spenser was forced to flee to Cork, whence he went to London to plead the cause of the Munster colonists. He died soon afterwards and was buried in Westminster Abbey. Any student of Spenser should see *Observations on the Faerie Queene* (1754), T. Warton, London; *The Life of Spenser* (1879), R. W. Church; *Outline Guide to Study of Spenser* (1894), F. L. Carpenter; and *The Allegory of Love* (1936), C. S. Lewis, Oxford.

SPIEGELMAN, KATIA
Birth date unavailable.

This young American writer has only published two novels as yet, but each suggests she is very much one to be followed closely in the future. She lives in Brooklyn, New York, and her works have appeared in both New York and London. Her first novel, Soul Catchers (1990), was the story of an innocent fifteen-year-old girl who finds herself in a boarding school where she is initiated into the conflicting values and moral confusions of the 1970s. It has been called "the tale of a generation's coming-of-age." This was followed by Peculiar Politics (1991), which sets out to chart a course through the confusion and self-deception of personal relationships in the latter part of the twentieth century in New York's yuppieland, as Spiegelman sees it—a situation where there are no longer any strict rules enforced by society to regulate and guide sexual behavior, so that anything and everything seem permissible. The author concentrates on the relationships of two contrasting couples and how their lives are interlinked and made chaotic by the presence of the mysterious and licentious Mike Mauvais. The story contains an intricate web of sexual promiscuity and emotional confusion. The characterization is extremely well done and the author makes her roguish story explore the frightening problem of how to cope in a world where love is bereft of its traditional boundaries and meanings.

STERNE, LAURENCE
Born 1713. Died 1768.

This Irish novelist and humorist was born at Clonmel in Tipperary. He entered holy orders and was given the living of Sutton near York, England, and later he had a prebendary's stall at York Minister. His best-known work is undoubtedly The Life and Opinions of Tristram Shandy, nine volumes in all, which was published between 1759–67. This was the story of life in and around a parsonage, but it is a remarkably discursive work, some passages distinctly Rabelaisian in tone, containing piquant character studies, while he sometimes rambles off to discuss such diverse subjects as metaphysics, swearing, and ontological doctrine. His style is lesiurely at one moment, rumbustious and farcical the next. Even when long-winded, he is amusing, as for example when writing about "that particular aperture of Phutatorius's breeches, for which, to the shame and indelicacy of our language be it spoke, there is no chaste word throughout all Johnson's dictionary—let it suffice to say—it was that particular aperture which, in all good societies, the laws of decorum do strictly require, like the temple of Janus (in peace at least) to be universally shut up."

At other times, as in Tristram Shandy, he is more forthright: "It had ever been the custom of the family, and by length of time was almost become a matter of common right, that the eldest son of it should have free ingress, egress and regress into foreign parts before marriage—not only for the sake of bettering his own private parts, by the benefit of exercise and change of so much air—but simply for the more delectation of his fancy, by the feather put into his cap, of having been abroad."

His other works include *The Sermons of Mr. Yorick*, and *A Sentimental Journey through France and Italy* (1768). He was highly popular in London society. See also *Memoirs of the Life and Family of the Late Reverend Laurence Sterne*, Laurence Sterne, London, 1775.

STEVENSON, JOHN HALL
Born 1718. Died 1785.

A gregarious Englishman with a passion for forming clubs, Stevenson's original name was John Hall. He was educated at Jesus College, Cambridge, after which he founded a secret society known as the Demoniacs who met at Skelton Castle, a fifteenth-century ruin that he had inherited. This Yorkshire Castle was the scene of many wild pranks and jests during the 1730s and Stevenson had it renamed Crazy Castle. Despite his marriage to Anne Wharton of York, his whole life was one of nonstop dissipation and fornication. In 1761 he wrote *Fables for Grown Gentlemen*, a number of salacious tales that no doubt he had read to his fellow members of the Demoniacs. This was followed by *Crazy Tales* (1762). Stevenson sometimes wrote in a breathless manner, often switching from prose to verse. His various writings were published in three volumes after his death under the title of *The Works of John Hall Stevenson* (1795).

For some reason Stevenson, who had been a member of the equally secretive "Hell-Fire Club" at West Wycombe, took a virulent dislike to Sir Francis Dashwood, the founder of that club. It may have been envy or the fact that Dashwood was a Tory, whereas Stevenson was a Whig, but Stevenson took this dislike so far that he made Dashwood quite unfairly the target for some of his most erotic verse. This he did in a lengthy poem entitled The Confessions of Sir F—— of Medmenham and of the Lady Mary, his wife. Referring to Dashwood he wrote:

> Like a Hotspur young cock, he began with his mother,
> Cheer'd three of his sisters one after another;
> And oft tried little Jen, but gain'd so little ground,
> Little Jen lost her patience and made him compound.
> Jen played on the flute with her fingers so white
> And twinkled her eyes and kept time very right.
> Then he served up his cousin, a delicate blade,
> And old Bridget his aunt for the sake of her maid.

This poem is verbally infelicitous, banal, and, though describing some unusual sexual permutations, has neither the rhythmic and onomatopoeic merit of Restoration wit, nor the picturesquely rounded humor of Rabelais. One must also entirely reject the outrageous allegations of incestuous conduct made by Hall Stevenson. See chapter 4.

STRAPAROLA, GIOVANNI FRANCESCO
Born circa 1495. Died 1557.

One of the earliest Italian novelists, Straparola was born at Caravaggio (Cremona) and later lived in Venice. His work *Piacevoli Notti* (Pleasant nights) is remarkable as the first European collection of tales based largely on folk lore. He was also noted for his erotic work, *Les Nuits Facétieuses*, translated into French, Paris, 1573.

SUDERMANN, HERMANN
Born 1857. Died 1928.

This German dramatist and novelist was born at Matzicken in East Prussia and is perhaps best known for his novel that was translated into English as *The Song of Songs* (1908). His novels in German were *Frau Sorge* (1888), *Der Katzensteg* (1890), and *Eswar* (1894). *The Song of Songs* was condemned by some for its erotic undertones, but praised by others. Plays by Sudermann included *Die Ehre* (1889), *Sodoms Ende* (1891), and *Heimat* (1893).

SUSANN, JACQUELINE
Born 1918. Died 1974.

This American writer was one of the first modern female authors to explore sexuality in explicit and provocative language. She struck out successfully in the 1960s during the so-called sexual revolution of that period with her first best-seller *Valley of the Dolls*. What is surprising is that it was not until the last ten years of her life that she really came into her own: in a sense this was a tragedy as she died relatively young. *Valley of the Dolls* (1966) perhaps gave a too highly dramatized version of the career-fixated young American females of the period, the high-rolling background to their lives, and the manner in which they reacted both to work and to the men around them. However, it did provide a salutary warning of the sense of hidden doom by which such lives could be undermined. Here were females resolutely pursuing a path to supremacy in their careers, but failing miserably in their choice of sexual partners who, as often as not, were wealthy and influential, but at the same time erratic and unsatisfactory partners. All this, Susann showed, led to disillusionment, despair, and, finally, drugs—the "dolls" implied in the title of her book.

Other novels by Jacqueline Susann were *Once is Not Enough* and *The Love Machine*. One critic said of them that "the reader is beguiled into an enjoyable state of shocked titillation and invited to make moralistic judgments. Like women's magazines, they incorporate a great deal of consumer information, beauty tips, fashion comments, and advice on etiquette." However, this same critic later asserted that Susann used sexual gratification and the description of designer commodities "to support weak, flash-ridden plots." Another criticism was that Susann used too many heroines in her novels. The answer to this is that by doing so the author established what really were current trends, something that would have been much more difficult to convey with only one heroine.

SWIFT, JONATHAN
Born 1667. Died 1745.

Born in Dublin, this greatest of Irish satirists became confidential secretary to Sir William Temple at Moor Park, Surrey, England, in 1689. Five years later he took orders and was given the living of Kilroot near Belfast, but he did not last there for long. He returned to work for Sir William Temple for a period, after which he went back to Ireland and was presented with the small living of Laracor and a prebend in St. Patrick's Cathedral, Dublin. In 1704 he published anonymously a work entitled *The Battle of the Books* and *A Tale of a Tub*. He began to take an interest in politics, first as an associate of such Whigs as Addison and Steele, but later transferred his allegiance to the Tory Party. His name is, of course, first and foremost associated with that work popular with all ages, *Gulliver's Travels* (1726). As a satirist, especially in defense of his beloved Ireland, he was not merely one of the most savage of his kind, but also the most practical in publicizing political errors and failure to act by the government of the day. In his work, *A Modest Proposal*, for example, he sardonically proposed to alleviate the misery of the Irish people by making use of their children as food!

Three women played a part in his life. First of all in his early life he had a passing courtship with a Miss Waring (whom he referred to as "Varina"). Esther Vanhomrigh adored Swift and he in turn gave her friendship, but it was the third woman who was not only the delight of Swift's life, but around whom he built up some wildly erotic tributes in writing in his *Journal to Stella*. This work was descriptive of his life in London and was not intended for publication. Its most recent edition in two volumes, edited by Harold Williams, appeared in London in 1948. Authorities on Swift disagree widely on the interpretation of much of his lengthy correspondence with "Stella" whose real name was Esther Johnson, a girl he had probably known from the age of nine. It was not until after his death that scholars began to edit and interpret (some of his letters to Stella were written in a code of his own) this correspondence in the form of the *Journal to Stella*.

The letters between Swift and Stella began in 1710. When it comes to the nursery dialogue between the pair, while it is obvious that Swift and his "Stella" are moving toward greater intimacy, the reader is often baffled, as in the following extract: "Does Md never read at all now, pee? but oo walk plodigiously I suppose, oo make nothing of walking to too to to ay, to Doni-brooke. . . . Nite deelest Sollahs; farwell deelst Rives; rove poopoodfr farwell deelest richar Md, Md Md FW FW FW FW FW Me Me Lele, Me, lele lele richar Md."

Swift first addressed Esther Johnson as Stella in 1719 when he sent her this poem:

> Stella this day is thirty-four,
> (We won't dispute a Year or more)
> However Stella be not troubled,
> Although thy size and Years are doubled,
> Since first I saw Thee at Sixteen
> The Brightest Virgin of the Green.

Swift, it should be added, was not very good at dates and it is almost certain that he knew her from the age of nine. Never can a man have doted on a woman so much without any apparent intention of marrying her. Yet he wrote of going to bed to dream of Stella and of hoping "never to spend Christmas or New Year away" from her. In the last nine years of his life Swift suffered from an extreme mental illness, and some have argued that Swift's baby talk in his letters to Stella was merely an indication of approaching insanity. This theory, however, can almost certainly be discarded on the grounds that in those early days he was highly regarded in some political circles. It is most probable that Swift was trying very cleverly as a writer to bridge the age gap between himself and Stella. Swift attempted to lisp his words in childlike fashion as he wrote them, for he once said to Stella, "When I am writing in our language, I make up my mouth just as if I was speaking it." Thus he wrote "rover" when he meant "lover" and "vely" for "very" and "ourrichar Gangridge" for "our little language."

SWINBURNE, ALGERNON CHARLES
Born 1837. Died 1909.

"The libidinous laureate of a pack of satyrs" was the way one of his critics described Swinburne. This was the reaction of Victorian prudery and those who damned the erotic themes that Swinburne so often chose. Born in London, Swinburne started to write verse before he was even in his teens. When eventually he went to Oxford University (Balliol College) after he left Eton he made friends with Dante Gabriel Rossetti, William Morris, and Burne-

Jones. Having spent his youth and early manhood in Bonchurch in the Isle of Wight, in 1865 he went to Italy where he wrote his first masterpiece, *Atalanta in Calydon*. Returning to London he produced *Bothwell* (1874), *Erechtheus* (1876), and *Poems and Ballads: Second Series* (1878)—the first series appeared in 1866. By this time he had become acknowledged as one of the greatest poets of his time, so much so that he was an influence on many of his contemporaries.

He became obsessed with the theme of Mary Stuart, queen of Scotland, as such works as *Bothwell* and *Mary Stuart* (1881) indicate. He was frequently attacked for the manner in which he expressed erotic themes, but he replied to this by saying that he had in his *Poems and Ballads* "striven to express that transient state of spirit through which a man may be supposed to pass foiled in love and weary of loving, but not yet in sight of rest, in those violent delights which have violent ends in free and frank sensualities, which at least profess to be no more than they are." Curiously, British critics of Swinburne attack him more for what they see as French influences on him (especially that of Baudelaire) than anything else, always recalling his "Ave Atque Vale," which was written in memory of the French writer. One can see in some of Swinburne's verse eroticism mixed up with something very close to Masochism, especially in his poem "Dolores":

> Ah beautiful, passionate body
> That never has ached with a heart!
> On thy mouth though the kisses are bloody,
> Though they sting till it shudder and smart
> More kind than the love we adore is
> They hurt not the heart nor the brain
> Of bitter and tender Dolores
> Our Lady of Pain.

It may be that his somewhat unsatisfactory sex life had a considerable effect on his verse. Stories were told of how he paid women to whip him when he was living in various parts of London. That such stories were undoubtedly true seems to be confirmed by the fact that Swinburne contributed to the *Whippingham Papers* (1888), which was in effect a history of flagellation and flagellomania. In this pamphlet he wrote that "no propensity to which human nature is addicted . . . holds firmer root than flagellation." Nevertheless Swinburne provided much poetry that showed his genuine love of beauty and worship of love even if he sometimes expressed such through the eyes of a rebel. This is especially true of the chorus from *Atalanta* in which he declares:

> The ivy falls with the Bacchanal's hair
> Over her eyebrows hiding her eyes;

The wild vine slipping down leaves bare
Her bright breast shortening into sighs.

TIBULLUS, ALBIUS
Born circa 55 B.C. Died 19 B.C.

A member of an ancient Roman family, in 31 B.C. Tibullus accompanied
Messala into Gaul, where the Acquitanians had revolted, and afterwards celebrated his patron's victory with various parties and feasts. He next followed
Messala as far as Corcyra, but he was taken ill there and returned home. His
poems are mainly on the subject of love, marked by an unusual combination
of sincerity of feeling and realism, some of them being distinctly erotic. There
was also much dwelling on failure and lovesickness in Tibullus's verses, as for
example the following:

> Ah me! Ah me! love-tortured and love-torn!
> My darling yields not; arts and wiles are vain:
> Spare, dear youth, spare! nor hold me up to scorn,
> Lest lovers treat my precepts with disdain.

There was an English translation of his verses by Cranstoun, London, 1872.

TOLSTOY, COUNT LEO NIKOLAYEVICH
Born 1828. Died 1910.

Even to consider bringing Tolstoy into the concept of an erotic writer may
seem like lèse-majesté to some and like tilting the windmill to others. Nevertheless, the fact remains that the very sound of the name Anna Karenina is
still somewhat an erotic stimulant. What other heroine down the ages has
struck such chords of the harsh realties of love as well as the sweeter moments
as poor, doomed Anna? The important point is that the more one delves into
this book and the story behind it, *Anna Karenina* (1874–76), translated into
many languages, the more it becomes a study in the arts and problems of all
kinds of love affairs. So gripping is this work that it can cause a reader to
pause and rethink his or her life, or to feel he or she must learn more from
it. This book is a thinker's eroticism rather than eroticism itself.

Tolstoy was one of four brothers born on the family estate south of Moscow.
In 1844 he went to the University of Kazan to read oriental languages, but
he did not graduate and for some years thereafter led a dissolute life, something
that was reflected in *Anna Karenina*. This book is autobiographical at least to
the extent that it shows how early on there was a conflict in Tolstoy's life
between his feeling of the need for freedom and experiment as a creative artist
and an ethical code that would work. Tolstoy went to the Caucasus and joined

the army. Some time after this he resigned from Russian Orthodox religious beliefs and converted to what he called "a religion of love." He claimed that his new belief was based on a literal interpretation of the Sermon on the Mount. This resulted in his work, *A Confession*, Moscow (1879–82) and in 1901 he was excommunicated by the Orthodox Church.

Anna Karenina was Tolstoy's second great novel, and it is interesting to note that he at first thought of calling it either "Two Couples" or "Two Marriages." Here again one begins to get the impression that Tolstoy was trying to give some advice on the problems of lovemaking. It is the story of Anna, who falls in love with Count Vronsky, a handsome young officer, and abandons her child and husband to be with him. When he tires of her she kills herself by leaping under a train. Tolstoy became intrigued with the character of Karenina and his attitude toward her changed even while he was writing his story. His first notes on her were such: "She is unattractive, with a narow, low forehead, short, turned-up nose—rather large . . . but . . . There was something in the kindly smile of her red lips that made her likable." At that stage Tolstoy saw his creation as "the Devil, the agent of evil." But the story of Tolstoy's heroine and how she developed is almost more erotic than the book itself. The truth is that after a hostile and critical start to his theme Tolstoy began to fall in love with Anna Karenina. He started to change her whole physical appearance. So it was that he put into his revised version this description: "Vronsky was drawn, not by her beauty, although she was a very beautiful woman, nor by the unobtrusive elegance she radiated, but by the expression of utter sweetness in her charming face. . . . Her eyes and her smile revealed vast stores of repressed vitality."

It took Tolstoy four years to write *Anna Karenina*. In this work, as if to balance up the story of Anna, he developed his subplot, that of the happy marriage of Konstantin Levin and his young wife, Kitty, reflecting to a large extent Tolstoy's own quest for a meaning to life. The author himself revealed in his *Confession* something of the anguishing time he spent working on *Anna Karenina*. There is a strong clue as to what was going on in Tolstoy's mind while writing this book when in answer to Vronsky's comment about there being "only one happiness . . . for me in life, the word you so dislike—yes, love," Anna replies: "The reason I dislike that word is that it means too much for me, far more than you can understand."

Alexis Suvorin, one of Russia's most respected literary critics of that age, wrote of *Anna Karenina* that "the author has spared nothing and no one. He portrays love with a realism that no one in our country has yet approached."

At the end of his days Tolstoy made over his fortune to his wife, but continued to live under her roof in relatively spartan fashion despite the fact that relations with her had become acutely difficult. Then, at the age of eighty-two, he left home suddenly one day and died at the railway station.

TWAIN, MARK [SAMUEL LANGHORNE CLEMENS]
Born 1835. Died 1910.

This American author and humorist adopted "Mark Twain" as his pen name. Born in Missouri, he worked first as a printing compositor, then as a clerk, a teacher, and a miner before he qualified as a riverboat pilot on the Mississippi River. It was partly as a result of this last experience that he chose the name of "Mark Twain," taking it from the call of the leadsmen on the Mississippi steamers—"Mark Twain," meaning "mark two fathoms (deep)." When the Civil War ended he started writing and lecturing, becoming editor of newspapers in Virginia City and San Francisco, California. A lucky break gave him the opportunity to travel in Europe and the Middle East for the purpose of writing descriptive sketches. This undoubtedly played a great part in the making of his name as a writer, notably with his book, *The Innocents Abroad* (1869), which had an enormous sale.

It has been said that various people challenged Mark Twain to write an erotic work, if only as a joke. Whatever is the truth of this, in 1876, in between writing *Tom Sawyer* and *The Adventures of Huckleberry Finn*, he composed *1601–Conversation as It Was by the Social Fireside in the Time of the Tudors*. "Easily as scatological as it is sexual," wrote Ralph Ginzburg, "*1601* gave Twain, the bad boy of American literature, an opportunity to employ almost every verbal indecency of the English language." (See *An Unhurried View of Erotica*, Ginzburg, London, 1959). Yet long afterwards Twain claimed he had written this short work for the amusement of his friend, the Reverend Joseph Twitchell, of Hartford, Connecticut! Twitchell had not only conducted Twain's wedding service, but had christened all his children. The book first appeared in pamphlet form and was not printed in hardback until 1880. A reprint was made by the Mark Twain Society and published in Chicago in 1939.

1601 purports to be a record of conversations between Queen Elizabeth I of England and such others as Ben Jonson, Sir Walter Raleigh, Francis Bacon, and William Shakespeare, while throwing in for good measure a fictitious character, the duchess of Bilgewater. Much of the talk is on clandestine affairs, but when a loud fart is heard, the queen demands that the culprit should reveal himself. Shakespeare pays tribute to this faux pas with the words "Heaven's artillery hath shook ye globe in admiration of it."

Mark Twain not only studied pornographic literature when he visited Berlin on his travels, but also various works of Tudor Restoration writers in London when he lived at 23 Tedworth Square in 1897. He wrote *Following the Equator* while in London. This visit to London followed a somewhat checkered career in the latter part of his life. After having been editor of the *Buffalo Express* he became a partner in the publishing house of Webster and Company. The failure of that firm involved considerable financial loss. He fought back and by both lecturing and writing books eventually recovered enough to pay off all his debts.

While making his lecture tours Twain visited Paris and there in 1879 he gave a talk to members of what was known as the Club de l'estomac. The title of the speech was "Some Thoughts on the Science of Onanism." Later that year the speech he then gave was published in Paris.

TYNAN, KENNETH PEACOCK
Born 1927. Died 1980.

Throughout his life Tynan sought to outshine his contemporaries by outraging public opinion and making his name synonymous with a series of shocks. "Oh, Tynan again!" was a constant refrain in literary and theatrical circles in the 1950s. Born in Birmingham, England, he was the only son of Sir Peter Peacock and Letitia Rose Tynan (whose name he took): this was a relationship quite separate from Peacock's accepted household in Lancashire. Tynan was educated at King Edward School, Birmingham, and Magdalen College, Oxford. His career started off as a theater critic whose constant aim was to draw attention to himself rather than the play about which he was reviewing. Despite that, he received strong support in some theatrical circles, notably when Sir Laurence Olivier asked him to be literary manager of the National Theatre that was then being set up in the temporary home of the Old Vic Theatre.

Tynan married first of all Elaine, daughter of Samuel M. Brimberg, of New York. She, too, was a writer under the name of Elaine Dundy. His second wife was yet another writer, Kathleen Halton. Tynan had anticipated the sexual liberation of the 1960s ten years beforehand so that by the time he produced *Oh! Calcutta!* he had come into his own, readily naming his recreations in *Who's Who* as "sex and eating." *Oh! Calcutta!* was staged first in New York, then in London. Its title, which puzzled many people, was really part joke and part coverup for the real title that was the French *Quel cul t'as!* meaning "Oh, what an arse you have!" The only clue to this lay in the poster used to advertise the show—a picture of a naked odalisque lying in her side to reveal a rounded backside based on a painting by the French painter, Clovis Trouille. *Oh! Calcutta!* was really a mixture of attractively presented nudity on the stage and humor of a rather low standard. Its production in London created a furor with a threat of prosecution. It opened at the Round House, a small theater at Chalk Farm and later was transferred to the Royalty Theatre for two years and then to the Duchess Theatre for seven. One critic said of it that "much of what is seen is beautiful and most of what is heard is dreadful." Previously the *New York Times* critic, Clive Barnes, had said it was "the kind of show to give pornography a dirty name." Tynan himself said of the production that his aim was to "remove sexual embarrassment and shame" and "to titillate well, to give the fullest, most delicate sensual pleasure."

VATSYAYANA, THE MAHARISHI
Born circa 350. Died circa 400.

The Maharishi's full name was said to be Mallanaga of the Vatsyayana sect and his work, *The Kama Sutra*, was supposed to have been written some time before A.D. 400. The book lists sixty-four yogas or arts of love and consists of detailed suggestions for both sexes on how to be sexually attractive and how to retain such attributes. The Maharishi, a devout religious seer, decreed that his book was "not intended to be used merely as an instrument for satisfying our desires. . . . An intelligent and prudent person, attending to Dharma and Artha, and attending to Kama also, without becoming a slave to his passion, obtains success in everything that he may undertake." *Kama* in Sanskrit may be translated as "scripture" or "doctrines." The work was not discovered by western scholars until the latter part of the nineteenth century, when the book was laboriously translated into English by piecing together broken Sanskrit texts from various Indian libraries. As a result of this the Kama Shastra Society was established and the *Kama Sutra* was published in 1883. In both the original text and translations Vatsyayana's work is an admirable balance between a genuinely erotic approach to sexual intercourse and formal advice, resulting in freedom from salaciousness on the one hand and prurience on the other. See chapters 2 and 5.

VERLAINE, PAUL
Born 1844. Died 1896.

This French lyrical poet, born at Metz, was from youth onwards passionately devoted to a worship of beauty in all its forms. His earliest works were *Poèmes Saturniens* (1866) and *Fêtes Galantes* (1869). Shortly after this he had the misfortune to become attached to the poet Arthur Rimbaud of the Decadent School: they quarreled, Verlaine aimed a pistol at his friend and for this crime was sentenced to two years' imprisonment at Mons. For a while after this Verlaine turned to religious themes. Then he blossomed out once again in his former style with such works as *Romances sans Paroles* (1874), *Amour* (1888), and *Bonheur* (1891). Subtlety, exquisite rhythm, and delicacy of expression were the hallmark of his most erotic works, some of which were privately printed, in particular *Hombres* (1891), and *Femmes* (1890), both published in Paris. In the former book he wrote about homosexual love (undoubtedly influenced by Rimbaud) and in *Femmes* heterosexual love. Always in his verses there is some uplifting thought, even though sadness may be a theme:

> —*Ton coeur bat-il toujours à mon seul nom?*
> *Toujours vois-tu mon âme en rêve?—Non.*

VIDAL, GORE
Born 1925.

This American novelist and playwright was educated at Phillips Exeter Academy in New Hampshire. He graduated in 1943 just before joining the army as a private soldier to serve in the Pacific theater of operations in World War II. He started writing novels as soon as the war was over, publishing his first, *Williwaw* in 1946. This was followed by *In a Yellow Wood* (1947), *The City and the Pillar* (1948), and *The Season of Comfort* (1949). For a while Vidal took a keen interest in politics and was a Democratic Liberal candidate for Congress in 1960. When the Democrats came to power he was appointed to President Kennedy's Advisory Council on the Arts (1961–63). He was also cochairman of the New Party from 1968–71.

The main reason for Vidal's inclusion in this series of biographies is his book, *Myra Breckinridge* (1968), which was so successful that it was filmed the following year. In this book Vidal succeeded in making a somewhat outrageous theme both amusing and genuinely erotic. It was not only a parody, indeed almost a send-up of the pornographic novel, but it examined some uncertainties about identity and sexual roles generally, relying very much on first-person narrative, but maintaining the reader's attention by a conscientiously well worked out plot. Peter Webb in his work, *The Erotic Arts*, London, 1975, said of *Myra Breckinridge:* "The film fell a long way short of the success enjoyed by the book, in spite of the acting talents of Raquel Welch, Mae West, and John Huston. The novel got away with being outrageous in a way which was impossible for the film; the written word was explicit enough to fire the sexual imagination. . . . The crucial scene when Myra rapes with her dildo the handsome young stud on the examination table lost most of the erotic power of Vidal's description."

Vidal, who has lived lately in Ravello in Italy, has written a number of plays, including *Visit to a Small Planet* (1956) and *The Best Man* (1960).

VILLON, FRANÇOIS
Born circa 1431. Died 1485.

It is with some hesitation that I have included Villon in this book, as he is very much a borderline case in an assessment of whether or not he can be

included in the erotica genre. His original name was Corbueil or De Montcor-
bier or Des Logues and he was believed to have been born in a brothel.
Certainly he was brought up in one and he had a detailed knowledge of what
went on in such places and in the lives of prostitutes. In 1455 he was banished
for killing a priest in a street brawl, but a year later received a pardon and
returned to Paris to write his best-known poem, *Le Lais* (or *Petit Testament*).
In 1457 he was sentenced to death for yet another criminal offense, but
somehow he once again escaped by submitting to what was known as "the
ordeal by water," after which he was banished.

Villon received a pardon after the accession of King Louis XI and he then
produced his *Testament* (or *Grand Testament*), the subject of which was the
vanity of human nature. He frequently took as subjects for his verse women
of the streets and brothels and lowlife generally. but he managed to show in
his work compassion and sorrow, sometimes setting out to warn prostitutes of
the fates that awaited them as in this verse addressed to the *filles de joie*:

> And Blanche the Cobbler, never miss,
> For now you must consolidate.
> Take right and left and do not wait;
> I beg you, spare no man, but haste:
> For aged trulls are tarnished plate,
> Like money clipped and then debased.

Among his other poems were the "Ballade des Dames du Temps Jadis," and
"Le Jargon." He always praised the women of Paris and in his "Ballade aux
Femmes de Paris" in comparing them to those of other countries, he wrote,
"O Prince, to Paris women grant / The ribbon of this chatter game; / No
matter how Italians rant, / There's none can touch the Paris dame." Much of
his work has been translated into English by poets such as Algernon Charles
Swinburne, and Payne, Lang, and M'Carthy.

VOLTAIRE [FRANÇOIS MARIE AROUET]
Born 1694. Died 1778.

The son of François Arouet, an official of one of the high courts of France,
Voltaire was born in Paris and educated at the Jesuit Seminary of the College
Louis-le-Grand. That beautiful Parisian courtesan, Ninon de l'Enclos, gave
him lessons in social deportment and left him a legacy when she died. Thus
Voltaire at a very early age entered the leading intellectual circles of Paris. It
was not long after this that a stream of satires poured from his pen, paving
the way to his becoming a challenger of tradition, an intellectual noncomfor-
mist and a radical philosopher. For a while he studied for the law, but on the
death of King Louis XIV he wrote a tactless satire on the regent, the duke of
Orleans, for which he was imprisoned (1717).

When released, his play *Oedipe* was produced at the Theatre Français and was a great success. It was at this stage that he changed his name from Arouet to Voltaire. Other plays such as *Artémire* and *Marianne* followed, then once again he found himself imprisoned in the Bastille for being too outspoken. On his release from prison he went to England in 1726 and during the next few years made friends there with both statesmen and other writers. He returned to Paris and once again took up his literary cudgel against both political and religious intolerance, most notably in his *Lettres Philosophiques* (1733). In 1740 Frederick the Great of Prussia invited Voltaire to visit him and two years later he accepted the offer. Members of the French Court seem to have been impressed by this relationship, and in 1743 sent Voltaire on a secret mission to Prussia, for which service, as a result of the influence of King Louis XV, he was elected a member of the French Academy. In 1751 he again visited Frederick the Great in Berlin and then spent three years in Prussia, having apartments assigned to him in Potsdam, a pension of twenty-thousand francs and a chamberlain's gold key solely for the purpose of correcting King Frederick's writings.

After an unsettled and migratory life Voltaire finally settled down at Ferney near Geneva where he spent the last twenty years of his life. He died while on a visit to Paris. The curé of St. Sulpice refused to bury him so his remains had to be buried in the Abbey of Scellières. Later the body was transferred to the Panthéon.

Two erotic works of Voltaire were *Zadig* (1747) and *Candide* (1759). In the former Voltaire made use of a story that originated in China, was developed in Greece as "The Matron of Ephesus," used by Petronius in *The Golden Ass*, and later re-created by La Fontaine. It was the story of a widow seduced by a soldier while keeping vigil at her husband's tomb. In *Candide* Voltaire still indulged in philosophy while allowing his hero to be involved in earthquakes, murder, rape, and all manner of other troubles. Much of his philosophizing in this book was done by Candide's tutor, Pangloss, described as a "professor of metaphysicotheologicocosmolonigology." As to what exactly this meant, perhaps the best clue comes when seventeen-year-old Cunégonde, daughter of the house, while walking in a park sees Dr. Pangloss in the bushes, giving a "lesson in experimental physics to her mother's chambermaid." What Miss Cunégonde sees filled her with a desire to experiment herself, which later she does with Candide.

WILDE, OSCAR FINGAL O'FLAHERTIE WILLS
Born 1854. Died 1900.

The second son of an Irish surgeon, Sir William Wilde, and his wife, the poetess Jane Francesca "Speranza" Elgee, Oscar Wilde was born in Dublin, where, at Trinity College, he displayed considerable talents at an early age. He went on to Magdalen College, Oxford, where he won the Newdigate Prize for his poem, "Ravenna." He was a brilliant wit, a master of the epigram and had all-round literary talents from poetry to drama, but he was also an eccentric and a Bohemian who made pleasure his aim in life, and his campaign of "art for art's sake" caused many critics to regard him as a buffoon. He made a great success with his lecture tours of America and received a good deal of publicity for the remark he made at customs when he arrived in the USA: "I have nothing to declare but my own genius!"

His inclusion in this guide is mainly justified by his play, *Salomé* (1893), which was refused a license by the Lord Chamberlain. As a result it was rewritten in French and performed in Paris in 1894. It was largely on account of its biblical background that *Salomé* was refused a license in Britain. Nevertheless the play is steeped in colorful eroticism and sensuality, especially in the temptation of Jokanaan the Prophet by Salomé and the *Dance of the Seven Veils:*

> Jokanaan, I am amorous of thy body. Thy body is white like the lilies of a field that the mower hath never mowed. Thy body is white like the snows that lie on the mountains. . . . The roses in the garden of the Queen of Arabia are not so white as thy body. . . . Let me touch thy body. . . . Thy mouth is redder than the feet of those who tread the wine in the wine press. . . . Thy mouth is like a branch of coral that fishers have found in the twilight of the sea, the coral that they keep for the kings! . . . There is nothing in the world so red as thy mouth . . . Suffer me to kiss thy mouth.

Then, later, when at Salomé's request the head of the dead Jokanaan is brought to her on a shield, she cries: "Ah! Thou wouldst not suffer me to kiss thy mouth, Jokanaan. Well, I will kiss it now. I will bite it with my teeth as one bites a ripe fruit."

In 1895 Wilde instituted an action against the marquis of Queensberry for libel, but the evidence that Queensberry produced in court concerning Wilde's homosexual behavior with boys was so overwhelming that the poet was immediately arrested and tried. In those days the laws on homosexuality were stringent in the United Kingdom and Wilde was sentenced to two years' imprisonment with hard labor. He was harshly treated by his wife, who insisted on changing her name and that of her son from Wilde to Holland, as well as by friends and by the authorities, who withdrew his plays from theaters where they had previously been performed. His few remaining years were spent in relative poverty in exile in Paris, where he was buried in the Père La Chaise cemetery. He is still highly regarded in various European countries for his poems and especially his essays, while his play, *The Importance of Being Ernest,* is perhaps the one classical farce in the English language.

One alleged work of Wilde's is in the British Museum Library's erotica private case section. This is *Teleny; or, The Reverse of the Medal,* said to have been written in 1893. It has been described by Leonard Smithers, a highly literate undergound publisher of the day, as "undoubtedly the most powerful and cleverly written erotic romance which has appeared in recent years." He should have explained, however, that it is a homosexual novel. It appeared briefly in 1901 under the auspices of Charles Carrington, a publisher of many translations of erotic work. In 1966 the work was published in London, with an introduction by the late H. Montgomery Hyde, and an unexpurgated edition also appeared in California in 1968. But it is only attributable to Wilde and there is as yet no confirmation of this fact.

WILKES, JOHN
Born 1727. Died 1797.

John Wilkes was one of the most remarkable and underestimated men of his age. History has not been kind to him and there is still a tendency to lay far too much stress on his licentious private life and too little on his political ability. Educated at Leyden University, Wilkes, the son of a London distiller, rejected his Calvinist upbringing and became a confirmed agnostic. As member of Parliament for Aylesbury he was launched into British politics under the banner of the Temple-Pitt faction of the Whigs. He was a close friend of Sir Francis Dashwood, chancellor of the Exchequer, and as a result became a member of Dashwood's secret society, named the Knights of St. Francis of Wycombe, but known by outsiders as the Hell-Fire Club. Members used to meet for drinking bouts and wild parties in the caves under West Wycombe Hill, close to Dashwood's estate.

However, Wilkes did not care for all the members of this secret society: in particular he made an enemy of the fourth earl of Sandwich, then First Lord of the Admiralty. It is said that Wilkes was expelled from the society in 1763 on account of a prank he played by letting loose a baboon in a black robe with horns placed on its head during one of the society's parties in the caves. This is, however, by no means certain as Wilkes's marginalia in his own personal copy of *The History of the Late Ministry* suggests otherwise. About this time Wilkes disagreed with the foreign policy of the British government and attacked it in speeches and pamphlets. In June 1762, he founded *The North Briton,* a paper that existed for the sole purpose of satirizing the government. This paper was suppressed for a seditious libel and Wilkes was arrested. Though he was discharged by the judges on the grounds of privilege as a member of Parliament, in the autumn of the same year he was expelled from the House of Commons for printing (even though it was done privately) an "impious libel" entitled *An Essay on Women*. This resulted in his being out-lawed for some years during which he lived in France and Italy.

From a printer named Michael Curry, who had done some work privately for Wilkes, came a single copy of *An Essay on Women* that was received by a clergyman named Kidgell who passed it on to the authorities. There must be at least a score of versions of this work in existence, some of them palpable forgeries. The manuscript of a poem of the same title as that of Wilkes's work is in the British Library's Manuscripts Department. It was printed under Wilkes's name during his lifetime, but some literary experts deny that it is his work. The manuscript opens thus:

> Awake, my Sandwich, learn all meaner joys
> To Charles and Bob and those true poetic boys.
> Let us, since life can little more supply,
> Then just to kiss, to procreate and die.

"Charles and Bob" is an obvious reference to Charles Churchill and Robert Lloyd, both members of the Knights of St. Francis of Wycombe. Continuing in much the same vein, the *Essay* speaks of:

> The grasp divine, th'emphatic, thrilling squeeze,
> The throbbing, panting breasts and trembling knees
> The tickling motion, the enlivening flow,
> The rapturous shiver and dissolving—Oh!

One could hardly call this pornographic or a subject for prosecution. Various alleged "genuine copies" of the *Essay* have been published from time to time, including one printed in Paris and sold as a pamphlet in 1773 and translated in London ten years later. It included this jingle:

> The King was in his counting house, counting up his wealth;
> The Queen was in her boudoir, playing with herself.
> Poor Wilkes he was in Paris, solaced by Corradini,
> While Despencer down at Medenham languished *in limine*.

"Despencer" refers to Sir Francis Dashwood (he was also Baron Le Despencer) and "Corradini" was WIlkes's mistress in Paris. "*In limine*" was an eighteenth-century Latin phrase for the entrance to the womb.

There are grounds for believing that Wilkes's *Essay* was revised by the poet, Paul Whitehead, whose amendments must have been a delightful potpourri of the sublime and the salacious, for Whitehead could not portray a whore without making her seem a virgin. It was also suggested that the *Essay* had originally been intended solely for the delectation of members of the Order of "Saint" Francis. There was a rumor that *An Essay on Women* was dedicated to a celebrated courtesan named Fanny Murray who had been Lord Sandwich's mistress. One copy of the work, which is in the Dyce Library at South Kensington in London begins with the words "Awake my Fanny" instead of "Awake my Sandwich." Even in the eighteenth century cordials for women (mostly laced with cheap gin) had for years been sold under fanciful titles. Suddenly such names appeared as "Fanny Murray's Pick-me-up," "Fanny Murray's Nettle Juice," and "Gin and Fanny Sandwich."

In 1768 Wilkes returned to London in defiance of his outlawry and was elected member of Parliament for Middlesex. He was again expelled from the House of Commons and imprisoned for two years. But, volatile and undismayed, he fought his way back into public life. On his release from prison he championed the city of London in its contests with Court and Parliament, was elected lord mayor and upheld the power of the law during the Gordon Riots. Old antagonisms faded and in 1774 he was reelected to represent Middlesex and he remained a member of Parliament until his retirement in 1790.

Wilkes wrote several numbers of a periodical known as the *Monitor* between numbers 340 and 380 and the first forty-six numbers of the *North Briton*. Collections of his *Letters* were published in 1804 and 1805 and of his speeches in 1777 and 1786. An *Essay on Women* remains in the British Library. See also *The Extraordinary Mr. Wilkes: His Life and Times*, Louis Kronenburger, London, 1974.

WILMOT, JOHN (EARL OF ROCHESTER)
Born 1647. Died 1680.

The second earl of Rochester, John Wilmot became one of the poet favorites at the court of King Charles II and his taste for the erotic, and sometimes the obscene as well, was in many ways a reaction against the severe restrictions of the puritanical regime under Oliver Cromwell. He not only had great talent, but he was also the patron of many other writers of his day, including Dryden and Otway. One of his works, *Farce of Sodom*, dealt with the various amorous imbroglios at the court in his time. He was educated at Wadham College, Oxford, and eventually became ranger of Woodstock Forest. It was at Woodstock that he died and he was buried in Spelsbury. For a short period in 1665 he was imprisoned in the Tower of London by Charles II for abducting the heiress, Elizabeth Malet, who later became his wife. He was also the author of *A Satire against Mankind* (1675). A fairly complete edition of his *Poetical Works* was published in London in two volumes in 1731–32.

In the Victoria and Albert Museum in London are to be found in manuscript form two volumes of *The Earle of Rochester's Verses for Which He Was Banned*. These are often crude in the extreme as the titles of some of the poems suggest—"One Writing against His Prick" and "Description of Maidenhead." In the bawdy *Farce of Sodom*, a play that was acted before King Charles II, Wilmot introduced characters with such names as Buggermaster General, Queen Cuntigratia, King Boloximian. The last-named king of Sodom declares: "My laws shall act more pleasure than command, / And with my Prick I'll govern all the land."

WILSON, EDMUND
Born 1895. Died 1972.

The son of a lawyer and politician, Edmund Wilson was born in Red Bank, New Jersey, and was educated at Princeton University, where he graduated in 1916. After a brief spell as a reporter on the *New York Sun* he served as an enlisted soldier at a base hospital in France in World War I and later in the Intelligence Corps of the United States Army. On being demobilized he became managing editor of *Vanity Fair* from 1920–21, after which he settled down to write plays, poetry, and various critical works.

His book, *Memoirs of Hecate County*, New York, 1946, was banned by the Court of Special Sessions as being obscene. Reviewers pointed out that the volume contained some outstandingly distinguished short stories and that it was only one highly erotic story that had given the book notoriety.

For a while Wilson declared himself to be a Communist, but later he became disillusioned with this creed and turned away from it. He married four times, his third wife being the writer Mary McCarthy, author of *The Company She Keeps* (1942), which also acquired a certain notoriety. Wilson's other work includes such plays as *The Crime in the Whistler Room* and *This Room, This Gin, and These Sandwiches* (he was ever one to choose unusual titles), and *The Little Blue Light*. *Notebooks of Night* (verse) appeared in 1942 and he spent several years researching for his work *The Dead Sea Scrolls*.

YAMADA, AMY (MRS. AMY DOUGLAS)
Born 1959.

At the age of thirty-six Amy Yamada startled literary circles in Japan and elsewhere with her book, *Bedtime Eyes*, New York (1985). This revealed in explicit and frank terms a relationship between a young Japanese woman and a black American soldier. It was a story based in part at least on her own observations while visiting American military bases in Japan, when she was— to quote her own words—"a black music freak." Ada Yamada in describing those days says: "Books by black authors were the only things I was reading in those days. Through jazz I got interested in popular black music."

Amy Yamada lives on the western outskirts of Tokyo near to the U..S. military base of Yokota. Her husband, Craig R. Douglas, works at the base. They were married in New York in 1990. Since *Bedtime Eyes*, which apart from being a best-seller was made into a feature film, she has written more than twenty books and won both the Bungei Prize and the Naoki Prize for her works. A notable short story of hers, "Kneel down and Kiss My Feet," has been included in the Kodansha International Anthology, *Monkey Brain Sushi*, published in Tokyo, 1991. She stresses that she would like people to understand that "I write about blacks not because it makes for sensational stories, but because they are very much part of my life. . . . I think my values are very different from those of a lot of people. In my novel, *Chewing Gum*, there's a phrase that goes: 'I like teardrops that look like jewels more than real jewels.' I mean that and I found a man who understands that."

YU, LI
Born 1610. Died 1680.

Li Yu was one of the most distinguished Chinese writers of the seventeenth century as novelist, short-story writer, playwright, and critic. He was a master of what can only be described, his English translator says, as "comic invention." He himself put it this way: "Everything I have ever written was intended to make people laugh." His first play, *Lianxiang* (Women in love), took the very rare theme in Chinese literature of a love affair between two women. Eventually the women were united as wives to the same man. Later Li Yu described a love affair between two men in *Wusheng xi* (Silent operas).

Yu was a designer and inventor as well as a writer. He lived in a period when the erotic novel and play were at their peak of popularity in China. In 1657 he published what has become a classic of Chinese erotic literature, *Rou Putuan* (the carnal prayer mat). It tells the story of how, before he takes his monastic vows, the scholar Vesperus, student of Zen, seeks enlightenment on "the carnal prayer mat," devoting his whole life to sexual exploration and amorous adventures. It is, however, the comic spirit of the work that predominates. There is the passage in the book where Vesperus and Jade Scent, possibly in need of instruction in the variety of ways of making love,

> got up and dressed and then looked at the erotic album again until they became excited and had sex once more. From that day forward they were perfectly adjusted and more deeply in love than ever. After looking at the erotic pictures, Jade Scent was converted from puritanism to libertinism. When making love at night, far from practicing the Doctrine of the Mean she favored the novel and exotic. She was quite amenable to Dousing the Candle and Fetching the Fire from the Other Side of the Mountain, and so insistent was she on putting her tiny feet over her husband's shoulders that next morning he had to exert Herculean efforts to get them down again.

Li Yu makes much of the subject of erotic pictures as a means of sex education. Some of the titles of these pictures are comical enough: "The Releasing of the Butterfly in Search of Fragrance Position" and "The Lost Bird Returns to the Wood" position. *Carnal Prayer Book* has been banned inside China from time to time over the centuries. The fullest text of the work is preserved in the Institute of Oriental Culture of Tokyo University. The Harvard-Yenching Library at Harvard University has two copies of the fullest printed edition. In 1990 Professor Patrick Hanan of Harvard University translated this work into English. He is also the author of a study of Li Yu in his book, *The Invention of Li Yu*, Harvard, 1988.

ZOLA, ÉMILE
Born 1840. Died 1902.

Zola was the supreme enemy of hypocrisy and double standards, frequently putting himself at risk by his talent for uncovering such facts. Born in Paris, he started writing early on, publishing his first work, *Contes à Ninon* at the age of twenty-four. He also wrote various papers on literature and art, particularly attacking the censorship of explicit sexuality in paintings when eroticism was deliberately hidden. Zola considered such paintings to be false and illusory on the grounds that in effect they heightened their erotic influence. What Zola had in mind was the portrayal of nudes in the guise of angels or in paintings that were given a veneer of religious atmosphere. In this connection it is worth noting the comments of Lord Clark of Saltwood in his work, *The Nude*, London & New York, 1956: "All good nude painting and sculpture is sexually stimulating. . . . No nude should fail to arouse in the spectator some vestige of erotic feeling. . . . If it does not do so, it is bad art or false morals."

Zola's most powerful novel was undoubtedly *Thérèse Raquin* (1867). This was followed by his series of books detailing what he called *Les Chronicles* of the Rougon-Macquart family (1871–75) and *L'Assommoir*, a powerful novel depicting the horrors of alcoholism in the most realistic and lurid style. In *Nana* (1880) he applied his realistic style to detailing the life of a prostitute on the streets of Paris, tracing the story of Nana from when as a girl of fifteen she lured men behind the dark corners of the outer boulevards to her later days when she walked the principal boulevards and the heights of Montmartre, finding the so-called gentlemen frequently more brutal and filthy-minded than the average worker. He also touched on an erotic theme in *Germinal* (1885). Zola's passion for supporting just if not always popular causes did not help his career. More than once he was recommended as a candidate for a seat in the French Academy, but he was never successful. His attacks on the claims of miracle working at Lourdes and elsewhere did not endear him to many, while he suffered so severely from his campaign to restore the good name of Captain Dreyfus that for a while he had to seek sanctuary in London.

PART THREE

. . . .

7

A Final Look at the Art

O ne aim in this *Connoisseur's Guide* has been to include as many different examples of erotic literature as possible to enable the reader to make individual decisions as to which of these might be followed and studied.

It must be stressed that individual judgment is vital in a genre of this kind. Indeed, it might be right to say that there is not just one genre, but at least half a dozen. One must also realize that a great deal of erotic literature in the world is still either hidden away, or has not yet been brought to light. In other words, there is ample scope for a great deal more study, or detective work, in this type of literature.

There has always been a considerable amount of anonymous authorship of erotic work, but it should be stressed that this trend is as evident today as ever it was in the past. Diligent studies of many modern works have shown that it is far from easy to track down the identity of some of these modern authors. Not only do they use pseudonyms, but their true identities are very carefully hidden for one reason or another. Because of this many such writers are not included here in the A–Z section of biographies. It is only right, therefore, that some reference to these authors should be made in this final chapter.

It is necessary to pay tribute to some of the smaller publishing houses in the Western world that, in early days at least, against heavy odds, gradually made some splendid erotic works available to the public at a time when the vast majority of Western publishers would not handle them. True, such publishers very often had to publish pornography to supplement such experiments in order to keep themselves afloat, and were heavily criticized for doing so.

Who were these pioneering firms of today? Who among them still exists? First and foremost there was Maurice Girodias's the Paris Olympia Press, created on the model of the Obelisk Press, which was the brainchild of his Manchester-born English father, Jack Kahane. The story of that experiment has been told by Patrick J. Kearney in his book, *The Paris Olympia Press*.[1] "It may be said that Maurice Girodias cushioned himself to some extent by publishing English books in France," admits Kearney, but, as he points out, "even in Paris he [Girodias] was far from secure."

Later the Olympia Press published in New York, and, of course, in the meantime imitators of Girodias sprang up all over the place, such as the Opera, Oceanic, Pall Mall Presses, the Armor Publishing Company, and Patrick Garnot's Unique Continental Collection. There was also the Luxor Press, whose books werre published between 1963 and 1975; many of these were erotic classics, others were studies in sexology. Some of the titles of the books were unusual, to say the least. One was *Armand Coppens: The Memoirs of an Erotic Bookseller* (1969), which claimed to be the story of this bookseller's "numerous encounters and experiences with people whose lives are as bizarre, perverse and promiscuous as those of the characters in the books he sells." Yet another (this time published by the Canova Press) was *The Age of Perversion*, by Jason Douglas, described in its blurb as "a period piece of the swinging and kinky sixties."

While the operations of such small publishing houses undoubtedly brought to the force such writers as Joyce, Nabokov, Beckett, Henry Miller, and other writers of repute, some of them gave erotic literature a bad name by the blatant pornography they turned out. It was perhaps inevitable that once a more tolerant era for literature was introduced, standards would deteriorate. A vast amount of some of the new publications never arose above the level of pornography. Then one has to remember that Girodias described himself and his authors as "a family of vagrants trying to survive in postwar Paris."[2]

It was in 1964 that the Freedom of Speech Movement was launched at the University of California at Berkeley. That there was a need for such a movement had long been evident as far as literature was concerned. Yet while a number of first-class writers were either rejected or prosecuted for having had their books published, a great deal of inferior material was printed with hardly a murmur. One such example was *Peyton Place*, by Grace Metalious, first published in 1957, which one critic claimed was "addicted to a strident and ultimately risible vulgarity that infects much of what she wrote." At the same time there were many attempts to resurrect the works of the Marquis de Sade, Leopold von Sacher-Masoch, and others who concentrated on exploiting a mixture of sex and violence, not least of such works of the underground presses of the nineteenth century as *Experiences of Flagellation: Remarkable Instances of Whipping Inflicted on Both Sexes with Curious Anecdotes of Ladies Fond of Administering Birch Discipline.* This resurrected nonsense was written anonymously, having been originally published privately in London in 1885.

Many of the modern novels of erotic substance are still published anonymously, or under pseudonyms. It is not always possible to identify the pseudonyms because in some cases false trails are laid either by author or publisher. This charge has even been made against the late Maurice Girodias: it has been alleged that he gave misleading information about the identity of some of his pseudonymous writers.

Among such authors are Pauline Réage (Dominique Aury), who wrote *Histoire d'O*, later translated as *The Story of O* by Baird and Denny Bryant, with an essay by Jean Paulhan, Paris, 1954. This work, with the addition of a note on it by André Pieyre de Mandiargues, was later published in New York in 1965. Here again is a case of eroticism being marred by "O's" masochism, as the following quotation from it will show:

> Thus he would possess her as a god possesses his creatures whereupon he lays hands guised [sic] as some monster or bird, as some invisible spirit or as very ecstasy. . . . The more he subjected her to, the more important to him she would become. The fact that he gave her to others was proof thereof; proof in his eyes, it ought to be proof in hers, that she belonged to him. He gave her so as to have her immediately back, and recovered her enriched a hundredfold in his eyes, as is an ordinary object that has served some divine purpose and thereby become infused with sanctity.[3]

Sometimes a pseudonym has been used by a number of writers. That of "Marcus Van Heller" was used on thirty occasions, with twelve titles appearing in Paris over a period of some years and no less than eighteen in New York. Patrick Kearney states: "Needless to say, they were not all written by the same pen. Of the twelve Paris novels, however, the first eight were written by John Stevenson." These last books included *Nightmare* (1960), *Adam and Eve* (1961), and *With Open Mouth* (1956). Much of Van Heller's prose is so blatantly crude that it does not add up to anything truly erotic. There is no doubt that, though Girodias and one or two other bold publishers regarded the quality of writing as important, commercial pressures sometimes forced them and certainly others to overload the market with too many books that fell far below satisfactory standards.

Another author using a pseudonym was Norman Rubington, who wrote under the improbable name of "Akbar del Piombo." His work included *L'Anti-came, ou les Aventures de Sir Edwin*, Paris, 1960, later published in New York as *Fuzz against Junk*, and *The Fetish Crowd: A Trilogy*, Paris, 1965, a book that included three bawdy and explicit novels in one volume, their titles being *Who Pushed Paula?*, *Cosimo's Wife, and The Traveller's Companion*. Some idea of how authors stretched their imagination for themes on which to spin supposedly erotic stories may be gleaned from the fact that in 1962 the Olympia Press published *The Sexual Life of Robinson Crusoe* by Humphrey Richardson (real name Michel Gall). This was supposed to be a picture of Crusoe's life on a deserted island with only his Man Friday and animals for company.

There was a reaction during this period on the part of women writers who objected to men's domination of this kind of a market. It is true that there were some females whose work of this sort was published by the Olympia Press, not only Pauline Réage, but Harriet Daimler and Angela Pearson.[4] Also it is noteworthy that Girodias published Valerie Solanas's *The SCUM Manifesto* in the 1960s: this referred to the Society for the Cutting Up of Men. But it was not until the late 1970s and 1980s that women began to enter the field of modern erotic literature in increased numbers. Prior to this they had either had to adopt pseudonyms to protect themselves not only from virulent critics, but to avoid ostracization. It had not only been writers such as Radclyffe Hall who had been victimized, but such female authors as Norah Cordner James (1900–1979). Her first novel, *Sheeveless Errand* (1929), was published in the USA and other countries, but was ruthlessly suppressed in Britain. Shops containing it were raided. Later an expurgated edition was published. Nobody seems quite sure today why it was censored, but the theory is that the objection was to one single word in the book!

Significantly, the new school of female writers touching on erotic themes made it clear that they had a desire to teach as well as to tell a story. One female critic of Erica Jong's *Any Woman's Blues* made the surprising comment: "In the wake of the feminist movement a real threat emerged: women stepped into the male arena and wrote about sex."[5]

In the 1920s and 1930s it was, of course, the men who tried to write erotic novels and preach at the same time. Yet neither Samuel Beckett, James Joyce, nor D. H. Lawrence succeeded in satisfactorily achieving this. No doubt the modern female author took note of this failure. Frieda Weekely, the German wife of a Nottingham University professor with whom Lawrence eloped and later married, may have been in his opinion "my woman of a lifetime." but she saw him as "missionary work," someone who "needed rescuing from his own dividedness between spirit and flesh."[6]

William Scammell has summed up Lawrence as well as anyone, calling him "a preacher *manqué*" like Joyce (though they hailed from opposite ends of the religious spectrum).[7] Lawrence thought on occasion that he was taking up the cudgel on behalf of women: in a letter he declared that one of his aims as a writer was "to do my work for women better than the suffrage." That may sound surprising to some of today's shrill feminists who regard him as the worst type of chauvinist pig.

The men who yearned to teach and preach, like James, Beckett, Joyce, Lawrence, and even Erskine Caldwell and Henry Miller on occasions, often spoiled the erotic touch in their writings by doing too much teaching. If they failed, it was partly because their messages were often confused. It may well be that this role will in the future be undertaken, possibly much more effectively, by female writers. It must be said that when it comes to such teaching the women get down to the nitty-gritty of the argument far more directly than the men. Such writers as Simone de Beauvoir in nonfiction paved the way, and they have been followed more recently by novelists such as Anne Cumming, Ann Oakley, and even Katia Spiegelman and Jaci Stephen. These have taken the feminine approach to erotic literature much further even than Erica Jong (see A–Z section for CUMMING, ANNE, and OAKLEY, ANN). Katia Spiegelman both in *Peculiar Politics* and *Soul Catcher* has shown a real talent in this direction. In her poignant book, *Soul Catcher*, London, 1989, she told the tale of Kate Steiner, an innocent fifteen-year-old who suddenly finds herself at boarding school, where she is initiated into the conflicting values and moral confusion of the age.

Miss Jaci Stephen is somewhat different. She writes quite frequently about sex, notably in the London magazine, the *New Statesman*, has actually offended the susceptibilities of her feminist readers according to the editor, Steven Platt, who says that during the seven years she has worked for the magazine he has been bombarded with complaints about her from females. The result has been that readers have been invited to give their opinion as to whether she should stay or go.

Switching to another kind of query altogether, but certainly one likely to be raised again and again, judging from today's output of books, is the question of whether the word processor is hampering or stultifying some of today's literary erotica. Harold Brodkey is said to have spent twenty-five years on the writing of his first novel, *The Runaway Soul*, London, 1991. This tells the story of a Jewish boy growing up in St. Louis in the 1940s and becoming some kind of "famous writer" in the next decade. The book tells of his sexual awakening and the reader is taken through his life from schoolboy masturbation (why do so many modern writers have to delve so far back when writing erotic novels?), homosexual experiments, to arousal at fifteen by an older girl and on to the day when he acquired a mistress. David Holloway, the literary editor of the London *Daily Telegraph*, when reviewing this book, raised the query about word processors:

> Particularly during the night of adult passion, I was yearning to yell at Wiley [the book's hero] and his lady to stop talking and get on with it. Yet it would have been futile, for all the while they *were* getting on with it—on the bed, off the bed and half on the bed. This novel seems to me the ultimate casualty of the word processor.

Every day, one imagines, Brodkey summoned up his text on the screen and inserted bits—an extra half-dozen adjectives here, a patch of italics there, and endless afterthoughts. Adding, adding, but never taking enough away.

One thing that does seem certain is that there are no longer any writers on love techniques to compare with Nefzawi and other splendid Arab and Indian composers of love manuals, nor of the somewhat less didactic but totally charming "pillow books" of the Japanese and word charmers of the Chinese. Today the emphasis is much more on psychological understanding and self-analysis. Some of the new school of such writers seem essentially commercially minded, such as Miss Tuppy Owens's various works, *The Safer Sex Maniac's Bible*, London, 1989, *Two Girls and You*, and *Take Me, I'm Yours*, this last named said to be "a unique guide to the seduction of women." As for *The Safer Sex Maniac's Bible*, the author has claimed that it gives "the background and way forward to understand and find all kinds of eroticism. . . . You can take the appropriate section wherever you are going anywhere in the world to make sure you find the places that are sizzling." What exactly, one might ask, does the author mean by "sizzling"? The reader may well think this sounds very much like stepping into the maze of erotica once again.

Yet another of such works is *Twelve Steps to Heaven*, described as "a woman's first impression of sex." Rather more interesting, however, are those writers who try to combine eroticism, alternative medicine, and, occasionally, the paranormal. Here is a path that, if cautiously and seriously followed in a disciplined fashion, might lead to something new and worthwhile. One must remember that Flaubert gave us the idea of wearing a mask in amatory affairs. Apparently he influenced Jules de Gaultier so much that he adopted a process of "Bovarysm" by which one must impose a more or less fictitious personality upon oneself, and do one's best to act the imaginary part consistently, whatever may be the real state of one's psychology. *Sexual Secrets*, London, 1991, by Nik Douglas and Penny Slinger, touched upon some of the sexual secrets and what the authors call "mysteries" of the East with various "secrets of inducing and maximizing the experience of ecstasy." Another intriguing work is Margo Anand's *The Art of Sexual Ecstasy* that almost guides one into the sphere of meditation and alternative medicine for enhancing sex life. Not perhaps a classic, it can usefully be considered within the terms of exploring erotic literature. At least this book stresses that "sexual pleasure is a delight of the heart, an ecstasy of the spirit." Margo Anand's suggested techniques in lovemaking range from massage, visualization, breathing exercises, and what she calls "ritual and movement to enhance pleasure and deepen intimacy."

Yet another of the new female teachers of erotic arts is Dolores Ashcroft-Nowicki, who has devoted her life to a study of esoteric arts generally. Her work, *Tree Ecstasy*, London, 1990, tells how sexual energies can be used for self-healing and why sex and religion are, in her opinion, inextricably mixed. Here the author reminds us that many writers of erotic works over the centuries have been priests, monks, bishops, and sometimes even cardinals.

It may well be that in this age of stress and tension as unavoidable occurrences of daily life such writers will point us in new directions and, in doing so, bring back something of the more relaxed and spiritual eroticism of past ages. Recent study of Tantrism and Reichianism, not only in universities around the world but in various groups of people, suggest that sometime in the near future these two cults may be merged and result in a new type of erotic novel. Tantrism is one aspect of ancient Indian religion that has attracted interest in the Western world today. The Tantra cult aims at creating ecstasy by means of inflating one's inner sexual energy; it involves meditation, a special kind of yoga, and various rituals. Reichianism, which gets its name from Wilhelm Reich (1897–1957), is in some ways a modern form of Tantrism. Reich, who started life as a psychoanalyst in Vienna and a disciple of Freud, soon turned away from what he regarded as the negativism of his mentor. In its place he invented what he called "orgone philosophy." His book, *The Function of the Orgasm*,[8] angered the puritanical Freud and Reich left Vienna first for Berlin, then for Norway and Sweden, and finally for America. Here, in a place he called Orgonon, he set up his own laboratories and research center into the science of what he called *orgone* or *life energy*. He believed that he could develop an orgone energy accumulator that would help people in their sex lives. However, the authorities regarded his experiments as dangerous and in 1954 he was arrested after what he alleged had been "a long conspiracy to defame and discredit me."

Though Reich is long since dead, his theories have been taken up by some self-styled amatory therapists. One of his students, Alexander Lowen, developed the theory of *psychomanipulation*, or *bioenergetics*. In a book he published in USA in 1958, *Physical Dynamics of Character Structure*, Lowen propounded the theme that where orthodox psychoanalysis was inadequate, there was a failure to recognize the need to release physical as well as emotional tension: it was essential, he argued, to "learn the language of the body," which was the title he gave to his book when it was reissued in paperback.

This may be some way off the subject of erotic literature, but people like Reich, Lowen, the Maharishi Mahesh Yogi, and others of today who have written on Tantric philosophy, transcendental meditation, and similar cults have all, either directly or indirectly, contributed to new teachings on sexual matters. Looking to the future, it may well be that eventually novels, plays, and even poetry may develop a new form of eroticism out of such cults.

To support what must seem to some readers as a digression from the main subject, I should like to quote from a letter I have received from a female

author who is planning a novel that she says is "based on Reichian theories."
I am not permitted to give her name, but this is what she has written to me:

> In the Reichian philosophy a therapy session provides a space for
> the safe discharge of emotions. Breathing plays an important role in
> this. The release of such emotions results in more energy and more
> relaxed breathing. Reich's theory is that this relaxed state aids better
> concentration and can be most positively applied to one's sexual
> life. Orgone energy is a natural energy that is present in the atmo-
> sphere that can be trapped. Reich made a trap for it in the form of
> a large box, his orgone accumulator, the sides of which were layered
> with wool and steel. It has been claimed that it can cure such
> diseases as cancer. People who have sampled the orgone box have
> described the following sensations—warmth all over, a feeling of
> aliveness and radiance and a quite astonishing sexual awakening.
> The whole subject lends itself to a new kind of erotic writing.

So maybe one day soon we shall hear of a book called *The Magic of the
Orgone Box* or *A Tantric Miracle*.

In Britain the abolition of the outdated system of submitting plays to the
lord chamberlain before they could be performed has improved the prospects
for would-be dramatists. What is astonishing is the way in which in the past
the lord chamberlain would veto many innocuous plays simply because he
objected to a few lines of dialogue. In 1912 Eden Phillpots had his play, *The
Secret Woman*, banned, despite the fact that it was merely the adaptation of
a novel of the same title that he had published in 1904. Nobody had objected
to the book that was only mildly erotic. There were many similar instances.

Rather more surprising (though in this case the lord chamberlain cannot
be blamed) was the news in November 1991 that forty-one years after his
death George Bernard Shaw was to have the complete version of his play,
The Philanderer, performed onstage at the Hampstead Theatre, London. In
advance of this performance it was stated that Shaw wrote this play in 1893
when he was only thirty-seven and that the hero of the title was based on
himself. Up to 1991 the rare stage productions of *The Philanderer* had always
been of a revised text. The last act of the play had been censored by Shaw
himself and had never previously been seen. The story behind all this was
that Shaw's friend, Lady Colin Campbell, to whom Shaw first read the play,
advised him to throw the last act into the fire. She had been through the
divorce courts and was an experienced judge of public opinion and morality
at that time. She thought that the play's comic assault on the imprisonment
of wedlock and the expediency of divorce was far too advanced for the 1890s.

Shaw, who was anxious to have the play produced at all costs, reluctantly
accepted her advice. However, instead of burning the last act, he simply

rewrote it, and long afterwards the act in question found its way into the British Museum where it lay unread and unpublished for years. The revised play was never a success on the stage even though Shaw hinted that the act he had omitted was "a combination of mechanical farce with realistic filth which disgusted me." Many years later he changed his view and said that it would not "shock a convent in Connemara these days."

When the original play was finally performed at the Hampstead Theatre critics were almost united in saying that while *The Philanderer* retained "its capacity to entertain and provoke," it was "unlikely that anyone today will find the piece unspeakably improper."[9]

This poses the question as to whether Shaw's real reason for taking out his final act was a different one altogether from what he said at the time. For the play in effect gives a fascinating picture of Shaw himself as "the Philanderer" and in the London production, as a reviewer mentioned, "With his beard and Irish accent, Clive Owen leaves no doubt that Charteris is a portrait of the dramatist as a young man."[10]

The original version of *The Philanderer* with that missing fourth act included is undoubtedly an improvement on Shaw's personally censored play. The latter seems almost stilted in comparison with this livelier and more realistic production. The narrative, more unpleasant in character than erotic, finds the philanderer scheming to palm off a girlfriend on to a Mayfair doctor in order to leave himself free to carry on a liaison with a "new woman." In retrospect it rather looks as though Shaw suddenly became disgusted with his own philandering hero.

One cannot help feeling that with further diligent research many other previously censored plays could be beneficially revived. In trying to appreciate this play one has to bear in mind that Shaw once wrote: "What people call love is impossible save as a joke between two strangers meeting accidentally in an inn or a forest."[11]

It is surely significant that in the 1990s there are still rather more erotic works of the past printed and sold than of modern books of this kind. Not only new publications of ancient love treatises, but translations in modern language of works by the ancient Japanese and Chinese. Somehow there could be a lesson in this: certainly it suggests that new developments in such literature are needed to satisfy people's needs. Tomorrow's women writers may achieve this and then it will be up to the male writers to learn and digest and find new themes of their own.

In conclusion it is worth mentioning the indisputable fact that in the past quite often a single line of poetry, or a fascinating novel, has inspired somebody's love affair, or drawn two people together. For this reason alone one must hope that the uplifting type of erotic literature will survive. Two instances in support of this theory are worth citing. There is the case of the effect that some verses of a poet who died in 1991 had on one particular female. The poet was the rumbustious George Barker (see BARKER, GEORGE, A–Z section). Elizabeth Smart, the Canadian novelist, decided she wanted to marry him long before they met, making her decision solely on what she had read of his poems. She would ask friends at parties: "Do you know George Barker? If so, I'd like to meet him and marry him." Eventually in 1940 they met and had a celebrated affair together over a lengthy period. Elizabeth Smart told the story of their relationship in her novel, *By Grand Central Station I Sat Down and Wept,* New York and London, 1945.

The second similar case is that of Georgette Leblanc who, in her book, *Maeterlinck and I,* describes how a friend once gave her a copy of Emerson's essays to read. In the Emerson book was a preface by Maeterlinck that Georgette read and reread. "By morning," she says, though she had not seen the celebrated author of *Blue Bird,* "I was sure that in all the universe he was the one man I could love." Shortly afterwards she went to Brussels because she wanted to meet Maeterlinck. Thus can literature sometimes become a guiding light for one's whole life, for that meeting was swiftly followed by a most romantic elopement.

Glossary of Erotic Terms

AGAPEMONITES: A British society of what was called "spiritual brides," set up in the nineteenth century by Henry Prince, a doctor of medicine, at Spaxton in Somerset, England. It was supposed to be an Abode of Love and took its name from the early Christian love feasts. After Prince died and was buried in the gardens of the Agapemone, John Hugh Smyth-Pigott, an ex-curate of the Church of England, became head of the sect, taking the title of the "Heavenly Bridegroom." An imitation of this sect was later set up in the United States of America and named the Agapemone of America, with branches in Arizona, Nebraska, and California.

AKHATAYMITA: The ancient Peruvians carried out a series of erotic festivals each year that ranged from that of Vestal Virgins and Virgins of the Sun, marked by a sacred fire lit at the summer solstice to the Akhataymita around which orgies were held.

AMORET: This term has been used to describe a love song, a love affair, and a lover's knot. Thomas Heywood in his work, *Love's Maistresse* (1633), wrote: "He will be in his amorets, and his canzonets, pastorals, and madrigals." The phrase also owes much to the Amoret in Spenser's *The Faerie Queene*, in which Amoret is the twin sister of Belphoebe and both were begotten by the Sun: "pure and unspotted from all loathly crime that is ingenerate in fleshly slime." Spencer later describes Amoret as "Lodestarre of all chaste affection."

ANACREONITIC: This was a phrase given to describe what becomes a cult—anacreonitic verse, named after the Greek poet, Anacreon. The phrase referred to all verses about love and wine. There were many copiers of Anacreon and some verses attributed to him have undoubtedly been composed by others.

ANANDRYNE: This was a lesbian cult founded by Madamoiselle de Fleury in Paris in the eighteenth century. Its president was an actress, Marie Antoinette

Raucourt, who had charge of the cult's priestesses. Her duty was to initiate the novices (known as *Les Désirantes*). The cult's premises were decorated with busts of Sappho and other females along with altars upon which fires burned.

ARCANA: Derived from the Latin word for mystery, Arcana is the code word used in the British Museum's Library for its repository for erotic verse.

ARMOUR: Usually prefixing the words "to fight in," and referring to a condom. (See PEPYS, SAMUEL in A–Z section.)

ATUM-RE: An ancient Egyptian myth relating to the creation of the world refers to the sun-god Atum-Re ("Lord of the Phallus") creating the first couple in the world, Shu and Tefnut, by masturbation.

BRIDAL ROLL: A custom for a newly wed couple to be given a scroll of written instructions on sexual intercourse that they took to bed with them on their marriage night. Pillow books, put under the pillows of each for reference, was an alternative.

BROTHER STARLING: One who stays with the same female.

BUNDLING: A custom now obsolete, at least in the Western world, but which was once practiced in New England in the USA and in Wales in the United Kingdom. Engaged couples were permitted to go to bed together fully dressed to spend the night, the object being for them to get to know each other better without indulging in intercourse. Washington Irving wrote of "stopping occasionally in the village to eat pumpkin pie . . . and bundle with the Yankee lassies." (*See* TROUSER WEEK in glossary.)

BUSSING: Kissing in an erotic manner. It comes from the Latin *basium* and the French *baiser* and usually means the intermingling of tongues while kissing.

CALMETTING (sometimes referred to as CALUMETTING): This is said to have been a Brazilian custom originally, though it has also been much practiced among Indian tribes in North America. Lady Augusta Hamilton in her book, *Marriage Rites*, London, 1822, speaking of the Shawanese Indians near the mouth of the Great Kenhaway River, says that "going a *calumetingus* is a piece of gallantry. . . . As all property is in common, and the doors are open day and night, the lover, taking advantage of this, lights his calumet, enters the cabin of his mistress and presents it to her; if she extinguishes it, she admits him to her arms; if she suffer it to burn unnoticed, he returns disappointed, knowing that while there was light she will not consent to his wishes."

CAREZZA: An ancient and unusual Italian custom that has found its way to other countries. Translated, it means "intercourse without any coital movements whatsoever," and, seemingly, no orgasm. It is claimed by supporters of the custom that it gives deep spiritual satisfaction through sublimation.

"Cherry Case": Erotica kept in the USA Armed Forces Medical Library in Washington is stowed away under this heading.

Chinese Love Tongs: See **Golden Lotus Society.**

Cinaedic Verse: Ancient Greek and also Latin poetry that takes as its themes pederasty and incest as well as other forms of intercourse. The Latin word for this was *cinaedus* and Marcus Valerius Martialis, the Latin poet (circa A.D. 80), sums up the condition of the cinaedic in this verse: *"O quanta scabie miser laborat! Culum non habet, est tamen cinaedus."*

Code of Courtly Love: This was the celebrated code of chivalry among the upper classes in the Middle Ages. It was devoted to patriotism, the Church, fighting the infidel, obeying the feudal overlord, and yet still, with a certain amount of hypocrisy, allowing scope for clandestine love affairs. The troubadours and others who exploited the romantic aspects of chivalry did so with a keen eye on the wives left behind while their husbands were away fighting the Crusades. A lady left in charge of her husband's castle could give hospitality to anyone she chose, and a wandering minstrel was always popular. Hence the constant theme of unrequited love and unfulfilled desire throughout the troubadours' songs. C. S. Lewis in his work, *The Allegory of Love*, Oxford, 1936, sums up the code so closely associated with the troubadours as follows: "The sentiment, of course, is love, but love of a highly specialized sort, whose characteristics may be enumerated as Humility, Courtesy, Adultery and the Religion of Love. The lover is always abject. Obedience to his Lady's lightest wish, however whimsical, and silent acquiescence in her rebukes, however unjust, are the only virtues he dares to claim. . . . He addresses her as *midons*, which etymologically represents not 'my lady,' but 'my Lord.'" A hundred years ago Léon Gautier, a French scholar who had devoted his life to the study of the literature of chivalry, worked out what he described as "The Decalogue, or Ten Commandments" concerning the conduct of a knight. (*See also* The Ten Commandments of Love in this glossary). Andreas Capellanus, a twelfth-century writer produced a manual of courtly love, *De Amore Libri Tres*. (*See* capellanus in the glossary, also chapter 3).

Coffee House: A phrase used in Captain Grose's *Classical Dictionary of the Vulgar Tongue* and described as referring to "prolonged or interrupted coitus."

Cottage Love: This became a popular cult in the latter part of the eighteenth century, largely as a result of the patronage of Queen Marie Antoinette of France. The concept was that of a tiny cottage or pavilion in a forest glade where ladies of the court could dress up as rustics or shepherdesses, and seek the simple and carefree life with a congenial male companion, away from the world of protocol and strict rules of etiquette. It was the custom among these ladies to leave copies of their favorite romantic novels lying around with certain passages underlined, thereby indicating their desires to any quick-witted man. The man's reply could take various forms, sometimes a brief message indicating a rendezvous tucked inside the book, or another book alongside with passages marked, together with a map showing where the rendezvous was to be. This cult was immortalized in *The Happy Hypocrite*, Max Beerbohm, London, 1896.

DECADENT MOVEMENT: The Decadent Movement in the late nineteenth century was to a large extent linked with the cult of Decadent Art that was obsessed with sex. Aubrey Beardsley (*see* in the A–Z section), the Marquis de Bayros, and Mihaly Zichy were among the painters indulging in Decadent Art, and Beardsley and Oscar Wilde counted among writers of the cult. So-called Decadent literature was rather different in that much of its emphasis was on sexuality and death. There was a feeling among some artists and writers of the latter part of the nineteenth century that they were in some way alienated from society and at the same time opposed to the kind of society represented by the Establishment. In the type of erotic writing in which some indulged in this period there was a tendency to create female characters who were sinister and sometimes even satanic rather than idealistic and virtuous. In many respects the Decadent Movement was a reaction against the Church in European countries and against Victorian puritanism and prudery in Britain. (*See* BEARDSLEY, AUBREY and WILDE, OSCAR in the A–Z section.)

"DELTA": This is the code word given to the section containing erotica in the Library of Congress, Washington. It is derived from the Greek symbol for the female organ.

DEMI-VIERGE: Literally, this means "half-virgin" and is referred to by those who indulge in petting—i.e., the kind of sexual relationship in which everything is permitted with the sole exception of penetration. In recent years in America Demi-Vierge became the name of a cult devoted to virgin worship.

EROTIC COLLECTIONS: Most of the major libraries of the world from the Vatican, the British Museum, the Library of Congress, the Bibliothèque Nationale in Paris, the Institut für Sexualvissenschaft in Berlin (said to have been partially destroyed by the Hitler government) and the Institute for Sex Research at Indiana University, have collections of erotic works. There are many other private collections of such works in various universities and organizations.

EROTIOGRAPHOMANIA: The desire to write about, draw, or paint subjects relating to sexual intercourse such as are to be found on doors, walls, trees, and in public lavatories. A book on this subject, *Atropophyteia* by Dr. Friedrich Krauss, was privately printed in Leipzig several years ago.

FACE MAKING: A term sometimes used for coitus, presumably because facial expressions are most marked and evocative in such situations.

FLO BUMTICKLER: A name given to female flagellants in the last century. It originated from the work, *Lady Bumtickler's Revels, a Treatise on the Use of Flogging in Venereal Affairs*, which was one of a series of books published in London in 1872 under the somewhat deceptive title of *The Library Illustrative of Social Progress*. In this period a number of works touching on the subject of flagellation were surreptitiously printed. One female flagellant named Margaret Anson in 1857 wrote her life story entitled *The Merry Order of St. Bridget*, this being the name of a secret club.

FLORAL LANGUAGE: Flowers as symbols of coded love messages have been used all over the world down the ages. In Algiers in the early part of the nineteenth century there was a subtle code in which flowers played a vital part. Lady Augusta Hamilton explained it thus in her book, *Marriage Rites:* "The flower-gentle, placed by a violet, shows that the lover hopes, when the husband is gone away to sea, to meet such a return to his passion as will fully compensate for the evils his presence occasions. The orange flower denotes hope; the marigold despair; the amaranth constancy; the tulip reproaches with being unfaithful; the rose is an encomium of beauty." Bernardin de Saint-Pierre, author of the popular novel, *Paul et Virginie*, built a love cottage on an island near Paris where he lived with the young sister of his publisher, and used a code of flowers for communication. A red rose on the lunch table at his beloved's place was an invitation to spend the afternoon lovemaking, but three white roses indicated a call to milking the cows!

"GARDEN": From the earliest times and certainly among the Greeks there has been a tendency to associate a beautiful woman with the qualities of an attractive garden. The Romans referred to a garden when actually meaning a female. The Roman god Priapus was called the *Cultor Hortorum*, or patron of gardens. The exact meaning of this phrase is evident when one studies a poem entitled "Priapus": "What my garden has, you may take with impunity: if you give us what your garden has."

GOLDEN LOTUS SOCIETY: This was a Chinese tong, or secret society, which took its name from a character named the Golden Lotus in a famous Chinese novel of the sixteenth century written by a Confucian scholar. (*See* chapter 2). The tong, which was highly secretive, existed to propagate the idea that love should be considered the highest form of art. It seems to have kept its correspondence between members in code. Numbers are a vital factor in most

Chinese secret societies and the *Hung* ritual is bound up in them. The numerals between one and ten are divided between the principles of *Yang* and *Yin*, the odd numbers being called "perfect" and the even numbers "imperfect." Numbers were a vital part of this society's secret code, e.g., "Oh, for you to tell me of 0001 and 0002 and to keep whispering such wickedness."

GOVERNESS: This word is used by the Danes as a description for a woman who whips men, or indulges in similarly sadistic practices.

"HELL-HOLE": This is the name given to the repository of erotica in Harvard University Library.

HERMAPHRODITIC CONCEPT: The ancient Greeks had an obsession about the idea of hermaphrodism, the conception of persons with either indeterminate sexual organs or having organs belonging to both sexes. It became a fetish and almost a subject for specialized worship. The word comes from Hermaphroditus, son of Hermes and Aphrodite, who became the hermaphroditic god. This led to the worshiping of a male-female divinity, at which ceremonies men and women wore clothes of the opposite sex. It used to be said that all those who bathed in the Salmacis Fountain in Caria would become hermaphrodites. At the festival of Apodysia, dedicated to the philosopher Leucippus (fifth century B.C.), men wore female clothing and women dressed as men.

HINDU ART OF LOVE: This refers to the erotic Hindu book by Vatsyayana, giving instruction in the techniques that he believed enhanced the whole process of sexual intercourse. The work is described by Ralph Ginzburg as being "generally considered the most beautifully and sensually written sex instructor in the world."

INDORSER: A somewhat obscure term for a pederast.

IRRUMATION: A bizarre form of sexual perversion practices by Greeks and Romans.

KAMA KALPA: An ancient Hindu series of rituals applying to women in love: the equivalent for women of the *Kama Sutra* for men. (*See* chapter 2).

LAMBITUS: Another word for cunnilingus.

L'ENFER: The name given for the repository of erotica in the Bibliothèque Nationale in Paris (otherwise "The Hell Collection"). There is even a book, by one Perceau, entitled *L'Enfer de la Bibliothèque Nationale*.

LUPANARIA: A title given to public brothels.

MASOCHISM: This word, now generally accepted as describing the alleged sexual pleasure a person finds in suffering from pain, particularly by a sexual partner, owes its origin to Leopold von Sacher-Masoch (1835–95), author of *Les Batteuses d'Hommes*, tales of flagellation. His obsession with the subject of self-inflicted pain giving pleasure equally led to the noun *masochist*.

MUCKERS: This was the popular name given to a society founded as the Pietists by Archdeacon Ebel in Germany in 1836. It was based in part on the teachings of Père Enfantin who wanted to found a religion linked to sexual practices. The society referred to members as "brides called by the Lamb," or "spiritual wives," and indulged in "spiritual love feasts." The idea was that a man, whether unmarried or unhappily married, had a "sacred duty" to seek out a "bride of the soul" and that he should have the right of courting her whether she be unmarried or another man's wife. In a book entitled *The Nine Spiritual Rocks*, privately produced, this society laid down that their members had arrived at a state of perfect freedom, that passions were no longer snares but sanctified by heavenly power and that sin was a thing of the past. Ebel's three female disciples were described by him as follows: Countess Ida was his first "wife," representing the principle of light *(Licht-natur)*; Emile von Scrotter was his second "wife;" representing the principle of darkness *(Finsternissnatur)*; while Frau Ebel, his third and legal wife, represented the principle of union *(Umfassung)*. All three women lived in one household with the archdeacon.

MULLOI: In celebrating the Feast of the Thesmophoria in Syracuse centuries ago (a feast conducted by women) symbols representing the female organ, filled with honey and sugar, were carried in procession.

MYLITTA: The ancient Babylonians gave the name of Mylitta to invoke the goddess Aphrodite. Worship of Mylitta became a cult. Herodotus in his history of the Persian Wars described one strange custom by which every Babylonian woman must once in her life go to the precinct of Aphrodite and wait there until summoned to have intercourse with a stranger. Once having taken a seat in the precinct no woman could leave until she had been claimed by a male stranger. Contact would be established by the stranger throwing a coin into her lap and saying, "I summon you in the name of the goddess Mylitta." It has been recorded that while the attractive women rarely stayed in the precincts for many minutes, some had to wait a year or more before they could fulfill what was a particularly harsh law.

NEST OF LOVE: The first man formally to establish an Abode of Love was Barthélemy Prosper Enfantin early in the nineteenth century. Being French, he did not call it an abode, nor, despite his insistence that this was the basis or home of a new religion, did he term it a temple. Barthélemy, a wine salesman, named his establishment the Nest of Love, and became the first man to try to make a religion out of love since the days of the ancient Greeks. Enfantin set this up in a mansion at Menilmonyant, described as "a gigantic harem where every woman was a bride and every bride the property of Enfantin." In 1832 he was arrested and sentenced to a year's imprisonment for outraging public morals.

NEW HAVEN PERFECTIONISTS: This sect was an early American version of the cult of spiritual wifehood started in Europe by Ebel and Enfantin. It was started in the 1830s by John Humphrey Noyes, a Congregationalist who spent his time traveling and preaching. In a beerhouse at Manlius, a village in Onandaga County, the gospel of spiritual wives was proclaimed. Young factory girls were flattered and thrilled into acceptance of the utopian delights promised them. Similar sects about this time were the Bible Communists and the Pauline Communists, with both of which Noyes was associated. Léonore Labillière, who had left Enfantin's Nest of Love to proclaim his gospel of "spiritual brides" elsewhere, wrote to Enfantin in 1838, saying, "Perfectionists, American Paulines, Bible Communists, Shakers, all have their own peculiar interpretation of free love."

PALATINE ANTHOLOGY: This refers to some fifteen books of Greek erotic verse and epigrams. The most notable contributor to this anthology was Asclepiades of Samos (c. 280 B.C.), the tutor of Theocritus, who gave rise to the word *asclepiadic*, which defines a certain metrical verse he invented. Thirty-nine epigrams of Asclepiades are included in this anthology.

PALLADES: The name given in ancient Greece to maidens who were consecreted to "serve Zeus" by playing the role of courtesans. Those so chosen were usually the most beautiful and of the most respected parentage.

PLATONIC LOVE: This has been given a variety of meanings over the years and is somewhat casually dismissed by some as simply meaning love without sex. The Greek philosopher Plato, who gave his name to the phrase, described it as follows: "Each of us when separated is always looking for his other half: such a nature is prone to love and ready to return love. And when he finds his other half, the pair is lost in an ecstasy of love and friendship and intimacy, and one will not wish to be out of the other's sight: these are people who pass their lives with one another. The entire yearning which each had for the other does not appear to be the desire of intercourse, but of something else, which only the soul desires and cannot tell, and of which there is only a dark and doubtful presentiment." This passage comes from Plato's *Symposium*. It may well be that it was the last part of this sentence that caused Samuel Richardson to take a more cynical view when in *Pamela; or, Virtue Rewarded* (London, 1840), he commented: "I am convinced, and always was, that Platonic Love is Platonic nonsense." It is probable that Plato was referring to the nonsexual love of one man for another rather than of a male for a female, though sometimes one doubts whether Plato even differentiated between one sex and another. What is clear from the rest of his *Symposium* is that he visualized love as ascending from the individual to contemplation of a universal ideal.

POMPEIAN GRAFFITI: Pompeii, which suffered so harshly in the Vesuvius eruption and the earthquake of A.D. 79, has nevertheless survived as a tradition of what the ancient world could produce in works of art. As many as 3,500 paintings were eventually recovered from the rubble. Also preserved were the graffiti and scribblings on the walls of many erotic themes. Some of these graffiti are surprisingly elegant. One such is: "To try to separate lovers is to try to contain the wind in a goatskin or stop the flow of running water." Some scribblers have expressed anger, as, for example, the person who wrote that he could "whip Venus's buttocks with a switch. She stabbed me in the heart and I would gladly break her head with a sword." Sometimes the graffiti were terse: "Serena has had her fill of Isidore."

PSYCHOMACY: Literally, this word means a conflict between body and soul, a definition that is almost as obscure as most of those given for Platonic Love. Undoubtedly it derives from *The Psychomachia*, an allegorical poem by Clemens Prudentius Aurelius, a Spanish Latin poet (c. 348–410), who seems to suggest that life is one long battle of the virtues against the vices, making an attempt to introduce a Christian theme into his work. In doing so Prudentius descends to the use of what today would be called crude melodrama, for example:

> On comes the foe and bears a torch of pine
> Instinct with burning sulphur, and intends
> To assail with fire and dash with noisome smoke
> Her modest eyes and face.

REGISTRUM LIBRORUM EROTICORUM: A bibliography of some five thousand erotic works in English, French, German, and Italian, compiled by Rolf D. Reade (a.k.a. Alfred Rose) and published in London in 1936. (Reference in the British Museum is Mus. Brit. P.C. 29a 76.)

RIDING ST. GEORGE: A phrase denoting the female astride the male in lovemaking.

ROMANTIC LOVE AND ROMANTIC LOVE COURTS: In the Middle Ages the concept of romantic love was promoted by poets, troubadours, and jongleurs (jugglers). It was the propagation of the theme of idealized love and made a symbol of chivalrous conduct. However, such codes still allowed a great deal of latitude. A knight could actually kidnap the lady of his choice in some circumstances, provided he did this in what was called "a courtly manner," bowing to her as he did so! Courtly love, as it was termed, appeared suddenly in Languedoc at the end of the eleventh century. It was such a hodgepodge of ideas that C. S. Lewis summed up its characteristics as "a feudalization of love," yet, admitting that there was "an unmistakable continuity" connecting the Provençal love song of the eleventh century with "the love poetry of the later Middle Ages" (*The Allegory of Love,* London, 1936). A Court of Love adjudicated on amatory problems. Grant Uden in A *Dictionary of Chivalry,* London, 1986, states "in a typical case, the Court was asked to decide which man was really the favored suitor if a lady listened to one, squeezed the hand of another and touched the foot of a third with her toe. Often the tribunal consisted of ladies."

SADISM: Though this word has long since been accepted by dictionaries as the finding of sexual pleasure by inflicting pain on someone else, it is perhaps necessary to say a few words about it here. *Sadism, sadist,* and *sadistic* all owe their origin to the Marquis Donatien Alphonse François de Sade (1740–1814), the author of *Justine* and other works that touch on the subject and practice of sadism. He was its chief propagandist.

SAINT SIMONISM: This was the philosophy of social and religious reform propounded by Claude Henri, Comte de Saint-Simon, in the 1820s, but after his death degenerating into what was a plea for universal sexual promiscuity under the title of "The Enfranchisment of Women." (See also NEST OF LOVE.)

SANCTIFICATION OF LOVE: This has been practiced in different ways by both Christians and Moslems down the centuries. In Italy prostitutes both before and after an assignation briefly prayed, "Pardon me, Madonna," to the Virgin Mary, and Moslems still invoke Allah before intercourse with the words: "*Bismillah er rachman er rachhim*" (in the name of Allah, the merciful, the gracious).

SHAKERS: A sect formed about the same time in the United States as the Newhaven Perfectionists and the Bible Communists in Europe. They believed in conducting their own theories of free love by daring one another to go to bed without having intercourse, a custom that they called *bundling* (see BUNDLING). Religious revivalism produced some remarkable customs and the morbidity of the relationships between men and women of the Shakers sect was so marked that a large percentage of them suffered from nervous breakdowns. John Humphrey Noyes in his *History of American Socialism* wrote: "They bundled, it is true, but only to prove by trial their power against the flesh; in other words, their triumphant Shakerism. . . . The women led the way in the bundling."

SOIXANTE-NEUF: A French expression for tersely describing the form of intercourse where the partners' heads are at opposite ends to one another, aptly summed up by regarding the symbol "69."

SOUL BABES: Members of the Agapemone of America (see AGAPEMONITES) in the 1930s were called Soul Babes. In a letter cited in *Temple of Love* (Donald McCormick, London, 1962) a lady in Arizona writes: "We have elected twelve Sisters and a mission has been entrusted to us by our Top Man who has given us your name and address. We are commanded to seek and to enroll six Soul Babes each, which will give us a further membership of seventy-two. The duties of a Soul Babe are simple. She must swear allegiance to our society and our Top Man. She must use no makeup of any kind during the period of probationship. Each day she must read the *Soul Babes Handbook.*" The society was in some ways rather like a pen friendship club that led to "soul friendships" paving the way to "Trial marriage." It was described by one member as a community of "sympanymphs and sympafauns," who drank what they called "Soul Tonic" in loving cups at special marriage feasts. This "tonic" was said to have been doctored with ginseng.

STORK FOUNTAIN: The famous Stork Fountain in Amagertorv, Copenhagen, not only stresses the stork as a symbol of fertility, but small pillars around it also symbolize in the fashion of ancient Greece phallic worship. A number of erotic odes in various languages have been written about this fountain.

TEMPLE OF LOVE: There have been many temples of love, or devoted to love, down the ages, but perhaps the greatest of all is the Thirteenth-century Temple of Love (or Black Pagoda, as it is sometimes called) at Konarak in India. This partly ruined building is covered with erotic sculptures depicting all manner of sexual activities, even showing women coupled with animals, presumably because the Hindu belief was that the goddess had to be fertilized by all animals in order to ensure that all species were continually produced. It was in this temple that the cult of Tantrism was taught and practiced. Tantra is a Hindu cult that puts forward the idea that sexual activities can in some way inflate a person's inner sexual energy so that the ecstasy induced can be devoted to religious causes. Tantrism is a mixture of yoga, meditation, mantras, and ritual. In some ways it is similar to theosophy.

TEMPLE OF VENUS: This was built on a peak of Mount Lebanon about the second century. It is described by the Roman historian Eusebius, who was appointed bishop of Caesarea by the Emperor Constantine, as follows: "A school of vice for libertines of all kinds has been established high up on Mount Lebanon. . . . There are womanish men who are not really men at all as well as unlawful unions of women and abominable deeds are conducted in this temple. . . . No respectable man is to be found in the temple."

TERPSICHOREAN EROTICISM: Terpsichore was one of the Nine Muses of ancient Greece, the muse of dancing and lyric poetry, and the dancing cult for furthering the cause of eroticism was named after her. Dancing was regarded as being a stimulus to love and there was a wide range of erotic dances, some of which have been detailed by Aristophanes and Lucian. One such was the Dance of the Heart, a wildly lascivious performance.

"THE CAGE": In New York's Public Library the section containing erotica is called by this name.

"THE PEARL: This was a magazine devoted to erotic writing that circulated in London in the nineteenth century (so called because anything greatly treasured in that era was always referred to as "a pearl of great price"). Its full title was *The Pearl, A Journal of Facetiae and Voluptuous Reading* and its first issue was in July 1879. There were eighteen issues of the magazine before it suddenly ceased publication in December 1880. Apart from featuring erotic stories and jokes it also contained some gossip of the day. The journal was reproduced in the USA in recent years (see *The Pearl, a Journal of Voluptuous Reading*, New York, 1968).

"THE TEN COMMANDMENTS OF LOVE": These were drawn up by a Spanish medieval sage, Juan Rodrigues of Granada. His advice was essentially practical, urging the need to avoid dismal thoughts, while stressing the necessity of serving one another and rejecting all behavior that might be dishonorable.

TINKER: This was a word used in earlier centuries both to describe a person in search of amorous adventure and amorous encounters, sometimes called *tinkering.* It appears frequently in books, usually describing some male wandering in quest of cuckoldry. Such titles are *The Beverley Maid and the Tinker* (Bodleian Library, Oxford), *Room for a Jovial Tinker* (Roxburghe Ballads), and *The Tinker* in *Merry Drolleries*, London, 1661.

TROUSER WEEK: A custom in Finland in days past that an engaged couple could sleep together during the last week before their wedding on the understanding that they kept their trousers on. (See BUNDLING).

VENUS CULT: Apart from the notorious Temple of Venus on Mount Lebanon there were several temples set up in her name by devotees of what became known as the Venus Cult. This extended to the Aegean Islands, Thessaly, Corinth, Olympia, the coasts of Asia Minor, and as far into the Mediterranean as Sicily and Southern Italy. The cult set out to promote erotic love in all its various forms.

WARTIME LOVE CODES: In wartime the most normal, pedestrian, and unimaginative of people turn to codes and ciphers when it comes to affairs of the heart. This started to some extent in World War I, but it was not until World War II that it flourished as an art. It was censorship that largely contributed to this use of code. Men in the services knew they could not indulge in any obvious code for the simple reason that the censorship would remove it. But they delighted in doing their utmost to baffle the censors (they knew it would force them to find out exactly what they meant), but it was also owing to a certain coyness and desire to mask their innermost feelings. Often the man doing the censoring of letters was the writer's immediate officer, and men did not like to feel he would be reading their letters and guffawing over some sentimental gesture. The censor would be confronted with "Yours, Bill, SWALK," or "Goodbye my love, YTHF," or "Jitterbug alongside me, Helen, IYIMD." For the sake of later generations who may know nothing of these things, SWALK meant "Sealed with a loving kiss," YTHF spelled out "Yours till Hell freezes," while IYIMD fondly confessed "Inside you in my dreams." Sometimes an officer acting as censor would ask for an explanation of some such initials, but in due course most officers acting as censors not only guessed or learned the meanings, but often used them in their own letters home or to girlfriends. Gradually it was realized that the very fact that such sentiments were being set out in code enhanced their meaning and gave such code words an eroticism of their own, especially WMCHW—"Wish my cock had wings." War-time codes led to postwar codes that became a new means of communication within certain small circles after the war. They became the accepted symbols of such people. One such was IWSRD ("I want specially romantic date,") while another (sometimes used by radio hams) was RUNAIRWM ("Are you on air with me?").

Notes

Introduction

1. Ralph Ginzburg, *An Unhurried View of Erotica*, London, 1959.
2. Alan Craig, *The Banned Books of England*, London, 1937.
3. Ibid.
4. Richard Aldington, *The Eaten Hearts*, London, 1930.
5. John Cleland, *Memoirs of Fanny Hill*, London, 1750.
6. In an introduction to *The Perfumed Garden of the Shaykh Nefzawi*, by Sir Richard Burton, London, 1963.
7. Ibid.
8. Such practices of writing in code were as prevalent among the old as the young. This was a practice which continued from courtship to old age with the ancient Indians who used to kiss by code. These kisses were known as "the straight kiss," "the bent kiss," "the turned kiss," and "the pressed kiss." Each had a different meaning. There was also "the kiss of intention," which simply meant kissing the reflection of a person that one loves in a mirror, in water, or even the shadow of that person on a wall.
9. Christina Georgina Rossetti (1830–94), sister of Dante Gabriel Rossetti, who also wrote "Better by far you should forget and smile, / Than you should remember and be sad." In the quotation she goes on to say, "Sing no sad songs for me," and the title of her poem is "When I am dead."

Chapter 1

1. See ANACREON OF TEOS in the A–Z section, also Anacreonitic in the glossary at the end of this book.
2. See AELIANUS CLAUDIUS, in A–Z.
3. See PLATONIC LOVE in the glossary.
4. See OVID in A–Z.
5. Ibid.
6. Some of Ovid's translations into English have been made in what can only be termed Chaucerian English, or a nineteenth-century copy of such. This quotation has been put into more modern English by the author of this book.

7. See CATULLUS, GAIUS VALERIUS in A–Z. Among the worthwhile editions of his works is that of R. Ellis, London, 1889, which contains valuable notes.

8. See PLAUTUS, TITUS MACCIUS in A–Z. Shakespeare's *Comedy of Errors* was based on Plautus's *Menaechmi* and Molière's work, *L'Avare*, on *Aulularia*.

9. See APULEIUS, LUCIUS in A–Z.

10. See AUSONIUS, DECIMUS MAGNUS in A–Z.

11. Ioannes Secundus in his work the *Epithalamium*. See SECUNDUS in A–Z.

12. This quotation is taken from Albius Tibullus's address to Priapus, the phallic god. See TIBULLUS, ALBIUS in A–Z.

13. See PETRONIUS, GAIUS in A–Z. Also *Quo Vadis* by Henrik Sienkiewicz, Warsaw, 1896.

14. See examples of this in Ausonius, DECIMUS MAGNUS A–Z.

15. See MARTIAL, in A–Z. Martial verged between the erotic and what would today be called the pornographic. He dealt in great detail with incest—e.g., "You ask, Fabullus, why Themison does not have a wife. He has a sister."

Chapter 2

1. See NEFZAWI, in A–Z. Also *The Perfumed Garden of the Shaykh Nefzawi*, London, 1963.

2. E. Windsor, *Hindu Art of Love*, New York, 1946.

3. This translation is an adaptation and variation on translations by Burton and others. See also *Ananga-Ranga: Traite Hindou de l'Amour Conjugal*, with an introduction by B. De Villeneuve, Paris, 1910. Also *Anananga-Ranga: The Hindu Art of Love* (in English, Paris, 1940).

4. See *Anthologie Erotique d'Aamarou*, Paris, 1831.

5. An English translation of this work was published in Paris in 1931. A French version, entitled *Le Collier du Pigeon* by Léon Bercher was published in Algiers in 1949.

6. This work was translated by E. L. Fackenheim and published by the Pontifical Institute of Medieval Studies, Toronto, 1945.

7. See also *Les Louis Secrètes de l'Amour*, after Omar Haleby, with a commentary by P. de Regla, Paris, 1893.

8. *Tales from the Arabian Nights: Selected from the Book of the Thousand Nights and a Night*, translated by Richard F. Burton, New York, 1978.

9. Ibid.

10. Chiang Yee, *Chinese Calligraphy: An Introduction to Its Aesthetic and Technique*, London, 1938.

11. Lin Yutang, *The Importance of Living*, London, 1938.

12. Ibid.

13. *The Golden Lotus*, translated from the Chinese novel, *Chin P'ing Mei*, 4 vols., New York, 1954.

14. *Babbage Papers*, British Museum, London, Add MS 37205 65–227 ff, Charles Babbage Papers, Department of Manuscripts.

15. Eighteenth-century poem by Fei Su-Huang, cited in *Anthologie de la Poésie Chinoise*, Paris, 1969.

16. See Wu Wu Meng, *Houses of Joy*, Paris, 1958; and Eric Chou, *The Dragon and The Phoenix*, London, 1971. It should be mentioned that in *The Paris Olympia Press*, by Patrick J. Kearney, Wu Wu Meng is stated to be a pseudonym for Sinclaire Beiles.

Chapter 3

1. C. S. Lewis, *The Allegory of Love*, Oxford, 1936.
2. *Passetyme of Pleasure*, Stephen Hawes. See HAWES, STEPHEN in A–Z.
3. See FLEMING, PAUL in A–Z. Hofmann von Hofmannswaldau lived from 1617–79, but there is still some argument about the authenticity of some of his alleged works.
4. See CODE OF COURTLY LOVE in glossary.
5. The earliest surviving copy of this work is in the British Museum, printed in 1626, and its title is *The First and Best Part of Scoggin Jests, Gathered by Andrew Borde, Doctor of Physicke*.
6. Sir Nicholas L'Estrange (1603–56), *A Naughty Nickname*. His manuscript collection contains more than six-hundred items and when some of them were published under the title of *Anecdotes and Traditions Illustrative of Early English History and Literature in 1839*, the editor, W. J. Thoms, said that the "greater portion" of L'Estrange's work, "is unfit for publication."
7. See DAFYDD AP GWILYM in A–Z.
8. Letter to the author from Dr. Johnston, August 29, 1991. Dr. Dafydd Johnston's book is *Canu Maswedd yr Oesoedd* (Medieval Welsh erotic poetry), Tafol, Cardiff, 1991.
9. George Saintsbury (1845–1933), *History of Criticism*, London, 1904–05. Dr. A. L. Rowse's book on the subject is *Shakespeare the Man*, London, 1973.
10. *The Roxburghe Ballads*, reprinted by the Ballad Society, London, 1869–80 (8 vols), edited by W. Chappell and J. W. Ebsworth.
11. *The Whore's Rhetoric* has been published by Ivan Obolensky, New York. It is believed, but not certain, that the original source was an Italian, Ferrante Pallavicino, though much of the English version is original.
12. This statement was contained in a letter from Freud to Dr. Friedrich Kraus, author of an erotic magazine called *Anthropophytheia* in 1910. It is cited by John Wardroper in his work, *Jest Upon Jest*, London, 1970.

Chapter 4

1. See A–Z section for further details on CLELAND JOHN, HAZLITT WILLIAM, and SWIFT, JONATHAN.
2. "Anatole France in Slippers," an article by Jean Jacques Brousson, cited by Frank Harris in *My Life & Loves*.
3. See *Correspondence of John Wilkes and Charles Churchill*. E. M. Weatherley, London, 1954.
4. See CHURCHILL, CHARLES in A–Z.
5. Wallace C. Brown, *Charles Churchill*, London, 1953.
6. Anonymous, *Nocturnal Revels*, London, 1779.
7. Commodore Edward Thompson, *The Temple of Venus*, 1763.
8. This would appear to be an adaptation of one of Wilkes's poems: see WILKES, JOHN in A–Z.
9. In *Fools and Jesters*, John Payne Collier, London, 1842, there is a reprint of Armin's *A Nest of Ninnies*.
10. These and many other similar items are to be found in both the Douce Collection and the Firth Collection at the Bodleian Library, Oxford University.
11. Sigmund Freud, *Jokes and Their Relation to the Unconscious*, London, 1960; also a paper on "Humor," vol. 21, Hogarth edition of Freud's Works, 1961.

12. *Daily Telegraph*, London, September 9, 1991: article entitled "Personal View: Literary Porn That Is One Long Yawn," by David Holloway.
13. A *Dictionary of the Sussex Dialect, and Collection of Provincialisms in Use in the County of Sussex*, compiled by the Reverend W. D. Parish, Lewes, Sussex, England, 1975.
14. Byron Farwell, *Burton: A Biography of Sir Richard Francis Burton*, London, 1963.
15. An *Anthology of 'Nineties Verse*, edited with an introduction by A. J. A. Symons, London, 1928. This work includes poems by Beardsley, Dowson, Le Gallienne, Arthur Symons, Oscar Wilde and many others.
16. *The Pearl*, volumes 1, 2, and 3, was printed in London in 1970, with a paperback edition in 1991. It was also published in New York in 1968 under the title of *The Pearl—a Journal of Voluptuous Reading*. *The Oyster* was published in London in 1991 in paperback.

Chapter 5

1. David Kahn, *The Code-Breakers*, London, 1968.
2. See OVID in A–Z. Also Ovid's *Ars Amatoria*.
3. See CAPELLANUS in A–Z.
4. See *William Lilly's History of His Life and Times*, written by himself to his "worthy friend Elias Ashmole," London, 1715.
5. Ibid.
6. These diaries of Senator Byrd are to be found in the Huntingdon Library and the Library of the Virginia Historical Society. Many passages have been brilliantly deciphered by Louis B. Wright and Marion Tinling, who admit that the "identification of proper names, which Byrd always wrote in shorthand, has proved particularly baffling."
7. See Harry Andrew Wright Winthrop in "Those Human Puritans," in *Proceedings of the American Antiquarian Society*, April 17, 1940.
8. See Restif de la Bretonne's *Monsieur Nicolas*, London, 1964, abridged translation by Robert Baldick.
9. See Donald McCormick, *Love in Code*, London, 1980.
10. See Maureen Duffy, *The Erotic World of Faery*, London, 1972. Also see DUFFY, MAUREEN PATRICIA in A–Z.
11. Lady Susan Chitty, *The Beast and the Monk*, London, 1975.
12. Wemyss Reid, *Memoirs and Correspondence of Lyon Playfair*, London, 1899.
13. Babbage Papers, British Library, Add MS. 37205 65-227 ff, Department of Manuscripts.
14. Ibid.
15. In a letter to the author from Mr. Vincent Dallison, who deciphered the diaries. He added that "in nearly all of the 1963 diary it had been lively, lucid, carefully spelt and with very few abbreviations. Later she began to spell erratically."
16. Ibid.

Chapter 6

1. *Maurice Girodias*, obituary, *Daily Telegraph* of London, July 5, 1990. In 1964, despite the fact that he had published works by Miller, Bataille, Beckett, Nabokov, and Genet, Girodias estimated that nearly seventy of the two hundred books published by Olympia Press had been declared unsuitable. He died of a heart

attack while giving a radio interview to promote his memoirs, *Une Journée sur la Terre.*

2. Ibid.
3. Introduction by H. E. Bates to Raymond Peynet's *The Lovers' Bedside Book,* and *The Lovers' Pocketbook.*
4. Ibid.
5. Introduction to *The Lovers' Pocketbook.*
6. Reports in the *Beckenham Advertiser,* England, June 6 and 20, 1957. The woman was imprisoned in an underground room beneath a shed at Lewisham, Kent, for three months.
7. Letter from John Fowles, January 27, 1983.
8. Ibid.
9. See HAZLITT, WILLIAM in A–Z.
10. Anne Edwards, *Wallis: The Novel,* London and New York, 1991.
11. Mario Vargas Llosa, *In Praise of the Stepmother,* London, 1991.
12. Susannah Herbert, review entitled "Orgies Are Compulsory, Talent Optional," Daily Telegraph, London, September 1991.
13. Cited in William H. Forbis, *Japan Today,* New York, 1975.
14. The French title of this book is *La Neige Était Sale.* Simenon wrote some 212 novels, mainly thrillers, and his very frank autobiography, *Intimate Memoirs* (1984), is well worth studying.
15. See MARIVAUX, PIERRE CARLET DE, in A–Z.
16. Charles Spencer, article entitled "Experiment in Sexuality," in London *Daily Telegraph,* September 1991.
17. Shaw's letter to Sylvia Beach is cited in Richard Ellman, *James Joyce,* Oxford University Press, revised edition, 1982.
18. Interview with Erica Jong by Martyn Harris, entitled "Changing Zip Code for the Nineties," *Sunday Telegraph,* London, August 5, 1990.
19. Ibid.
20. Richard Last, *A Climatic Whimper, Daily Telegraph,* London, October 23, 1991.

Chapter 7

1. Patrick J. Kearney, *The Paris Olympia Press,* Black Spring Press, London, 1987.
2. Ibid.
3. Pauline Réage, *Story of "O",* Grove Press, New York, 1965.
4. Harriet Daimler was the pseudonym for Iris Owens. Her books included *Darling, The Pleasure Thieves, Innocence, The New Organization,* and *The Woman Thing.* Angela Pearson is once again a pseudonym. One of her most notable books, published by the Odyssey Library in Copenhagen and later by Olympia Press's New York office, was *Scream, My Darling, Scream.*
5. Review by Maria Lexton, cited in article entitled "On the Critical List," *Sunday Times* of London, July 29, 1990.
6. John Worthen, *D. H. Lawrence: The Early Years,* Cambridge University Press, 1991.
7. Review by William Scammell of *D. H. Lawrence: The Early Years* in *The Spectator,* London, September 7, 1991.
8. Wilhelm Reich, *The Function of the Orgasm,* Farrar, Straus, and Giroux, New York, 1961. This was an especially influential book in the sense that it stressed

the vital importance of the role of sex in modern society, giving some controversial ideas about political repression of sex.

9. Review by Charles Spencer, entitled "Portrait of the Dramatist as a Young Man," *Daily Telegraph*, London, November 21, 1991.
10. Ibid.
11. Cited by Benedict Nightingale in a review of Shaw's play in *The Times*, London, November 20, 1991.

Select Bibliography

For Further Study of the Subject of Erotic Literature

Armitage, Gilbert. *Banned in England*, Wishart: London, 1932.

Ashbee, Henry Spencer (Pisanus Fraxi). *Forbidden Books of the Victorians*. Odyssey Press: London, 1970. This is an abridged edition of Ashbee's bibliographies of erotica, including *Index Librorum Prohibitorum* and *Catena Librorum Tacendorum*.

Blondeau, Nicolas. *Dictionnaire Erotique*. I. Liseux: Paris, 1885.

Craig, Alec. *The Banned Books of England*, Allen & Unwin: London, 1937.

Duffy, Maureen. *The Erotic World of Faerie*, Hodder & Stoughton: London, 1972.

Forberg, Friederich Carl. *The Manual of Exotica Sexualia*. Brandon House: California, 1965.

Freeman, Gillian. *The Undergrowth of Literature*. Panther: London, 1969.

Ginzburg, Ralph. *An Unhurried View of Erotica*, Secker & Warburg: London, 1959.

Jackson, Holbrook. *The Fear of Books*. Soncino Press: London, 1932.

Kearney, Patrick J. *The Private Case*. Annotated bibliography of the British Museum's "restricted" erotica book collection. Jay Landesman: London, 1981.

———. *A History of Erotic Literature*, Macmillan: London, 1982.

———. *The Paris Olympia Press*, Black Spring Press: London, 1987.

Legman, Gershon. *The Horn Book*. Studies in erotic folklore and bibliography. University Books: New York, 1964.

———. *Love and Death: A Study in Censorship*. A book that warns that violence not sex is the great danger to society. Hacker Art Books: New York, 1963.

Lewis, C. S. *Allegory of Love*. Oxford University Press: 1951.

Loth, David. *The Erotic in Literature*. Messner: New York, 1961.

Pierrugues, Pierre. *Glossarius Eroticum*. Paris, 1826.

Rabenalt, Arthur Maria. *Theater ohne Tabu*. Eroticism in the modern theater. Emsdetten: Verlag Lechte, 1970.

Rose, Alfred (Rolfe S. Reade). *Register of Erotic Books*. Jack Brussel: New York, 1965.

Saltus, Edgar. *Love throughout the Ages*. Camden Publishing Co.: London, 1930.

Tabori, Paul. *The Humor and Technology of Sex*. Julian Press: London, 1969.

Thesaurus Eroticus Linguae Latinae. Stuttgart, 1883.

Webb, Peter. *The Erotic Arts*. Secker & Warburg: London, 1975.

Wedeck, H. E. *Dictionary of Erotic Literature*. Peter Owen: London, 1963. Also *Philosophical Library* of New York, 1962.

Index